EDITED BY
Jeffrey P. Greenman and Gene L. Green

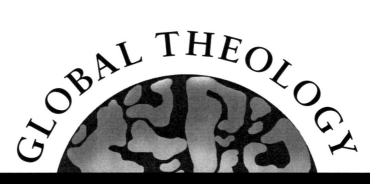

GLOBAL THEOLOGY

Exploring the Contextual Nature of Theology and Mission

IN EVANGELICAL PERSPECTIVE

IVP Academic

An imprint of InterVarsity Press
Downers Grove, Illinois

InterVarsity Press
P.O. Box 1400, Downers Grove, IL 60515-1426
World Wide Web: www.ivpress.com
E-mail: email@ivpress.com

InterVarsity Press® is the book-publishing division of InterVarsity Christian Fellowship/USA®, a movement of students and faculty active on campus at hundreds of universities, colleges and schools of nursing in the United States of America, and a member movement of the International Fellowship of Evangelical Students. For information about local and regional activities, write Public Relations Dept., InterVarsity Christian Fellowship/USA, 6400 Schroeder Rd., P.O. Box 7895, Madison, WI 53707-7895, or visit the IVCF website at <www.intervarsity.org>.

While all stories in this book are true, some names and identifying information have been changed to protect the privacy of the individuals involved.

Cover design: Cindy Kiple
Interior design: Beth Hagenberg

ISBN 978-0-8308-3956-8

Printed in the United States of America ∞

Library of Congress Cataloging-in-Publication Data

Global theology in evangelical perspective: exploring the contextual
nature of theology and mission/edited by Jeffrey P. Greenman and
Gene L. Green.
p. cm.
Includes bibliographical references and indexes.
ISBN 978-0-8308-3956-8 (pbk.: alk. paper)
1. Theology—Congresses.   I. Greenman, Jeffrey P. II. Green, Gene L.
BT80.G54 2011
230.09'051—dc23

2011051587

P	20	19	18	17	16	15	14	13	12	11	10	9	8	7	6	5	4	3
Y	28	27	26	25	24	23	22	21	20	19	18	17	16					

Dedicated to C. René Padilla

Pioneer in Latin American evangelical theology

With gratitude and appreciation

CONTENTS

INTRODUCTION 9
    Gene L. Green

PART ONE: SETTING THE STAGE

1. THE RISE OF GLOBAL THEOLOGIES. 19
    Andrew Walls

2. THE SIGNIFICANCE OF THE TRANSLATION PRINCIPLE 35
    Lamin Sanneh

3. THE CHALLENGE OF GLOBAL HERMENEUTICS 50
    Gene L. Green

PART TWO: NON-WESTERN THEOLOGIES

4. DOING THEOLOGY ON CHRIST'S ROAD. 67
    Samuel Escobar

5. SONGS OF HOPE OUT OF A CRYING LAND: An Overview of
    Contemporary Latin American Theology 86
    Ruth Padilla DeBorst

6. CHRISTIAN CHINESE THEOLOGY: Theological Ethics
    of Becoming Human and Holy 102
    Khiok-Khng Yeo

7. SOME INSIGHTS INTO INDIAN CHRISTIAN THEOLOGY 116
    Ken Gnanakan

8. AFRICAN THEOLOGY 134
    James Kombo

9. MIDDLE EASTERN THEOLOGY IN EVANGELICAL
    PERSPECTIVE 148
    Martin Accad

PART THREE: **NORTH AMERICAN THEOLOGIES**

10. NEW OLD PERSPECTIVES: Theological Observations
    Reflecting Indigenous Worldviews. 165
    Terry LeBlanc

11. "OUTSIDE THE GATE": Evangelicalism and
    Latino Protestant Theology 179
    Juan Martínez

12. ASIAN AMERICAN EVANGELICAL THEOLOGY 195
    Amos Yong

13. AFRICAN AMERICAN THEOLOGY: Retrospect and Prospect . 210
    Vincent Bacote

PART FOUR: **NEXT STEPS**

14. SOME IMPLICATIONS OF GLOBAL THEOLOGY
    FOR CHURCH, MINISTRY AND MISSION 225
    Mark Labberton

15. LEARNING AND TEACHING GLOBAL THEOLOGIES. 237
    Jeffrey P. Greenman

CONTRIBUTORS 253

NAME INDEX 257

SUBJECT INDEX 261

INTRODUCTION

Gene L. Green

• • •

During the twentieth century, the geographical center of the church moved South and East, so the heartlands of the Christian faith are no longer in the North Atlantic region but rather in Africa, Asia, Latin America and Oceania. The great missionary movement of the nineteenth and twentieth centuries has yielded a rich harvest of burgeoning churches in the Majority World who have embraced the Word of God in their mother tongue and are now, with Bible in hand, articulating Christian theology for themselves. They have received the gospel and Scripture, but are now becoming what Justo González has called a four-self church. That is, the global church is mature and therefore self-funding, self-governing and self-propagating. But it is also self-theologizing, with this fourth "self" being a sure sign of theological maturity and a phenomenon that the missionary churches in the West had not fully anticipated. While receiving a rich theological heritage from the Western church, Majority World churches have been asking questions about the way the gospel intersects their cultures and the shape of theology expressed in their mother tongues.

One of our authors, Prof. Andrew Walls, has been telling us for decades about the shift in the population center of the church and has urged us to listen as the church in the Majority World begins to undertake the theological task on its own and in dialogue with the theological traditions they received. Another of our writers, Lamin Sanneh, reminds us that not only is the Bible translatable into the languages of the world but so too the Christian faith. One does not have to become culturally Western in order to be a Christian. Christianity may be expressed in the languages of the world, through the music of the world and through the cultural idioms of the world. The current global engagements of Scripture and theology with culture are parallel to the way the early church took the message of Jesus rooted in the land of Judea and the Aramaic language and translated it both culturally and linguistically as it ran throughout the Roman world. This volume bears witness to another step in the process of theological development that began when the gospel first spread to Caesarea and Antioch through the ministries of Peter and Paul. The new story being told in these pages is just another chapter in the very old story.

If you have read the list of authors and seen the topics covered in the table of contents, you are already aware that this volume on global theology includes a rather surprising twist. Those who study Majority World theologies discover that the questions and issues raised there are often identical to those placed on the table among ethnic minority communities in North America. And, moreover, dialogue often occurs between these communities and those who are engaged in the wider global theological discussion. We wanted to capture some of that discourse by including voices not just from the Global South and East but also theologians from the Native North American, Asian American, Latino and African American communities. There is a surprise here since we discover that what we thought was "global" theological discourse is part of the discussion right next door. If we open the window we can hear the drum circle and the voices that exclaim "¡Gloria a Dios!" This global discourse brings us home again to a multicultural church that has also become self-theologizing. As a North American Christian community, we are all theologically enriched by the contributions of Terry LeBlanc, Amos Yong, Juan Martínez and Vince Bacote.

Over the years a number of observers have raised questions about the directions global theological discourse is heading, from liberation theologies to the more recent postcolonial theologies. Not a few in the Western church and Christian academy have wondered whether these theological developments are genuinely orthodox. Our distance sometimes pushes us to make hasty generalizations that do not reflect the varied texture of current global theological discourse. <u>Our concern in this volume is to introduce some of the important evangelical voices who are sometimes overlooked, yet who offer fresh theological contributions that are rooted in an evangelical embrace of Scripture and a commitment to mission within a vibrant piety.</u> Some will be surprised to hear from Samuel Escobar that liberation theology is not the only major theological development emerging from Latin America. In fact, the theology of *misión integral*, which was forged within the Latin American Theological Fellowship, *predated* Gustavo Gutiérrez's presentation of liberation theology and, indeed, was the central theological force behind the inclusion of the fifth paragraph on "Christian Social Responsibility" in the Lausanne Covenant of 1974. Many Western evangelicals have been shaped by Latin American evangelical theological reflection without being aware of it.

Some who pick up this volume may ask why there is any need to explore seemingly local theologies such as African or Asian American. Linking these theologies with a particular region appears to limit their usefulness and appeal, marginalizing them to a corner of Christian discourse. While I cannot answer for all the authors in this book, most would say (and many have said) that what has typically been regarded as theology for the whole global church actually has been, in many respects, Western theology, which has been assumed to be universal theology. Many authors question the premise that the theological heritage that they received from the West is somehow "neutral" and "universal." They recognize that Western theology has a Western accent despite its claims to the contrary. As Samuel Escobar remarked to me some years ago, "All theology is contextual." While all the authors of this volume embrace a high view of the authority of Scripture, they also recognize how God speaks to them where they live and addresses the needs and concerns raised among their communities. Unlike their Western counterparts, they openly acknowledge and celebrate their social location in relation to the gospel.

K. K. Yeo makes the argument that the development of global theologies is a necessary aspect of a truly catholic theology. Any careful reader of the New Testament, for example, will recognize the varied expressions of the faith expressed therein. While speaking with a single voice, they have different accents and emphases that respond to the particular contexts where they live and those of the communities they address. Not everyone in the New Testament speaks like Matthew or Paul. Martin Luther, for all his claims to Paul, developed his own contextual theology at the beginning of the Reformation. Andrew Walls has called these new global theological developments nothing less than a New Reformation. These contextual engagements also become a gift to the whole church as we listen to an African like James Kombo discuss the place of ancestors in Christian faith or a Latin American like Ruth Padilla DeBorst speak prophetically about poverty and justice. We hear their unique accent and theological formulations, and through them we all come to understand the faith more fully. This is an exercise of the one holy catholic and apostolic church.

Upon reading the essays, you will discover considerable rhetorical and theological variety among the voices, but with patient reading will come a deep appreciation for the different movements in this symphony. Some of the authors write with a studied and formal style, while others take us on a journey that leaves us white-knuckled and breathless—yet safe—at the end. The themes they address may be unfamiliar but they are their themes that offer us all insight into the biblical text and the way the church's theology develops. The differences in interpretive approaches will also become apparent quickly, a topic that I have addressed in a compressed summary of global hermeneutical trends. Some of the essays are careful surveys of the theological landscape, while others are more constructive pieces which map out some of the new directions in theological understanding. The reader looking for a predictable and uniform volume that speaks with a single voice best look elsewhere. But if the reader wants to discover the varied colors of the global theological tapestry, just start turning the pages. This volume reflects some of the rich and deep variety of evangelical theological reflection that is characteristic of this era. We are passing through a moment of discovery and excitement, a new terrain where all the mountains and valleys have not been fully mapped, as Martin Accad reminds us. Global theological reflection is a work in progress, and this volume reflects that reality.

But amid this variety, the reader will notice common themes emerging. The concern for doing theology to, within and from a particular community is a constant throughout, as is an appreciative critique of the Western heritage. Each wants to ask how culture and faith work together and attempts to foster a truly relevant faith. There is also a struggle in many of these essays to understand how the Christian faith relates to inherited cultural traditions and faiths, as the one by Ken Gnanakan from India. A question often asked by African theologians is, "Did the missionaries bring God to Africa or did God bring the missionaries?" We know the answer, but we do not expect the second question they ask: "If God brought the missionaries, where was he before they came?" The voices heard in these pages also place considerable emphasis on community in the theological process as they reject stark individualism. That community includes those who have not been common participants in theological discourse, such as the poor. These and other themes will make us aware that there is a dialogue emerging from South to South and between South and East, often bypassing the West. There are lessons here for us all, and a glimmer of the new networks of theological discourse that will characterize all future Christian reflection.

This volume takes the reader through the various regions of our world and explores many of the theological developments among North American ethnic communities. No author had sufficient pages to develop fully the themes at hand, so each has presented a brief bibliography for further reading. Anyone who wishes to explore additional dimensions of these current theological trends will want to have on hand the *Global Dictionary of Theology* published by InterVarsity Press.[1] This volume makes a valuable contribution, offering brief articles and bibliography for additional exploration. Most of all, it is important to read the works of emerging authors from the Majority World and minority communities, and not depend simply on Western summaries of their thought.

---

[1]William A. Dyrness and Veli-Matti Kärkkäinen, eds., *Global Dictionary of Theology* (Downers Grove, Ill.: IVP Academic; Nottingham, U.K.: Inter-Varsity Press, 2008).

And we must read further. The voices we hear in this volume are the echoes of the future. As Jeffrey Greenman and Mark Labberton remind us at the end, this is a discourse for the whole Christian academy and for the whole Christian church. Just as we have been in dialogue with Christians in the West through the centuries, now is the moment to begin the conversation with the global church and minorities within our borders so that we can all together come to a fuller understanding of how God is speaking through his Word to the church today where we live. From this time in history onward, theological discourse will never be the same. We are witnessing, and are part of, a new thing that God is doing. Given that, we hope that this book will become part of creative courses in our colleges and seminaries that explore the new accents of theology which we are hearing. And we trust that educational programs in the church will likewise help believers everywhere enter into this fresh conversation around the Word of God.

• • •

This volume emerged from the twentieth annual Wheaton Theology Conference held in April 2011 on the campus of Wheaton College in Illinois. There are many people to thank, without whom the conference and this volume would have remained a dream. Bob Fryling and Gary Deddo of InterVarsity Press have offered consistent support and wise counsel through the design of the conference and this volume. We are grateful to them and to InterVarsity Press for helping to defray the cost of bringing speakers from the corners of the globe to Wheaton. We also express our deep gratitude to Rebekah Canavan, whose logistical expertise made this and previous conferences run on well-greased rails. We likewise extend our gratitude to the many students of Wheaton College who served as hosts and offered their labors to make every participant in the conference feel most welcome. One in particular, Aubrey Buster, did a superb job of helping prepare this manuscript for publication. And, not least of all, we thank the administration of Wheaton College for their unwavering support and encouragement as we explored these themes of global theology together. Finally, we are grateful to our many speakers who took the time from overly pressed schedules to prepare and present their papers. Their joy brought us joy.

There is one person who was not on the program but whose name is written large in the heart of everyone who is involved with or watching the development of evangelical theology around the globe. Fortunately, he attended the conference since he was in the Wheaton area at that time, working as the general editor of a new Latin American biblical commentary. He has been a strong and influential voice at such venues as Lausanne and has written many volumes and articles that have mapped out the course of evangelical theology in Latin America. Moreover, he has worked tirelessly to assure that Latin American Christians have had sound biblical and theological tomes at their disposal. His labors have inspired evangelical biblical scholars around the globe as he has set a stellar example to follow. An Ecuadorian living in Buenos Aires, he is also a beloved son of Wheaton College (B.A. '57, M.A. '60, D.D. '92). We dedicate this volume to him, our esteemed brother, Dr. C. René Padilla—*siervo fiel del Señor Jesucristo.*

Part One

SETTING THE STAGE

1

THE RISE OF
GLOBAL THEOLOGIES

Andrew Walls

• • •

The Development of Theology in
Christian Mission and Life

Theology "is an act of adoration fraught with the risk of blasphemy."[1] Adoration must be the tendency of any word we use of God. Isaac Watts counsels reticence as the mark of adoration, recalling Isaiah's temple vision, where the seraphim covered their faces in the divine presence. And so:

> Be short our tunes, our words be few;
> A sacred reverence checks our songs,
> And praise sits silent on our tongues.[2]

This puts theology into a different category from most sciences, where the spur to development is intellectual curiosity. The laboratory space for theology is not in the study or the library. The major theological laboratory—workshop might be a more appropriate term—lies in the life situations of believers or of the church. Theological activity arises out of Christian mission and Christian living, from the need for Christians to make Christian choices and to think in a Christian way.

This compulsion to think in a Christian way becomes more power-

---

[1]"Notes of Recent Exposition," *The Expository Times* 64, no. 11 (1953): 322.
[2]Isaac Watts, "Eternal Power, Whose High Abode," *The Methodist Hymnal* (New York: Methodist Book Concern, 1905), p. 12.

ful and more urgent whenever the gospel crosses a cultural frontier, since the process of crossing cultural frontiers almost inevitably creates situations not previously encountered by Christians, and a different climate of thought poses intellectual questions not considered before. Crosscultural encounter is therefore a spur to theological creativity. In order to understand this it may be helpful to consider first what occurred when the church crossed its very first cultural frontier. The early stages of that encounter are recorded within the New Testament.

Theology in Jerusalem and Antioch

The mother church of us all, that of Jerusalem, is vividly presented for us in the early chapters of the Acts of the Apostles. It is salutary to remember that these first believers in Jesus, under the leadership of the apostles trained by him, did not think of themselves as Christians: they had not even heard the word. Apart from the consciousness that they were disciples of Jesus, they hardly needed a name. They knew that they were Israelites, and Israelites living in the climactic period of Israel's history, the messianic age, "in those days," in the age to come described by the prophets. The theme is grandly declared by Peter in the Pentecost address, when he announces that the great day of the Lord has arrived, a day so significant that one may speak metaphorically of sun and moon being darkened, the day when God's Spirit is poured out on humanity. The event that has triggered this outpouring of the divine presence is God's announcement and demonstration that Jesus of Nazareth, recently crucified at the hands of members of the community, and now raised from death, is indeed the Davidic Messiah promised in Scripture. It is now a time of decision, a time for repentance and identification with the Messiah, leading to forgiveness and sharing in the outpoured Spirit of God. It is a day of salvation, when the promises of Scripture are fulfilled (Acts 2:14-39). There is a grand inclusiveness in Peter's call to Israelites to seize the promise; it is to them and to their children, whether, like so many of the hearers, they live "far off" in the Dispersion, or at home in Palestine (v. 39). But Peter says not a word about the salvation of anyone outside the "House of Israel" and gives no hint of God's interest in any people but the Jewish.

In this church the thought of global theologies would be unintelligible. Theology was bounded by the history of Israel. The nature of the divine presence signified in the pouring out of the Holy Spirit might well provoke fresh theological reflection. The nature and timing of the restoration of the kingdom to Israel, the political dimension of the messianic age, would almost certainly become a matter of theological discussion in the church, for, though the Lord sidelined it, that question was at the top of his disciples' minds as, on the Mount of Ascension, they realized that a new era was about to open (Acts 1:6). For Jews there is no salvation without the salvation of the nation. In an entirely Jewish church the key category in Christology is messiahship, the word that gives that branch of theology its name; the records we have of Palestinian Jewish-Christian communities in the second century and later suggest that a purely Jewish Christology might have followed quite a different path from that familiar to us now. Without the need to respond to Greek questions it is unlikely that we would have the Niceno-Constantinopolitan creed today.

The theological high road on which we are now traveling was opened in Antioch, when some Jerusalem believers from Cyprus and Cyrene, refugees from the persecution that followed the death of Stephen, made the first great departure in mission policy by deliberately introducing Greek-speaking pagans to Jesus. Up to now, Jesus had been regularly presented as Messiah, a term all Jews recognized, rooted as it was in the history of Israel and speaking as it did to Jewish hopes and desires. But the term *messiah*, even when translated into Greek, would mean little to Gentiles used to the religious cults of the Hellenistic East Mediterranean. The evangelists in Antioch presented Jesus as "Lord" (Acts 11:19-21). This was perfectly acceptable in Jewish terms: in the Pentecost address, Peter speaks of God having made Jesus "both Lord and Christ" (Acts 2:36). But Antiochene Gentiles used *Kyrios* as the title of their cult divinities. Some might fear the pagan associations of the word, but by means of it Gentiles could begin to glimpse who the Lord Jesus Christ was, receiving ideas of a divine Lord that could never have come to them by means of the word *messiah* alone. The outcome was a bicultural church in Antioch, where observant Jews who recognized Jesus as Messiah shared with Hellenistic Gentiles who called Jesus Lord. Such a new sort of community needed a name, and so the name *Xristianoi*, Christians, was invented (Acts 11:26).

The bicultural conversation in Antioch about the Lord Jesus Christ would give plenty of scope for theological development. For Gentile believers the affirmation that "Jesus is Lord" was central to faith, and the gateway to understanding it lay in the titles of other divine lords, such as the Lord Sarapis. But how did this idea of the divine Lord square with the insistence of their Jewish friends that there is only one God whose name in Greek is also *ho Kyrios*, the Lord? Jewish believers, we may well guess, might discourage such questionings, believing that when thinking of the Godhead "a sacred reverence checks our songs." They might speak of the relationship between God and the Lord Jesus in such phrases as Stephen used, "Jesus is at the right hand of God." Stephen's hearers understood him, and killed him (Acts 7:54-60).

But in Greek terms it was no answer at all. Even discounting the anthropomorphic language (does God have a right hand?), it says nothing of the relations in terms of being or essence. Greek mythology had many stories of figures with divine fathers and human mothers. Were these stories true analogies? Is Christ, like Herakles, a mixture of divine and human?

Theological Development in a Hellenistic World

Crossing the cultural frontier into the Greek world of thought opened theological issues undreamed of in the Messianic Judaism of the Jerusalem church. And those issues could only be pursued in the Greek language, using Greek categories of thought such as *ousia* and *hypostasis* and Greek methods of debate, the intellectual materials to hand. This was the process that produced the great creeds and led to such declarations as "God from God, light from light, Very God from Very God, begotten not made, being of one substance with the Father" and laid the foundations of what we now think of as the classical doctrines of Trinity and incarnation. The theological process arose by asking Greek questions in the Greek language, questions that were neither raised nor settled by using Hebrew categories such as messiah. Subsequent crosscultural movements of the Christian faith open the way to theological discovery by raising questions in other languages that have no answer in the terms of another culture.

But long before the age of the great councils, the Christian invasion of Hellenistic Gentile society that began in Antioch was opening a still wider set of theological questions, many small in themselves but vital for believers living in Hellenistic culture. They arose out of the decision of the early church, ratified at the Council of Jerusalem described in Acts 15, that Gentile believers in Jesus were members of Israel by virtue of their faith in Israel's Messiah (Acts 15:13-41). They did not have to become Jewish proselytes or adopt the Torah and accept circumcision. The implications of this were huge, and no one could guess where they would lead. Hitherto, the pattern of life for followers of Jesus had been guided by the way of life of observant Jews. Jesus himself had lived under the law and had said he had come to fulfill it, not destroy it. His apostles followed that path; his brother James, the dominant figure in the Jerusalem church, was celebrated for his observance of the Torah. The life of the church reflected in the early chapters of Acts was a converted Judaism, in which Jewish life and thinking were transformed in the light of the messiahship of Jesus. Thus, instead of the exploitative society denounced by the prophets, these Israelites of the messianic age shared their property (Acts 2:44) and their meals (Acts 2:46), and cared for vulnerable people such as widows (Acts 6:1-7). The decision of the Jerusalem Council meant recognizing a different way of following Jesus. The Gentile new believers could not enter the temple, could not easily keep sabbath, and were not bound by the laws about food and ritual purity. Had they become proselytes, as Gentiles entering Israel had previously done, and as some conservative Jewish believers thought they still should, a great deal of theological activity would have been unnecessary. The pattern of Christian life would have continued to be essentially Jewish.

But the abandonment of Torah and circumcision opened up innumerable small theological questions, which forced Christians to make

choices. A new Christian lifestyle had to be devised under the guidance
of the Holy Spirit now poured out on Gentiles: a Hellenistic way of
following Jesus and a converted pattern of Hellenistic social and family
life. The New Testament epistles show this lifestyle under construction. First Corinthians is full of issues that demanded decisions depending on thinking in a Christian way. What, for instance, should
one do if invited to dinner by a pagan friend who might have got the
meat from a temple, where it would have been previously offered in
sacrifice to a pagan deity (1 Cor 10:27-30)? We see various questions
arising; will it hurt me if I eat it? Should I ask my host where he got the
meat? Suppose he tells me that it has come from the temple? These are
not straightforward questions; in his answers Paul ranges over such issues as the ontological status of pagan divinities, the nature of Christian liberty, the Christian duty of loving consideration for other Christians, and the different degrees of Christian maturity.[3] But it is clear
that Christians must come to a decision as to whether they are eating or
declining to eat that meat, and be prepared to explain it. As Paul puts
it elsewhere, "everything that does not come from faith is sin" (Rom
14:23).

The need for such thinking was new and arose from the fact that the
new believers were neither Jews nor proselytes; they were converts whose
task was to model converted Hellenistic social life as the old believers
modeled converted Judaism. The experience of old believers could be
little help to them. It would be unlikely that, observant Jews as they
were, they had ever been or ever would be invited to dinner by a pagan.
Crossing the cultural frontier created new theological issues that arise
from the need for a new sort of Christian life, where Christians might
go to dinner with pagans and speak about Christ at the table. Such theological issues were beyond the experience and counsel of the oldest and
the best and most experienced believers of a different cultural upbring-
ing. The new Christians were not proselytes, following the converted
cultural pattern of earlier believers; they were converts, needing, under
the guidance of the Holy Spirit, to turn the ways of their own societies

---

[3]The question arises in the context of earlier consideration of general issues about meals: 1 Corinthians 8:1-13; 10:14-26.

toward Christ. Conversion is less about content than about direction. It is about turning toward Christ what is already there.

Commonly, the first theological issues arise from the question, What should I do? How should I act as a Christian in this situation? They belong to the "Should I go to dinner?" category. But the "What should I think?" category of question inexorably follows as Christians seek to understand Christ in terms of the ways of thought and traditions of their culture. The theological process arising from the crossing of the Greek cultural frontier lasted several centuries. Second-century Greek Christian thinkers wrestled with the question of the relation between the Christian present and the Greek intellectual tradition. It is the crucial issue for Justin, the converted philosopher who taught Christianity as the true philosophy. We catch Justin's sense of liberation as he reflects on the prologue to the Fourth Gospel and recognizes in the word *Logos*, with its Stoic and Platonic connotations, the key to the critique of the Greek cultural past.[4] It shows him the divine creative *Logos* active among the great figures of that past in a way Paul, who was "circumcised on the eighth day, of the people of Israel, of the tribe of Benjamin" (Phil 3:5), never had to wonder about. Tracing the activity of the divine *Logos* in past ages showed him what could be affirmed in his heritage, what must be denied, what must be modified. Much Western discussion of Justin's *Logos* doctrine centers on its place in the evolution of the doctrine of the Trinity; it is hardly accidental that it is a modern African theologian, the late Kwame Bediako, who interprets Justin primarily in terms of his wrestling of the relationship to his own culture to the gospel, and who argues that second-century Greek theologians and mid-twentieth-century African theologians had exactly parallel concerns.[5]

The third century brings a new generation of Christian thinkers with dual education, thoroughly Greek in culture but educated in the Scriptures as Christians from childhood. In Origen we see a Christian seeking to reconceive the entire Greek intellectual inheritance to make

---

[4]Justin Martyr, *Apology I*, in *Ante-Nicene Fathers* (Grand Rapids: Eerdmans, 1978), 1:163-86.
[5]Kwame Bediako, *Theology and Identity: The Impact of Culture on Second Century Christian Thought and in Modern Africa* (Oxford: Regnum, 1992).

it serviceable for Christian purposes. And we see the Greek academy itself, once essentially hostile to Christianity, in process of conversion, the conversion of their Greek past. We cannot suppress our past; it gives us our identity. To lose one's past is to lose one's memory; to lose one's memory is to lose one's identity, to cease to be able to form confident relationships. The past cannot be suppressed, nor can it be left untouched by Christ. The past, with its identity-shaping cultural traditions, has to be converted, turned toward Christ. And that is a major theological undertaking.

Origen illustrates the importance of the theological task by asking how the Israelites were able to furnish the tabernacle, including the golden cherubim and gold vessels, in the wilderness. It was possible, he says, because they had spoiled the Egyptians. It was Egyptian gold that formed the cherubim that symbolized the presence of God, and the curtains of the tabernacle must have been of Egyptian cloth. The theological task, in Origen's view, is to take the things that are misused in the heathen world and to fashion from them things for the worship and service of God.[6] The theological agenda is thus culturally conditioned. The tabernacle and its furnishings follow a divine pattern, but the gold and the cloth, the intellectual materials that have to be used in following that pattern, are those already to hand. Each time the gospel crosses a cultural frontier, new issues will arise, first of the "What should I do?" and then of the "How should I think?" category, many never faced by Christians before. Each time the gospel crosses a cultural frontier, a fresh set of intellectual materials is available for the task. The theological workshop never shuts down; its work is never complete.

Theological Development Beyond the West

Our present theological situation is the product of one of the most extraordinary centuries of Christian history. It has been marked by the fastest recession from the Christian faith (by far faster than that brought about by the rise of Islam), coinciding with the most considerable as-

---

[6]Origen, "A Letter from Origen to Gregory," *Ante-Nicene Fathers* (Grand Rapids: Eerdmans, 1978), 4:393-94.

cension to the Christian faith in its history. The former has been centered in Europe, the latter concentrated in Africa and some parts of Asia. In addition, a theological and religious revolution has taken place in Latin America, which one might describe as the delayed impact of the sixteenth century on a continent that seemed to have bypassed both the Protestant and the Catholic Reformations of that century. The result of these extraordinary developments has been the cultural and demographic transformation of the Christian faith, raising the possibility of a theological explosion for which the nearest analogy we have is the theological explosion that took place in the early centuries of the Christian faith brought about by the interaction of the Christian faith with Greek and then with Latin thought. Western Christians are shaped by those centuries of early interaction (and, just in parenthesis, let us note here that the principal early Christian interaction with Latin language and culture took place in Roman Africa; Western theology is an African artifact). The result of the transformative developments of the twentieth century on Christianity is that the twenty-first century will face new theological issues that have little to do with Greek or Latin, and still less to do with the later developments of European and American thought. The issues will arise from the Christian interaction with the cultures and realities of life in Africa and Asia and Latin America.

The chapters that follow illustrate this from every part of the Christian world. For the moment let us notice that this situation is not new in Christian history. Global Christianity is not a product of the twentieth century. One might say that in the twentieth century Christianity reverted to type: that it is the previous five hundred years that were exceptional by linking Christianity so closely to Western culture and history and language. This experience has given Western Christians a somewhat skewed and limited view of the Christian past. When Western Christians talk of the early church, for instance, they are usually thinking of the church in the Roman Empire, since that story is formative for Western Christianity. But much of the early church lay outside the Roman Empire. It is easily forgotten that the emperor of China was studying the Christian Scriptures at almost exactly the time that the king of Northumbria in Northern England was placing the adoption of the Christian way before his council,[7] and that by the seventh century gospel preaching had spread across the whole Eurasian land mass from the Atlantic almost to the Pacific. Much of Asia had a millennium and a half of Christian history before the first Western missionaries reached there, and some parts of Africa have a continuous Christian history far longer than Scotland's. In those early centuries the gospel interacted with cultures other than the Greek and Roman, and theological developments took place in other cultures than these.

Consider, for instance, this second-century Syriac hymn:

A cup of milk was offered to me,
And I drank it in the sweetness of the Lord's kindness
The Son is the cup;
And the Father is he who was milked
And the Holy Spirit is she who milked him.[8]

The worshiping believer takes up the cup and makes contact with the solid humanity of the incarnate Son. But the content of the cup, the sweet and nourishing milk, comes from the Father—and to illustrate it we have the bold image of the Father as milked cow, the source of the nourishment we receive from the Son. But how does the Father's milk come to the believer? The Holy Spirit is the heavenly milkmaid, making available the Father's riches that we receive through knowing the Son. And *ruh*, the Syriac word for spirit, is feminine; so the Holy Spirit is spoken of as "she." Here is a powerful relational model of the Trinity; and I cannot think of anything in second-century Greek theology that puts trinitarian relationships so clearly. Here is theology as poetry reaching a point that theology as metaphysics took much longer to attain; in some respects, as feminist theologians might note, going further than Greek theology ever reached. Some of the greatest Syriac theological writers are poets. While they are aware of the Greek world, their cultural universe is much more complex. They encounter, for instance, Zoroastrian culture, with its cosmic structure of good against

---

[7]The Christian inscription dates the arrival of Alopen and his mission at the court of the second Tang emperor in A.D. 635; King Edwin's council (according to Bede, *Ecclesiastical History*) occurred not long afterward.
[8]Odes of Solomon 19:1-2.

evil and its developed doctrine of resurrection and final judgment. So Syriac theologians such as Ephrem explore the resurrection doctrine more thoroughly than their Greek contemporaries. They also pick up New Testament hints such as the reference to the spirits in prison (1 Pet 3:18-20), offering a basis for a theology of the ancestors. Besides theology as poetry, the Syriac Church offers theology as drama. Ephrem, for instance, more than once develops a dialogue, becoming increasingly strident and bad tempered as it goes on, between Death and Satan, each setting out his claims to superiority. Each claim gives both theological teaching and practical warnings for the Christian life. Finally the choir bursts out, "Blessed is he who has set these cursed slaves against one another, so that we may laugh at them at the last day as they laugh at us." The whole dialogue has displayed Death and Satan rejoicing in their power over humanity. But God in Christ has overthrown their power, setting them against one another. Christian believers, who experience Christ's victory, can laugh at Death and at Satan. And the congregation responds, "Praise to You Son of the Shepherd of All, who has saved His flock."[9]

In the ancient literature of this Asian Christianity with its resilient Arab missionaries, we can trace the experience of a church that had an emperor like Diocletian and knew persecution and suffering, but never had a Constantine, and never knew unchallengeable peace and security. In this respect we may recognize the resemblance to the church in parts of Asia today. It was also a church that, like Asian Christians today, lived amid religious plurality, where Christians had to interact with those of other faiths. Its theology faced issues arising from Chinese, Indian and Buddhist language, culture and religion, and it had to reckon with Islam, not as rival but as ruler. And away in the Nile valley, in a Christian Nubian state in Sudan (the significance of which is only now coming to light), in the Christian kingdom of Axum and on the Ethiopian high plateau, the Christian gospel was making its impact on African life and engaging with the traditional powers of Africa. One of the best ways of preparing for the new age of global theology may be to

---

[9]Ephrem, quoted in Sebastian Brock, *The Harp of the Spirit: Eighteen Poems of Saint Ephrem* (San Bernardino, Calif.: Borgo Press, 1984), pp. 70-73.

develop the study of the history and literature of the former age of
global Christianity. It is the joint inheritance of Western, African and
Asian Christians alike.

The First and Second Ages of World Christianity

In the first age of world Christianity there were Christian communities
across Europe and Asia and deep into Eastern Africa, representing a
multitude of languages and cultures and styles of government—major
constituents such as the Greco-Roman, Coptic, Syriac-speaking and a
host of others from Armenian to Axumite. There were regional centers
of the church, but no single center; no single church approached the
leadership role that Jerusalem had in the early apostolic age, a position
that disappeared in A.D. 70 amid the ruins of Jerusalem itself. But across
this vast and diverse area there was a sense of the community of Christians, of one church dispersed across the world (1 Pet 1:1). Alas, this
first age of global Christianity passed away, and Christian theologians
and Christian politicians must alike bear some responsibility for the
loss of the sense of an intercontinental and crosscultural community of
Christians. In the course of the sixth century the joint heirs of the first
age of world Christianity became strangers to one another, and the
alienation had its origin in the Christian accession to political power.

In general the churches East and West in the Roman and in the
Persian Empire and beyond it saw themselves as a single body. When
Constantine sought to bring the Arian controversy to an end by means
of a council of the whole church, he was seeking a solution to the problem of the unity of the Empire; but he knew that the church extended
beyond the Empire. Among those at the Council of Nicaea were church
leaders from outside Roman territory. But when the great Christological controversies of the fifth century threatened to tear the church in
the Roman Empire apart, no one thought to consult the Christians
beyond the Empire. Imperial domestic policy under successive emperors gave high priority to the unity of the church but thought little of the
possible concern in the matter of the Christians of Iran or Iraq, or of
the Armenians or the Ethiopians.

There are various ways of viewing the Definition of the Council of Chalcedon of A.D. 451. It can be seen as a landmark in the history of Christian doctrine, the culmination of the process of conversion of the Greek past that had begun when those "Greeks" in Antioch put their trust in the Messiah of Israel, calling on the Lord Jesus. It can be seen as a triumph of consensual theologizing, for it represents the agreement of theologians thinking in Greek with those thinking in Latin as to the parameters of Christology, marking out the area of safety, while leaving some room for movement. But alas, it has also to be seen as the prelude to a colossal ecumenical failure. For what followed was the dissolution of the first age of world Christianity. Consensus among the theologians of the cultural sphere that saw the fundamental division of humanity as that between "Greeks" and "barbarians" did not embrace the neighboring believers of the Coptic and Syriac speaking spheres.

The dissolution of world Christianity was not immediate. The root of the trouble was not so much in Chalcedon itself as in the process that followed in the succeeding century whereby successive Christian emperors sought to impose the Chalcedonian Definition, ultimately by force, on the church of the Empire. The resultant split divided the Greek and Latin-speaking Christians of the Empire from those who spoke and thought primarily in Coptic or Syriac. And the connections of Coptic Christianity of Egypt, the stronghold of the heirs of Antony, that rural, vernacular-speaking charismatic who began one of the earliest revival movements in Christian history, ran well beyond the Empire, deep into East Africa. They extended to the Sudanic Christian states of Nubia, and to the Christian kingdom from which the church of Ethiopia derives. And the Syriac-speaking Christians of the Roman Empire were but a fragment of a larger Syriac Christian world whose heart lay in the Persian Empire, with a missionary outreach stretching across Asia.

All Christians acknowledged the full divinity of Christ; all his full humanity. All acknowledged the perfect union of divinity and humanity in the incarnate Christ, but the issue concerning the nature of that union produced an era when theological swearwords such as *Nestorian*, *monophysite* and *Melkite* were hurled at fellow Christians, and theological positions set out in order to accuse others of holding them. Historians have sought in vain to identify any Nestorianism in the surviving records of the Nestorian missionaries in China, but the sense of a world Christian community that transcended all imperial frontiers became submerged. The world church split along linguistic and cultural lines. So bitter was the division that Syriac and Coptic Christians could welcome the Arab occupation of Syria and Egypt as liberation, and accept Islamic rule as preferable to that of oppressive fellow Christians.

The division had two long-lasting effects. First, it produced a separation of the Christians of Europe from those of Asia and Africa, and at a time when the latter were about to come under sustained pressure, making the geographical wedge created by the Arab invasions a virtual sealing off. Monophysite Africa went its own ways. Western Christianity followed a path of its own as it spread, taking with it the culture of the late Roman Empire, among the peoples of the North and West that the Romans called barbarians. Eventually Western Christianity came to think of itself as "Christendom." The term is really another word for "Christianity." But it stands for Christianity on the map, Christianity territorially expressed; it was thought of as almost coterminous with Europe. The effects of this identification were to go deep into the consciousness of Western Christians.

The second long-term effect was that, having once divided Christians along linguistic and cultural lines, it became easier to do so again. By the eleventh century the consensus of Greek and Latin Christianity manifested at Chalcedon had broken down, and the churches of Eastern and Western Europe had drifted acrimoniously apart. As European Christianity spread to the Americas and to enslaved Africans there, a new dimension was added to ethnic and cultural separation within the church, and in later centuries division along cultural lines and cultural isolation within the church were to become commonplace. The New Testament norm of the communion of different cultures in the church, necessary to each other and to the ongoing building of the new temple of the Spirit and the proper functioning of the body of Christ, has been buried very deep.

There is, however, now an opportunity to recover it. The position and the tasks of theology have been transformed by the events which have remade the Christian church in the course of the past century. A second age of world Christianity has dawned, indeed an age of global Christianity, with the faith established in areas that Christians of the earlier world church did not even know existed. Furthermore, movements of peoples, notably from Africa, Asia and Latin America to Europe and North America (a reversal of the process in earlier centuries that brought European peoples into the rest of the world, setting up the present—transient—world order), bring the possibility not just of contact but of communion, fellowship in the body of Christ, between Christians of different cultural and linguistic backgrounds. Like the earlier world Christianity, the new one is multicentric. Mission can begin anywhere and be directed anywhere, and creative intercultural and crosscultural initiatives may arise in Nairobi or São Paulo or Singapore as well as in Chicago. And theological interaction becomes possible on a scale previously inconceivable. There is now the possibility, if not of repairing the great ecumenical failure of the sixth century, at least of making a fresh start.

Just as when the gospel crossed the frontier into the Hellenistic world there was an explosion of theological activity that gave us the great creeds and the beginnings of what one may call classical theology, so the biblical and Christian interaction with the cultures of Africa and Asia has begun to open a whole range of new theological issues and the possibility of fuller and clearer thought on some old ones. Western theology will have much to gain, for it has long been confined by the Enlightenment worldview that it embraced in a particular phase of Western intellectual history. Much of humanity, much of Christian humanity, lives in a larger, more populated universe than the Enlightenment one. As a result Christians face countless situations to which Western theology has no answer, but in which Paul's language about the principalities and powers and Christ's victory over them has deep resonance. We can expect, and rejoice in, a vast expansion of theological activity. The theological workshop is likely to be busier than ever before, its workers more varied in language, culture and outlook. And we have in the great ecumenical failure of the sixth century a warning of what can happen if we close the door on our fellow laborers in God's workshop. The chapters that follow give a glimpse of what the theological age to come may have in store.

For Further Reading

Bediako, Kwame. *Theology and Identity: The Impact of Culture on Second Century Christian Thought and in Modern Africa.* Oxford: Regnum, 1992.

Walls, Andrew. *The Missionary Movement in Christian History: Studies in the Transmission of Faith.* Maryknoll, N.Y.: Orbis, 1996.

————. *The Cross-Cultural Process in Christian History: Studies in the Transmission and Appropriation of Faith.* Maryknoll, N.Y.: Orbis, 2002.

2

THE SIGNIFICANCE OF
THE TRANSLATION PRINCIPLE

Lamin Sanneh

• • •

The Bible in Our Mother Tongue

The Bible in the tongue of the people is a theological first step in the divine instruction of the human race, with the diverse, multiple languages of the world as the appointed and indispensable means God chooses to bring into existence communities of faith. As Adolf Deissmann put it, as the message of God to humanity, the New Testament was written in the simple style of the carpenter's and tentmaker's language, which rendered it suitable to be the book of the peoples of the world.[1] There is no such thing as a church without a language or without the Scriptures. In spite of the barriers of natural separation among us, often reinforced by cultural systems, through the spoken word God remains accessible to us as the bridge that allows the streams of our experience to flow toward a common purpose. God woos us in tones and accents that belong with our primal self-understanding. No one is born an orphan. Similarly, faith is born of a living trust issuing from an encounter with a personal God. On any credible view, Christianity is recognizable only in the embodied idioms and values of the cultures in which we find it, allowing Christians to speak and respond with the facility of the mother tongue and mother-tongue speakers with faith

---

[1] Adolf Deissmann, *The New Testament in the Light of Modern Research: The Haskell Lectures* (New York: Doubleday, 1929), p. 106.

and trust in God's promises. Christianity as a distinctive religion is in principle invested without prejudice or favoritism in the distinctions of national life, and not in spite of those distinctions.

The strife and bloodshed that accompanied Bible translation in the medieval and early modern periods are strikingly and mercifully absent today. Yet even in the darkest hour of persecution in the Middle Ages, the slender flame of interest in the gospel destined for the whole world was tended faithfully, as the story of John Wyclif (1328-1384) sadly makes clear. Condemned as a heretic, forty years after his death his body and bones were exhumed by ecclesiastical order and burned, with instructions for his ashes to be so disposed as to leave no trace of the man. Thomas Fuller (1608-1661), the historian, was moved to make amends for Wyclif's besmirched memory. "Thus this brook (the river Swift) hath conveyed his ashes into Avon; Avon into Severn; Severn into the narrow seas; they into the main ocean. And thus the ashes of Wyclif are the emblem of his doctrine, which now is dispersed all the world over."[2] That is how, as if in filial restitution, the Reformation opened with a clamorous appeal to the vernacular Bible only to subside in inflamed antipathy to popular repercussions of its effects. The premise of Bible translation to the effect that no culture is inherently impermeable or alien, and none ultimately indispensable or exceptional, carries implications for projects of religion, language and culture above and beyond the technical, whatever the inclination of the cultural establishment or of the translators.

We need to be sensitive in interpreting the cultural changes missionaries demanded of converts. The demands of mission have to be set in the milieu of mother-tongue stimulus: attitudes of missionary superiority persisted, but often only by force of habit. Fluent in the vernacular, converts viewed Westernization in the church differently. They recited the creeds but in accents of their own. The polemical tone of the Nicene Creed, with its triumphalist swipe at vanquished heresies, for example, dissolved into chastened prayer of intercession against the powers of the spirit world. The victory of Christ is victory over evil and spiritual

---

[2]Thomas Fuller, quoted in Donald Coggan, *The English Bible* (London: Longmans, Green, 1963), p. 17.

powers, and the creed should be testimony of that rather than of abstract theological advantage. The enemy is not someone else's theology: it is the nemesis of one's own spirit world, and is lodged in the many maladies that afflict body and spirit. With the power of Christ the enemy must be driven out and muzzled. That was how a leader of one of the charismatic movements drew the battle lines of the new spiritual warfare. He argued that, as the active agent, prayer is the "gunpowder" of the movement; the Holy Spirit, as the terror of the powers of evil, the gun; the Bible in the vernacular the ramrod. Spiritual warfare requires spiritual weapons, not a word game. For that reason, the vernacular Scriptures as written oracle were received and digested for spiritual combat. The splits, splinters and divisions prevalent in the new charismatic and Pentecostal movements are largely shaped by the contest for spiritual mastery over witchcraft, spirit possession, the evil eye, the curse, and dreams and dream interpretation, not by the machinery that suppresses heresies. In that spiritual contest the entire charismatic movement in its multifarious factions is at one. Adopted into the framework of the old divination rituals, the Nicene Creed becomes just liturgical fodder to the rules of engagement in this primal reckoning.

We need not go beyond our own doorstep to appreciate the power of the vernacular. A celebrated architect of language himself, Walt Whitman (1819-1892) echoes the primal sentiments of Scripture when he speaks in his *November Boughs* of the translated Bible as the fuel of the creative life. He affirms:

> I've said nothing yet of the Bible as a poetic entity, and of every portion of it. . . . How many ages and generations have brooded and wept and agonized over this book! . . . Translated in all languages, how it has united the diverse world! Not only does it bring us what is clasped within its covers. Of its thousands there is not a verse, not a word, but is thick-studded with human emotion.

The special character of the Bible, Whitman pleads, consists in its "incredible, all-inclusive non-worldliness and dew-scented illiteracy."[3] In

---

[3]Walt Whitman, "The Bible as Poetry," *November Boughs*, in *Complete Poetry and Collected Prose* (New York: Library of America, 1982), pp. 1140-42.

the mother tongue it is the Bible's special power to harmonize the individual and the universal, to blend pithy anecdote and general norm, so that simple parable teems with sublime truth. So much of the Bible is weighed down with tribal matters, so much of it is festooned with the fabric of country speech and with the ripe tones of close-lived experience that we forget that Scripture was designed for the primal ear and heart.

The theological view of language is far more radical in its unqualified welcome of language, any language, as fit for Scripture and faith, than a purely utilitarian view in which languages of scale weigh more heavily in the balance of merit. Before God, all languages are equal as much in their merit as in their demerit, for which reason none has an inbuilt advantage or disadvantage. All languages share in the consequences of fallen human nature, just as by virtue of Bible translation all languages share equally in the benefits of God's intervention in Christ. Scriptural translation is not an exercise in linguistic perfection; it is a willing and attentive inquiry into God's mind and purpose for us. "We never thought," the King James Bible translators declared of their historic translation,

> from the beginning, that we should need to make a new Translation, nor yet to make of a bad one a good one; (for then the imputation of *Sixtus* had been true in some sort, that our people had been fed with gall of dragons instead of wine, with wheal instead of milk;). . . . To that purpose there were many chosen, that were greater in other men's eyes than in their own, and that sought the truth rather than their own praise.[4]

Undeterred by the pitfalls of human fallibility, the biblical writers set to work with the unwavering confidence that their commission was from God. It is in that sense that the Bible is *sui generis*. A focus other than that may produce a technically correct translation, but not the Bible as the heritage of faith, as the Scripture that, in the words of Kepler, "speaks the language of everyman."[5] The translators of the KJV continue:

---

[4]Erroll F. Rhodes and Liana Lupas, eds., *The Translators to the Reader: The Original Preface to the King James Version of 1611 Revisited* (New York: American Bible Society, 1997), p. 54.

[5]Johannes Kepler, quoted in F. E. Manuel, *The Religion of Isaac Newton* (Oxford: Oxford

Therefore the word of God being set forth in *Greek*, becometh hereby like a candle set upon a candlestick, which giveth light to all that are in the house; or like a proclamation sounded forth in the market-place, which most men presently take knowledge of; and therefore that language was fittest to contain the Scriptures, both for the first preachers of the Gospel to appeal unto for witness, and for the learners also of those times to make search and trial by. It is certain, that the translation was not so sound and so perfect, but that it needed in many places correction; and who had been so sufficient for this work as the Apostles or apostolick men? Yet it seemed good to the Holy Ghost and to them to take that which they found . . . rather than by making a new, in that new world and green age of the Church, to expose themselves to many exceptions and cavillations, as though they made a translation to serve their own turn; and therefore bearing witness to themselves, their witness not to be regarded.[6]

Translating Christianity into Culture

Translation is a dynamic process, and in Bible translation the Spirit is the guiding agent of that process—this is as it should be if faith has any meaning at all. Bible translation is invested almost solely in the purpose and outcome for which it is undertaken, and only secondarily in the reputation of the translators. The reception and appropriation of the message has precedence over the means and motives of its transmission. Whether in the West or in the Third World, the consequences of the impact of the translated Bible are of far more significance than the intentions, as history bears evidence. It is for this reason that in their local appropriation, the central acts of faith were adapted to address existential needs. Such was the case with baptism, which was adopted to respond to the issues of rapid social change. Converts saw baptism as affording them the power of being sealed and armed for spiritual warfare, like acquiring a new suit of armor that allowed you to come into safe contact with the invisible teeming world of spirits. Belief in the super-

University Press, 1974), p. 36.
[6]Rhodes and Lupas, *Translators to the Reader*, p. 35.

natural was a prevalent feature of primal societies as it was, indeed, of the worldview of the societies of the Bible, including the Greek. Translation bypassed Europe's Enlightenment prerequisites to connect with the preindustrial sensibilities of hinterland populations, thereby allowing the Bible to speak with authority in its own original voice. There would have to be interpretation and hermeneutics, but that would be a matter of local cultural engagement, not that of the wordplay and mind experiment associated with individual effort. In its own sphere Bible translation opened up different and multiple ways of receiving Scripture and of being religious, including community-based experience.

Missionary Bible translation often reckoned with the fact that translation would not spare Enlightenment assumptions and motives, and would change the course of the Christian movement. Resistance or encouragement of translation had a differential result in terms of the marked effects it produced on local views. Encouragement served the goal of authentic discipleship, while resistance inhibited local talent, including the talent for religion.

The classical missionary doctrine that commerce, civilization and Christianity went together assumed that cultural diffusion was the appropriate way to establish the church, that converts were primarily cultural adherents and believers only by inference. Certain desirable cultural traits defined a gentleman—and a lady—as much as they did a Christian. Mission could, therefore, impose a cultural template on local populations in the interests of "normative Christianity" and its highbrow scruples. All that left converts falling well short of the Christian qualification, somewhat in the manner of the god-fearing Gentiles of the Jewish Diaspora. Bible translation struck at that root classical doctrine by adopting the non-Western frame as a necessary and sufficient basis of the transmission of the gospel. Non-European peoples were thereby given a charter of full membership, a situation reminiscent of its New Testament counterpart. As Peter assured his incredulous and browbeaten Gentile audience: "Once you were not a people but now you are God's people" (1 Pet 2:10). Contrary to custom and to millennia of hallowed tradition, Gentiles too, Peter challenged, are a chosen race, a royal priesthood, thanks to the God who called them out of darkness into his wonderful light. The fact is that uniformity of belief and culture was not what the Gentile breakthrough was about. Christianity as a dynamic translation movement looked to open frontiers, and this idea received greater recognition in the modern period than at any other time in the church's history.

In its most creative phases, Christianity has been an intercultural reality, and its doctrinal system remained plausible at all because of the rich variety of cultures upon which the church drew. Yet this is not the same as saying that pluralism received unvarying support by church officials, many of whom were in fact inclined to wage war against vernacular innovation. What can be said with confidence, even if it has not been said consistently enough, is that the expansion of Christianity had a lasting effect on renewal movements at the local level. That historical theme of renewal is what I propose to explore next.

This approach has two consequences for mission. First, Christian expansion was not at the expense of the authentic values of culture—it was a winnowing and not an iconoclastic movement. Cultural features that had been weakening by the time of the Christian encounter, either because of a lack of necessary stimulus or because of natural exhaustion, received the coup de grâce. Other elements worth preserving and capable of combining with the tide of Christian advance acquired a vigorous boost. Second, intercultural experience helped check the tendency toward cultural idolatry by promoting all cultures as fundamentally equal in the plan of divine providence. Adolf Harnack referred to it as the new "philosophy of religion." Whatever their proximity or disadvantage with respect to notions of chosenness, no people could be denied a place in the life of God through Jesus Christ, for the conscience was capable of reflecting the light of God (Rom 2:14-15). It was an insight based on faith in Christ and was at once affirming and challenging, evocative of "the kindness of God" and of "the severity of God."

Christianity translated naturally into the terms of all cultures, a facility that left the religion at risk of a cultural makeover. In the Roman Empire, for example, Christianity was subject precisely to that outcome. In its successful assimilation, the religion was defended more as a "Greek" philosophy than as the way of Jesus. In the early missionary literature the reader is struck by the lack of local detail and color, and by an unswerving dedication to abstract and dogmatic questions. This was particularly the case in places that had come under Roman imperial influence. When Christianity came into the ascendancy, it fostered the establishment of Latin in the West and Greek in the East, a distinction that had little to do with theological differences. The fact that Latin and Greek Christianity ended in a split says more about the force of culture than about the core claims of the gospel. As has been rightly remarked, "The effect of the church's use of the official languages of the empire was to ensure the survival of these long after the empire itself was only a memory."[7] Europe owed a good deal of its cultural cohesion to the church after the shock of the collapse of the empire in A.D. 410. Yet we have reason to wonder whether the triumph of Latin Christianity was at the price of suppression of vernacular variety.

The church provided the impetus behind the standardization of ecclesiastical practice and the institution of a common liturgy, and together these acted to suppress the vernacular in many places. Yet the comparative thinness of local details in the accounts was not because believers suspended all traffic with their culture, but because the stalwarts of doctrine chose to ignore or deprecate it. By contrast, modern missionaries were often more forthcoming, though not necessarily more enlightened, on the subject of cultural appropriation.

Christianity was a stimulus on the vernacular. In its formal, organized character, however, official Christianity tried to impose uniform rules that conflicted with vernacular needs. What is particularly interesting in this sphere is that, in spite of concerted official attempts, Christian vitality tapped into vernacular springs. The decision to "reform" local adaptation was often counterproductive. Yet we should not confuse the bureaucratic instrument with the cultural basis of religious innovation. It was not a case of "charisma" in need of "routinization," but of the concrete embodiment of faith in its relevant cultural form.

---

[7]W. H. C. Frend, *The Rise of Christianity* (Philadelphia: Fortress, 1984), p. 560.

Besides, reform is not restricted to bureaucratization. The domestication of the gospel involves, at one level, neutralizing its intrusive foreign impetus. Religion can bring about change by the influence it exerts rather than only by the instruments it controls.

Translation is a fundamental reconstruction of the message and an implicit rejection of imposition and uniformity. Furthermore, translation introduces a dynamic, even an ambiguous, ferment into questions of the essence of the religion. Whatever the answer to the question of the essence of Christianity, there is no way around the fact that the religion must adopt the cultural forms of its environment. It is only in the "feedback" of cultural response that we know when and how the message has struck home. In that event, the originating assumptions of missionary transmission were challenged and even overturned by the force of the new experience. Translation helped to bring us to new ways of viewing the gospel, commencing a process of rethinking that had an impact on both the personal and the cultural spheres. This locates the message in the specific and particular encounter with contiguous cultural systems, although it is important to stress that the encounter still leaves culture subordinate to God's truth. The fundamental principle of faith decision was the need for God's revelation in Jesus Christ to be grounded in the life and experience of believers in relation to the sources of their identity. As the book of Proverbs puts it, "The spirit of man is the candle of the LORD" (Prov 20:27 KJV), illuminating the place of habitation as God's own.

The ambiguous relation of Christianity to culture hinges on the necessity for the message to assume the specific terms of its context, on the one hand, and, on the other hand, the equal necessity to inveigh against cultural calcification. As a historical movement Christianity is parallel to culture, but in its truth claims it is not exactly proportionate to culture. The religion is not culture, but it is not other than culture.

The gospel is capable of transcending the cultural inhibitions of the translator and taking root in fresh soil, a piece of transplanting that will challenge the presuppositions of the translator. This is a critical position that Christians reached by being plunged willy-nilly into the world of translation. Any sensitive translator will be awakened to the realiza-

tion that a certain judgment is being reserved for the originating culture. New paradigms and vastly different presuppositions will rise to
replace privileged ideas and the certainties they enshrined. That can be
unsettling in the extreme, and only a supremely saintly missionary
would not invoke economic or political sanctions where this was possible to try to compensate for the loss of power entailed in this intercultural shift.

Yet, however strongly one might wish to resist the consequences of
translation, little can be done to stop the repercussions from spreading.
When one translates, it is like pulling the trigger of a loaded gun: the
translator cannot recall the hurtling bullet. Translation thus activates a
process that will supersede the original intention of the translator.
Mainly for this reason we need to distinguish between the motive of
mission and the consequences, between the "trigger," so to speak, and
the "bullet." We should distinguish between missionary intentions and
their complex bundle of cultural, political and economic considerations,
on the one hand, and, on the other hand, missionary methods and
practices in the development and deployment of the vernacular. It
would be wrong to set up too rigid a division between these two aspects, yet a distinction, however tentative, there must be in order to
make for greater clarity in the material.

When we consider the transformation that took place in the world
of Hellenism, we see that as Christianity penetrated into the culture it
succeeded in establishing Hellenistic cultural paradigms as a condition of the religion's own identity. We need to explore the philosophical and religious basis of this transformation and suggest how eventually it elicited movements to restrict the extension of Hellenistic ideas
and values to new societies that were being Christianized. As the
missionary range grew to embrace non-Greeks, the achievement of
Christian Hellenism—specifically, the seminal contribution of early
Greek converts and theologians such as Justin Martyr, Origen, Athenagoras, Clement of Alexandria and Cyprian of Carthage—inspired
corresponding efforts at intellectual innovation in new and different
settings. If Christ could be at home in Greek philosophy and thereby
reinvigorate the ideas and values of a pagan dispensation, there could

be no bar to his performing a comparable role among other peoples in other times. To deny that was to deny that Christ had no intrinsic merit except the merit he acquired in Greek, which was not what the Greek fathers said. Even at that level, translation did have the compelling, consistent logic of open and evenhanded affirmation. The jump from a Torah-bearing Jewish Jesus to a Lyceum-adopted Greek Christ is no more implausible than the jump to the vernacular Jesus of the hinterland provinces of Mesopotamia and the Nile.

The Contemporary Phase

The rapid and unprecedented expansion of Christianity from the second half of the twentieth century has thrown into high relief the impact of Bible translation on emerging societies beyond the West. The suddenness and scope of the expansion, however, may have concealed an acute theological lesson. Standard theological models of Christianity have presented it as a closed-circuit organism whose main pathways of communication have been laid in deep-cut, sealed channels. Faced with this imposing, immobile system, the task of the theologian was seen as codifying the religion, mapping the contours of its form and the lineaments of its function, predicting and prescribing for changes in behavior, preventing foreign matter from entering it, repairing deviations and aberrations, fixing the qualities that alone define—and do not define—the religion, and generalizing about how God works in the world. In this analogy, translation spawns syncretism, sects, heresy and apostasy, which are to Christianity what aberration, mutation, infection and suicide are to a mutable organism. The mind of the theologian mirrors the neurological design of a living organism: the mind is wired to resonate with the religion's built-in circuitry. This organic model of Christianity has been the most powerful and the most influential so far, especially because its promoters have had monopoly of the academy and the printed page. Scholars of many different stripes have tinkered with it at its various points, but few have questioned its central assumption that the science of Christianity is neurological in nature, universal in design and normative by intention.

Yet it is clear by now that the pace and scale of Bible translation have shown a far different reality. Translation is evidence that Christianity's neurological center is in flux, that its vocabulary is growing and changing, that historical experience has perspective-altering power, that the allotment of "neurons" continues because "neurogenesis" is a living process rather than a relic of evolution, that foreign influence may lodge in the system like oxygen in the bloodstream, and that Christianity's "localizationism" in the frontal lobe of establishment Christianity has shifted to the central cortex of world Christianity, where new and expanded tasks have stimulated tolerance and diversity in the religion. Translation has shifted the "genetic determinism" of Western Christianity by encrypting the religion with the most diverse cultural chromosomes of other societies. Old school theology appears as a relic in this environment, which may explain its reported decline in its once hallowed academic strongholds.

Where once the old theology adhered gallantly to etymological diagnosis and exegetical prescription, translation, by contrast, has embraced a mindset that faith need not be a clone to be genuine, that new idioms are not stray dialects, that God's intervention in the Word made flesh is ground for embracing all flesh—and the words for it—as clean. The translated Scripture is the charter of lived Christian experience, and mission the church's dynamic pathway. To tell Christians, for example, that "the Faith is Europe and Europe is the Faith," as Hilaire Belloc said, is to tell them that the West and the unmentionable others cannot change.[8] Bible translation, in contrast, is intelligent design for the historical human dilemma in its specific character, and theological science cannot discount it as mere accident. In a speech on the occasion of the bicentenary of the British and Foreign Bible Society in 2004, Archbishop Rowan Williams challenged the church to face the implications of Bible translation: "If scripture can be 'recreated' in different languages, the humanity of the saviour who speaks in scripture must be an extraordinary humanity, a unique humanity. . . . Every language and culture [have in them] a sort of 'homing in-

---

[8]Hilaire Belloc, *Europe and the Faith* (New York: Paulist, 1920), p. viii.

stinct' for God—deeply buried by the sin and corruption that affects all cultures, yet still there, a sleeping beauty to be revived by the word of Christ" in its specific vernacular idiom.[9]

Conclusion

To summarize the main arguments so far:

- Bible translation commences with the need to bring the gospel into the terms of familiarity, and that process brings the translation enterprise into alignment with field method and experience.

- Pitfalls are unavoidable in trying to master the vernacular, including the adoption of terms and concepts that are strange to the translator. This shows the important need for an intimate grasp of vernacular usage and concepts and familiarity with local usage.

- Translation may make commonplace passages of Scripture come alive, and also stimulate indigenous religious and cultural renewal.

- For the purposes of scriptural translation, language may serve an instrumental function and be contextual in character, with Christian mission acting to strengthen vernacular languages in their particularity and enormous complexity. Such confidence in the vernacular has encouraged the role of recipient cultures as decisive arbiters of the appropriation of the message.

- The internal developments that generally follow from the promotion of the vernacular have included the antielitist popular impulse of common usage, the advantage for society of the open and public nature of religious faith and organization, the premium that Bible translation places on pluralism in language and culture, and the political ramifications of the importance Christians attach to free and equal access to the things of God.

---

[9]Archbishop Rowan Williams, foreword to *Sowing the Word: The Cultural Impact of the British and Foreign Bible Society, 1804-2004*, ed. Stephen Batalden, Kathleen Cann and John Dean (Sheffield, U.K.: Sheffield Phoenix Press, 2004), p. x. First presented at the "Service to Celebrate the Bicentenary of the British and Foreign Bible Society," St. Paul's Cathedral, March 8, 2004.

This way of understanding the matter implies a reappraisal of the issue of the Western encounter with other cultures, which may partly be resolved by taking into account vernacular primacy in translation. In this light, mission is fundamentally consistent with indigenous cultural integrity, especially when we view mission as the *missio Dei*. There is a radical pluralism associated with vernacular translation wherein all languages and cultures are in principle equal in expressing the word of God. In this regard, the *sola scriptura* biblicism of evangelical Protestantism, inherited from the Reformers, relegated Western theological commentaries to a peripheral place in translation, thus suppressing an important source of the diffusion of Western cultural and intellectual values. By that procedure, translation acted to shield indigenous cultures from Western intellectual domination. Equally important, the stress on the Bible as alone sufficient to effect God's purpose conferred on the vernacular an autonomous, consecrated status as the medium of God's Word, a consecration often more in tune with indigenous attitudes toward language than the Enlightenment attitudes toward religion and culture.

Two general ideas may be highlighted in this description:

- The first is the inclusive principle whereby no culture is excluded from the Christian dispensation or even judged solely or ultimately by Western cultural criteria.

- The second is the ethical principle of change as a check on cultural chauvinism. Both of these ideas are rooted in missionary teaching of God's universal truth as that was revealed in Jesus Christ, with the need and duty to work out this fact in the mother-tongue medium rather than in cosmopolitan forms of cultural hegemony.

The analogy of the *logos* concept may be helpful in increasing our understanding of the idea launched in Bible translation that any and all languages may legitimately be adopted for God's Word, a step that allowed missionaries and local agents to collaborate, if sometimes unevenly, in the mission of the church. Bible translation redirected the course of mission history toward primary language populations to place them at the center of the Christian movement, with missionaries as only aiding and abetting the process. The changes and directions indicated by Christianity's expansion and development in multicultural idioms suggest not only a geographical shift but also a mental shift of the religion's internal contours. In spite of their eye-catching prominence, the stationary institutions of mission are a misleading indication of Christianity's immense potential in Bible translation, showing the need for a change of perspective to comprehend the religion's worldwide appeal. Missionary personnel who lived long enough among the people understood something of Christianity's unsuspecting affinity with the mother tongues of new converts, and that discovery amounted to self-canceling in the outcome of a vernacular-derived church. The significance of Bible translation lies in its outcome, and not simply in its originating agents.

For Further Reading

Robert, Dana L. *Christian Mission: How Christianity Became a World Religion.* Malden, Mass.: Wiley-Blackwell, 2009.

Sanneh, Lamin O. *Translating the Message: The Missionary Impact on Culture.* Maryknoll, N.Y.: Orbis, 1989.

———. *Religion and the Variety of Culture: A Study in Origin and Practice.* Valley Forge, Penn.: Trinity Press International, 1996.

———. *Disciples of All Nations: Pillars of World Christianity.* New York: Oxford University Press, 2007.

Venuti, Lawrence, ed. *The Translation Studies Reader.* 2nd ed. New York: Routledge, 2004.

3

THE CHALLENGE OF
GLOBAL HERMENEUTICS

Gene L. Green

• • •

Global theologians and biblical scholars are very aware that the place from which they interpret Scripture and carry out the theological task is not that of Western theologians or interpreters. Interpreters who are members of minority groups in the West realize that the same is true for them. The questions that have conditioned Western discourse about the Bible and society are different than those germane to their communities. Craig Blomberg has suggested that asking new questions that are not sourced from Western culture may be what the "globalization of biblical interpretation" is all about. "It is perhaps best," he muses, "to think of the globalization of biblical interpretation as the process either of asking questions of a biblical passage which are not traditionally asked within a particular interpretive community or of allowing new answers, more supportive of the world's oppressed, to emerge from old questions out of a more careful exegesis of the text itself."[1] Many Majority World biblical scholars and theologians would concur.

Western education and literature have not tackled the pressing questions surrounding interpreters living in contexts where poverty and the oppression of the poor and women are dominant features. Asian Christians ask questions about the faith in a pluralist culture, African theo-

---

[1]Craig Blomberg, "The Globalization of Biblical Interpretation. A Test Case—John 3–4," *Bulletin of Biblical Research* 5 (1995): 2-3.

logians grapple with the relationship between Christianity and African traditional religions, and Palestinian and Native North American theologians have deep concerns about land. Reading from their place involves asking new questions that find little or no expression in the received texts from the West. In discussing liberation theology, René Padilla asks, "My question is not: How do I respond to Liberation Theology in order to demonstrate its faults and inconsistencies? Rather it is: How do I articulate my faith in the same context of poverty, repression and injustice from which Liberation Theology has emerged?"[2] Both the Latin American Theological Fellowship, which Padilla helped establish, and Gustavo Gutiérrez, author of *A Theology of Liberation*, interpret Scripture in places where the rich held the land and advanced economically over the broken poor who labored for subsistence wages.[3] Elsa Tamez wrote her brief commentary titled *The Scandalous Message of James*, in which she read from that Latin American situation and highlighted the dominance of the problem of oppression and poverty in that epistle.[4]

Along similar lines the evangelical Old Testament scholar Yohanna Katanacho wrote a theology of the land from his perspective as a Palestinian Christian. In this work he witnesses how North American interpretations of the theology of the land have contributed to the marginalization and oppression of his people. Katanacho stands at the intersection of interpretation and social location as he examines the biblical teaching on *Haaretz*, "the Land," and concludes, "The biblical data demonstrates that the concept of the borders of Haaretz was fluid since its inception and that God wanted to reach to the ends of the earth."[5] Katanacho asks an old question anew and looks at the biblical evidence through a unique sociopolitical lens. His article presents a theology firmly rooted in Scripture that challenges dominant dispensa-

---

[2]René Padilla, *El Evangelio Hoy* (Buenos Aires: Certeza, 1975), p. 59.
[3]Gustavo Gutiérrez, *A Theology of Liberation: History, Politics, and Salvation* (Maryknoll, N.Y.: Orbis, 1988).
[4]Elsa Tamez, *The Scandalous Message of James: Faith Without Works Is Dead* (Maryknoll, N.Y.: Orbis, 2002).
[5]Yohanna Katanacho, "Christ Is the Owner of Haaretz," *Christian Scholar's Review* 34 (2005): 425-41.

tionalist perspectives on his land. Global biblical scholars provide us all with needed interpretive revisions and reformation.

Kevin Vanhoozer summarizes these global engagements as the "turn to context."[6] The characteristic feature of global biblical interpretation and theology is the unyielding commitment to understand the faith from and to a particular social context, always with self-awareness of the interpreter's place and a celebration of the fact that the faith is translatable into the languages of the world.[7] What occurs at the level of Bible translation also happens in the interpretation of Scripture and the development of Christian theology. The church in the Majority World has become a "four self church" engaged in a macroreformation. Justo González observes that

> when mission theoreticians in past decades spoke of the "three selfs" as a goal for younger churches, they included self-support, self-govern-ment, and self-propagation. They did not envision self-interpretation or self-theologizing. They expected theology to continue being what it was, for the meaning of the gospel was fully understood by the sending churches, and all that the younger ones had to do was continue pro-claiming the same message.[8]

And as the Majority World church self-theologizes, the attention turns to the meaning of the gospel in relationship to its context. Ken Gnana-kan and Sunand Sumithra seek a methodology that has "a sensitivity to the context that will be expressed in attempts to theologize relevantly."[9]

Some Western interpreters worry that such approaches may devolve into a contextualism that issues in relativism and a shifting pluralism. In some quarters this has occurred where "reading from this place"

---

[6]Kevin J. Vanhoozer, "'One Rule to Rule Them All?' Theological Method in an Era of World Christianity," in *Globalizing Theology: Belief and Practice in an Era of World Christianity*, ed. Craig Ott and Harold A. Netland (Grand Rapids: Baker Academic, 2006), p. 93.

[7]Lamin Sanneh, *Translating the Message: The Missionary Impact on Culture* (Maryknoll, N.Y.: Orbis, 2009).

[8]Justo L. González, *Mañana: Christian Theology from a Hispanic Perspective* (Nashville: Abing-don, 1990), p. 49.

[9]Ken Gnanakan and Sunand Sumithra, "Theology, Theologization and the Theologian," in *Biblical Theology in Asia*, ed. Ken Gnanakan (Bangalore: Theological Book Trust, 1995), p. 43.

means subsuming Scripture entirely to context. But Majority World theologians principally dialogue with context in concert with a high view of Scripture. The shift is not, *in most quarters*, to pluralism and uncommitted relativism, but to reflections that take seriously how God still speaks to us in our place through his Word. They long for an *engaged* faith, but not a faith devoid of substance beyond the issue of the moment. This is especially true of evangelical global and ethnic minority interpretation. Shoki Coe argues that doing theology from a historical context does not promote a "chameleon theology" but a truly catholic theology patterned on the incarnation: "the Son of God was incarnated within a specific human history and culture through which grace has been made available to all."[10] The Latin American Theological Fellowship expresses this reflex well: the Bible's "divine character makes it the supreme tribunal for doctrine and conduct. Its human character demands of us the constant re-reading and contextualization necessary for the diverse generations of disciples."[11] While upholding the normative role of Scripture, Majority World interpreters hear its prophetic voice speaking into their world.

But the varied Majority World readings also speak to us, as K. K. Yeo remarks, about "the limitations of our present knowledge." We currently have an "eschatological reservation" that reminds us that knowing is partial, or, as he says, "complete knowledge of the truth cannot be obtained." Yet there is hope as we lean toward the *telos* amid our varied cultural engagements and readings. "The ambiguities and uncertainties of our culturally-conditioned and religiously-relative historicities are partially clarified and expanded through the process of global interpretation."[12] So we read together with hope for a more com-

---

[10]John Parratt, ed., *An Introduction to Third World Theologies* (Cambridge: Cambridge University Press, 2004), p. 9; Shoki Coe, "Contextualization as the Way Toward Reform," in *Asian Christian Theology: Emerging Themes*, ed. Douglas J. Elwood (Philadelphia: Westminster, 1980), pp. 48-55.

[11]CLADE IV Declaration, May 2006, Fraternidad Teológica Latinoamericana, www.ftl-al. org/index.php?option=com_content&view=article&id=130&Itemid=71.

[12]K. K. Yeo, "Culture and Intersubjectivity as Criteria for Negotiating Meanings in Cross-Cultural Interpretations," in *The Meanings We Choose: Hermeneutical Ethics, Indeterminacy and the Conflict of Interpretations*, ed. Charles H. Cosgrove (Edinburgh: T & T Clark, 2004), pp. 99-100.

plete understanding of the faith in the present, which anticipates the full revelation on Christ's advent: "we shall know fully, even as we are fully known" (1 Cor 13:12, pluralized). Plurality in reading means that we must gather to read as a global Christian community, which, this side of the *eschaton*, requires humility instead of the *hubris* that regards one's own point of view as the only point of view.

But the role of context in interpretation goes beyond seeing things we would not otherwise see, asking questions we would not otherwise ask, and theologizing along lines we would not otherwise explore. The "turn to context" has meant developing *approaches* to interpretation that locate contextual considerations in a different place than they have traditionally occupied in the West. If Western theological reflection has been dominated by the quest for objectivity due to its roots in the Enlightenment, Majority World theologians take approaches to interpretation that favor intersubjectivity and engagement. The global theological community is not in the main modernist and foundationalist, but acknowledges contextuality to greater or lesser degrees. What is new, says Parratt, "is a dynamic search for self-identity, an identity which takes seriously the traditions and cultures in which it is located, but at the same time seeks to address the social world in which Christians now live."[13] Tamez expresses this Latin American longing: "When we look for lights to illuminate a miserable present, objectivity is impossible." Their experience is like "living under a sky without stars. 'Absence,' with its list of synonyms— lack, privation, omission, estrangement, separation, departure, abandonment, exclusion, withdrawal, desertion—seems to me to be the word to define this reality."[14] The question they ask is: How do we interpret in our places that cry for involvement instead of disinterested detachment?

An early movement toward self-conscious contextual reading was liberation theology. Gustavo Gutiérrez, a Peruvian priest living among

---

[13]Parratt, *Introduction to Third World Theologies*, pp. 7-8.
[14]Elsa Tamez, "Reading the Bible Under a Sky Without Stars," in *The Bible in a World Context: An Experiment in Contextual Hermeneutics*, ed. Walter Dietrich and Ulrich Luz (Grand Rapids and Cambridge: Eerdmans, 2002), pp. 9, 4.

the poor, penned the seminal expression of liberation theology. He witnessed "the irruption of the poor" and understood poverty as "institutionalized violence," which stood alongside the "violence of terrorism and repression."[15] Out of that context he redefined the *theological* task as "critical reflection on praxis in light of the word of God." The first act of theology is *praxis*, liberating engagement with the issues of poverty and oppression, and *then* comes "critical reflection," which is done "in light of the word of God." As he states, "Theology is reflection, a critical attitude. Theology *follows*; it is the second step" that "arises only at sundown."[16] Critical reflection on *praxis* in light of the Word of God then informs further *praxis*. The theological task is not simply to develop a set of abstract propositions, nor is it merely to promote social justice. One begins with "Christian praxis (commitment and prayer)," oriented by the life of the church, but the theological task does not end there since critical reflection is not dispensable. Theology joins with context in this dialogue with "the prevailing culture."[17]

Latin American evangelical theologians did not fully embrace this new way of doing theology since they saw in Gutiérrez's approach a subordination of the Word of God and an absence of evangelical proclamation.[18] But they shared a commitment to *praxis* as an essential component of the theological task. The language used was *misión integral*, which gave Scripture primacy but understood that true theology embraced both *praxis* and proclamation. They affirmed that the *euangelion* did not come in Word alone but in Word and deed, a view that issued in the Lausanne Covenant's affirmation on "Christian Social Responsibility."[19] They understood that one could not do theology from

---

[15]Gutiérrez, *Theology of Liberation*, pp. xx-xxi.
[16]Ibid., p. 11.
[17]Ibid., pp. xxxiv-xxxv.
[18]See the discussions in Samuel Escobar, et al., "A Latin American Critique of Latin American Theology," *Evangelical Review of Theology* 7 (1983): 57-62; Emilio A. Nuñez, *Teología de la Liberación* (Miami: Caribe, 1986), pp. 125-61; Samuel Escobar, *La Fe Evangélica y las Teologías de la Liberación* (El Paso, Tex.: Casa Bautista, 1987), pp. 132-57.
[19]René Padilla, "Evangelism and the World," and Samuel Escobar, "Evangelism and Man's Search for Freedom, Justice and Fulfillment," in *Let the Earth Hear His Voice: International Congress on World Evangelization, Lausanne, Switzerland*, ed. J. D. Douglas (Minneapolis: World Wide Publications, 1975), pp. 116-45, 303-26.

the balcony but only down on the road.[20] Engagement with the social context was not secondary for them, but they defined its place in the theological task differently than had Gutiérrez.

The hermeneutical approaches that map the relationship between the biblical text and the social context are varied. Some Western interpreters who have read only a small subset of Majority World theologies have dismissed the whole hermeneutical enterprise because some voices pilloried the faith by favoring context at the expense of Scripture. Evangelicals in the Majority World would share the concern about approaches that subordinate Scripture. At the same time, there are shared contextual commitments across the theological spectrum, however diverse the approaches.

While contextual considerations provide the framework for undertaking the interpretive task for many, others look to the context as another text to be read that provides source material for theology. As Parratt notes, "Theology . . . also implies a way of looking at the world, bringing to the task something of one's own historical and cultural experience."[21] If the goal of theology is engagement with one's culture, then understanding the complexities of one's place becomes an essential theological concern. In discussing an inculturation hermeneutic, Justin Ukpong focuses not only on the biblical text and its context but also on interpreters and their context. His hermeneutic attends to the "'reader-in-context,' that is, [the] reader who *consciously* takes his/her socio-cultural context as a point of departure in the reading, and who is part and parcel of the Christian community whose world-view and life experience he/she shares." On this understanding, the context of the reader becomes the "*subject* of interpretation."[22] The presupposition is that no exegesis can be done from a universal perspective. The interpreter perceives from somewhere and therefore cannot be contextually detached. Analysis of the interpreter's context "enables him/her to be aware of the influences that work on him/her as he/she goes about

---

[20]John A. Mackay, *A Preface to Christian Theology* (New York: Macmillan, 1941), pp. 27-54.
[21]Parratt, *Introduction to Third World Theologies*, p. 9.
[22]Justin S. Ukpong, "Rereading the Bible with African Eyes: Inculturation and Hermeneutics," *Journal of Theology for Southern Africa* 91 (1995): 5.

reading the text and to utilize them positively and thus exercise control over them." The goal is "understanding the text in a contemporary setting."[23] In this interaction between the ancient text in its context and the interpreter in contemporary context we find meaning. Meaning is not simply about the past. "Rather it is seen as a function of the interaction of the contemporary context with the text and its context," says Ukpong. Both "play an important role in the production of meaning."[24]

This interpretive move brings us into the large swells of Majority World hermeneutics. On the one hand, we see the situatedness of the interpretive communities and the longing to hear God speak to them. On the other hand, the concern arises that reading from a place may dissolve all sense of hearing "from beyond," as Thiselton says.[25] Reading cannot become a mere projection of self or self-discovery, as evangelical interpreters in the Majority World recognize. They reject a relativism that would acknowledge every viewpoint as true. On the other hand, they understand that we meet the horizon of Scripture along our varied cultural horizons. In this sense evangelical Majority World interpreters affirm that all theology is contextual, while embracing Scripture's transcendent revelation. They refuse to accept the supposed cultural detachment that has characterized Western reading strategies.

Majority World theologies have developed fresh expressions of the faith via reading the biblical text from within a self-conscious social context. For example, African theologians have understood Jesus in ways that resonate with traditional concepts modified in light of Scripture. African views of life turn some to regard Jesus as the Life-Giver, an easy move due to the way John 14:6 identifies him as "the life." The biblical understanding of Jesus as Mediator, as in Hebrews, resonates with African views on mediation and the place of ancestors as media-

---

[23]Ibid., pp. 7, 9. Ukpong's basic cultural assumptions from African cultures are the unitive view of reality as opposed to dualism; "the divine origin of the universe and the interconnectedness of God, humanity, and the cosmos"; "the sense of community," expressed by the affirmation *"cognato ergo sum* (I am related by blood/I belong to a family, therefore I exist)"; and an "emphasis on the concrete rather than on the abstract" (ibid., p. 9).

[24]Ibid., p. 10.

[25]Anthony C. Thiselton, *New Horizons in Hermeneutics: The Theory and Practice of Transforming Biblical Reading* (Grand Rapids: Zondervan, 1992), p. 550.

tors. Jesus then becomes the Ancestor.[26] This inculturation hermeneutic has found wide acceptance, so that in India, Jesus may be viewed as a Dalit,[27] and in First Nations theology, God is primarily known as Creator, resonating with the traditional indigenous concept of God.

In an inculturation hermeneutic, or translation hermeneutic,[28] understanding God's providence through time and culture leads many to recognize greater or lesser continuity between cultural traditions and God's revelation in Scripture, similar to Paul's approach to the Athenians in Acts 17:16-34.[29] The process also follows New Testament authors who utilized concepts from the Roman religion and the imperial cult to describe God the Father and Christ. These concepts were modified so that God, not Zeus, was the true divine Benefactor, and Jesus, not Caesar, was known as the unique Lord and Savior. Kwame Bediako patterns his approach to African theology on the way some church fathers adapted the gospel in the Roman world.[30] To be sure, when inculturation loses its moorings in Scripture, it may dissolve into a relativistic sea. But for most in the Majority World, and for all evangelicals engaged in these new hermeneutic developments, Scripture holds the central place.

A corollary to Ukpong's inculturation hermeneutic is the affirmation that the meaning of a text is not monolithic but multiplex. The goal is not simply the recovery of history but the actualization of "the theologi-

---

[26]See Kwame Bediako, *Christianity in Africa: The Renewal of a Non-Western Religion* (Edinburgh: Edinburgh University Press; Maryknoll, N.Y.: Orbis, 1995), pp. 210-33; Diane B. Stinton, *Jesus of Africa: Voices of Contemporary African Christology* (Maryknoll, N.Y.: Orbis, 2004), pp. 109-42. As the Ancestor, he is the head of both the living and the dead, since community is not broken at death. He leads an exemplary life and becomes the moral guide. An ancestor gives the community its identity as does Christ the Ancestor. The concept also becomes modified since ancestors are of only one tribe.

[27]Arvind P. Nirmal, *A Reader in Dalit Theology* (Madras: Gurukul Lutheran Theological College & Research Institute, 1991); Arvind P. Nirmal, "Towards a Christian Dalit Theology," *Asia Journal of Theology* 6 (1992): 306-9; Peniel Rajkumar, *Dalit Theology and Dalit Liberation: Problems, Paradigms and Possibilities* (Farnham, U.K.: Ashgate, 2010), pp. 115-26.

[28]On the language of contextualization, inculturation and translation, see T. D. Gener, "Contextualization," in *Global Dictionary of Theology*, ed. William A. Dyrness and Veli-Matti Kärkkäinen (Downers Grove, Ill.: IVP Academic; Nottingham, U.K.: Inter-Varsity Press, 2008), pp. 192-96.

[29]Kwame Bediako, *Jesus and the Gospel in Africa* (Maryknoll, N.Y.: Orbis, 2005), pp. 54-56.

[30]Kwame Bediako, *Theology and Identity: The Impact of Culture Upon Christian Thought in the Second Century and in Modern Africa* (Oxford: Regnum, 1999).

cal meaning of the text in the contemporary context." For that reason, "the biblical text is seen as plurivalent [*sic*] that is, capable of yielding many different but valid meanings depending on the point of departure of reading it."[31] For Ukpong this does not mean that anything goes in interpretation since the text is read as part of the whole of Scripture and is constrained by the theology of the Bible.[32] His hermeneutical viewpoint is that all meaning is interpreted meaning because no reader can be co-present with the original communicative event. At the same time, he understands that the canon constrains contextual reading.

Global interpreters do not view this as abandoning the biblical text but as recognizing that interpretation always involves hermeneutics, however much we may want to make method the king of all hills. Meaning is only known and is only useful if it has efficacy for one's community and our world. They regard the notion of disinvolved interpretation as a quixotic quest with little hope of true success. Even exegetes are culturally involved. Real readers are not "neutral and disinterested" but self-aware and forthcoming about their location. "This new development posits instead," says Segovia, "a very different construct, the flesh-and-blood reader: always positioned and interested; socially and historically conditioned and unable to transcend such conditions— to attain a sort of asocial and ahistorical nirvana."[33] Evangelical Majority World interpreters would challenge Segovia's assertion regarding our inability to "transcend" at all. Indeed, true human communication always involves self-transcendence. They would affirm with Segovia, however, his recognition of location and critique of supposed disengaged universals. Identity cannot be bracketed out.

The question of identity becomes a dominant consideration in one of the most assertive interpretive approaches in the contemporary landscape: postcolonial biblical interpretation. This hermeneutic examines

---

[31]Ukpong, "Rereading the Bible with African Eyes," pp. 9-10.

[32]See also Hans-Georg Gadamer, *Truth and Method* (London and New York: Continuum, 2004), pp. 299-306.

[33]Fernando F. Segovia, "'And They Began to Speak in Other Tongues': Competing Modes of Discourse in Contemporary Biblical Criticism," in *Reading from This Place: Social Location and Biblical Interpretation in the United States*, ed. Fernando F. Segovia and Mary Ann Tolbert (Minneapolis: Fortress, 1995), pp. 28-29.

how the Christian faith came to the Majority World and indigenous communities via those who were members of the colonial powers. The Bible had a role in the process of colonization as it provided justification for the colonizer's imperial dominance and became a tool in suppressing the indigenous culture while promoting the colonizer's values.

Colonization included suppressing traditional religions and often blocked the way against indigenized forms of the Christian faith. Schools became instruments to shift the cultural orientation of children away from their traditions and toward the perspectives of the colonizers. As Musa Dube says,

> The victims of imperialism become the colonized, that is, those whose lands, minds, cultures, economies and political institutions have been taken possession of and rearranged according to the interests and values of the imperializing powers. Imperialism . . . actively suppresses diversity and promotes a few universal standards for the benefit of those in power.[34]

The colonized then feel like aliens in their own land and alienated from themselves. They experience loss and the cruel reality of exploitation.

Once the colonizers leave, as in India or Africa, or stay, as in the case of North America, how do indigenous people deal with their cultural hybridity? They are still people of their ancestral culture yet transformed by the colonizers' cultural influence, which leaves its imprint. Postcolonialism recognizes that European theories are incapable of dealing with these complexities.[35] What then does biblical interpretation look like when throwing off cultural subservience? Enter postcolonial biblical interpretation and theology. Sugirtharajah defines the term *postcolonialism* as "a resistant discourse which tries to write back and work against colonial assumptions, representations, and ideologies."[36] And so it is in biblical studies. Instead of looking at

---

[34]Musa W. Dube, "Reading for Decolonization (John 4.1-42)," in *John and Postcolonialism: Travel, Space, and Power*, ed. Musa W. Dube and Jeffrey L. Staley (London: Sheffield Academic Press, 2002), pp. 297-98.

[35]See Bill Ashcroft, Gareth Griffiths and Helen Tiffin, *The Empire Writes Back: Theory and Practice of Post-Colonial Literatures* (London: Routledge, 2002).

[36]R. S. Sugirtharajah, *Asian Biblical Hermeneutics and Postcolonialism: Contesting the Interpretations* (Maryknoll, N.Y.: Orbis, 1998), pp. ix-x.

Scripture as a harmonious narrative, the postcolonial interpreter recognizes the ideologies contained in biblical texts and takes out the colonial assumptions that undergird the Bible. As he says, "the Bible continues to be an unsafe and a problematic text," so he looks for those voices in the text that oppose colonial domination. Postcolonial criticism challenges "the notion of the ruler and the ruled." Postcolonialism also advocates for "a wider hermeneutical agenda to place the study of sacred texts—Christian-Hindu, Christian-Buddhist, Christian-Confucian—within the intersecting histories which constitute them."[37]

So if traditional texts have been suppressed, how can postcolonial interpreters revive and draw from them? For some this means leveling the Bible and all other texts, while others use traditional texts as a lens through which to read the Bible. On the other hand, some postcolonial interpreters explore the nature of their received cultural traditions through the lens of Scripture. This move continues to give primacy to Scripture. What is the relationship between what God has revealed through "general revelation" and what we know through the Bible? In Africa, for example, Christian theologians debate the relationship between the faith and African traditional religions.[38] Can any continuity be found between what God has revealed in Scripture and in culture?

Postcolonial criticism has many manifestations, some that favor contextuality over all other considerations, and others that earnestly attempt to come to grips with the realities of hybridity. Not all who deal with postcolonial realities embrace religious pluralism or dissect the biblical text into colonial and resistant voices. On the other hand, the questions and concerns about the universalizing of Western theology and hermeneutics take on a new face within postcolonial discourse. Is the Western Christian academy's insistence on adhering to one particular method of biblical interpretation a form of hermeneutical neocolonialism? Is the absence or rejection of Majority World theologies from our reading and curriculums an assertion of Western dominance over all theological discourse? George Mulrain from Trinidad reminds us

---

[37]Ibid., pp. 100, 103-23.
[38]See Bediako, *Jesus and the Gospel in Africa*, pp. 20-33, 49-62.

that "being 'third' world does not mean that the theological insights of the people are third rate."[39] They should be read and discussed.

The hermeneutic revolution in the Majority World also redefines the participants in the theological discussion. All members of the church are involved in the interpretive process, not just the academy. "Reading from below" has become part of the vocabulary as women and men in the churches take up, read and interpret. In her book *Jesus of Africa*, Diane Stinton has laced together African Christology from church leaders and laypeople with more academic discussions.[40] Popular reading and academic reading are not divorced, or at least that is the goal. Those considered to be the least in theological discourse are given a place of dignity and honor, and here we recognize the Reformation principle of the perspicuity of Scripture.

"Reading from below" has another side beyond merely widening the circle of theological participants as it acknowledges the "hermeneutical privilege of the oppressed."[41] Latinos in the United States, González notes, interpret from a place of marginality, poverty, mestizaje/mulatez, exile and solidarity.[42] Doing theology "from below" means starting from the margins and facing injustice, then integrating that experience into reading Scripture. It also means abandoning individualism and affirming the role of community in interpretation. "If theology is the task of the church," González says, "and the church is by definition a community, there should be no such thing as an individual theology. The best theology is a communal exercise."[43] Reading from below means reading from the margins and in community.

"Reading from below" raises the question whether we will recognize that the responsibility for interpretation and theological development

---

[39]George Mulrain, "The Caribbean," in *An Introduction to Third World Theologies*, ed. John Parratt (Cambridge: Cambridge University Press, 2004), p. 179.

[40]Stinton, *Jesus of Africa*, and see Justin S. Ukpong, "Popular Readings of the Bible in Africa and Implications for Academic Readings," in *The Bible in Africa: Transactions, Trajectories and Trends*, ed. Gerald O. West and Musa W. Dube (Boston and Leiden: Brill, 2001), pp. 582-94.

[41]Miguel A. De La Torre and Edwin David Aponte, *Introducing Latino/a Theologies* (Maryknoll, N.Y.: Orbis, 2001), p. 76.

[42]Justo L. González, *Santa Biblia: The Bible Through Hispanic Eyes* (Nashville: Abingdon, 1996).

[43]González, *Mañana*, p. 29.

rests in the hands of the whole church and not one segment of it. John Mbiti lamented some years ago:

> We have eaten theology with you; we have drunk theology with you; we have dreamed theology with you. But it has been all one-sided; it has all been, in a sense, your theology. . . . We know you theologically. The question is, "Do you know us theologically? Would you like to know us theologically? Can you know us theologically?" . . . You have become a major subconscious part of our theologizing, and we are privileged to be so involved in you through the fellowship we share in Christ. When will you make us part of your subconscious process of theologizing?[44]

Or to contextualize one of his questions: Would you like to know us hermeneutically?

The approaches to Scripture and theology coming from the Majority World and minority communities here are not monolithic. We discover many interpreters who have been trained in the Western academy and write as if they were located in a Western seminary or university. Yet most are exploring new contextually oriented interpretive approaches, some of which challenge and excite, while others may give pause and cause dismay. Ignoring the discourse and not participating in it is the worst thing that we can do for the health of the whole church. The questions about text and context affect us all as we look forward to that day when revelation will be "face to face" (1 Cor 13:12). Until that day, we need the church, the whole church, to be together in conversation since now we "know in part" (1 Cor 13:9). The Majority World and ethnic minority churches are taking up the interpretive task, and they will move forward in light—and grope in darkness at times. But they are offering us all new theological and hermeneutical perspectives in this macroreformation that is accelerating at the beginning of the twenty-first century. The question is, will we interpret together?

---

[44]John Mbiti, "Theological Impotence and the Universality of the Church," in *Mission Trends No. 3: Third World Theologies*, ed. Gerald H. Anderson and Thomas F. Stransky (New York: Paulist Press; Grand Rapids: Eerdmans, 1976), pp. 16-17.

For Further Reading

Branson, Mark Lau, and C. René Padilla, eds. *Conflict and Context: Hermeneutics in the Americas.* Grand Rapids: Eerdmans, 1986.

De La Torre, Miguel A. *Reading the Bible from the Margins.* Maryknoll, N.Y.: Orbis, 2003.

Dyrness, William A., and Veli-Matti Kärkkäinen, eds. *Global Dictionary of Theology.* Downers Grove, Ill.: IVP Academic; Nottingham, U.K.: Inter-Varsity Press, 2008.

Ott, Craig, and Harold A. Netland, eds. *Globalizing Theology: Belief and Practice in an Era of World Christianity.* Grand Rapids: Baker Academic, 2006.

Part Two

NON-WESTERN
THEOLOGIES

4

DOING THEOLOGY ON
CHRIST'S ROAD

Samuel Escobar

• • •

In the 1960s when I started to think through my evangelical faith as I tried to carry on evangelism in Latin American universities, Marxism was the gospel that was preached on campus with more success. The Latin American culture with which my colleagues in the International Fellowship of Evangelical Students and I were confronted was influenced in different degrees by the Western thinkers that Jacques Ellul has described as "the masters of suspicion," namely Marx, Freud and Nietzsche. But due to the impact of the Cuban Revolution that had triumphed in 1959, the most influential was Marx. As evangelists in the universities we had to respond to the questions that came from Marxism. There was in the intellectual atmosphere an active probing into the meaning of history, and it was marked by the utopian expectations about communism as a way of life toward which the social revolution had to point out. For youth in those days, to take sides fighting for revolution was to move in the direction towards which history was moving.

Years before, when I faced personally the strong challenge of Marxism in university, I found out that the evangelical theological canon was no help in the struggle. I was baptized in 1951 during my first year in university. What prompted me to ask for baptism was that on the campus I was challenged daily by the commitment and the sacrifice of my militant Marxist colleagues. I was not convinced by their ideas or their creed, but the way they lived according to their ideas put to the test my own commitment to Jesus Christ. So I recommitted myself to Christ and asked for baptism. When I asked for help for my intellectual struggles on campus, the best my missionary-pastor could give me was a poorly translated Spanish version of the book *Christian Evidences* by E. Y. S. Mullins. Of course, for Mullins, a Southern Baptist writing at the end of the nineteenth century and the beginning of the twentieth, Marxism was a nonissue. A few years later, when the furor over Francis Schaeffer took over evangelical thinkers, my American InterVarsity colleagues could not understand why I found Francis Schaeffer irrelevant for our ministry in Latin America.

Three little books may be taken as an example of the kind of theological reasoning we responded with. Pedro Arana from Peru had been an active student leader, and when he graduated as a chemical engineer, he became an IFES traveling secretary in Peru, Venezuela, Ecuador and Colombia. When he went to study theology at the Free College in Edinburgh he had time to revise the text of evangelistic lectures he had presented to university students in those countries during the 1960s. Spanish editor José Grau published them in Barcelona in 1971, under the title *Progreso, técnica y hombre* (Progress, Technique and Man).[1] Before that, in 1967 Pedro had published a collection of my own evangelistic lectures under the title *Diálogo entre Cristo y Marx* (A Dialogue Between Christ and Marx).[2] This book was used as an evangelistic tool during the Evangelism in Depth program in Peru and ten thousand copies were sold during that year. The third book to which our colleague René Padilla contributed two chapters was *¿Quién es Cristo hoy?* (Who Is Christ Today?), another evangelistic book which had to be reprinted.[3]

By the mid 1960s, René Padilla and I in Argentina started to develop a christological outline that would allow us to build a basic Christian social ethics using incarnation, the cross and resurrection as a

---

[1]Pedro Arana, *Progreso, técnica y hombre* (Barcelona: Ediciones Evangélicas Europeas, 1973).
[2]Samuel Escobar, *Diálogo entre Cristo y Marx*, rev. ed. (Lima: AGEUP, 1969).
[3]René Padilla, Samuel Escobar and Edwin Yamauchi, *¿Quién es Cristo hoy?* (Buenos Aires: Certeza, 1973).

frame for our contextual theological effort. Then, while I was doing my doctoral work in Spain (1966-1967), I was invited to present a short paper at the World Congress on Evangelism (December 1966) convened by Billy Graham in Berlin. In Berlin, John Stott presented three Bible expositions about the Great Commission. I was specially touched by his exposition of John 20:19-23. Stott emphasized the fact that in this short version of the commission, "as the Father has sent me, so I send you," we have not only a command but also a model for mission. I could find there, coming from a different context, some of the points René and I had been working with in Latin America. Encouraged by that and by my conversations with Stott, when I was asked to present a paper in the Bogotá Congress on Evangelism (1969), a follow-up to the Berlin Congress, my paper summarized the work we had been doing with René during that decade.[4] Referring to the standing ovation it received, René said that it "threw into relief the fact that a significant sector of the evangelical leadership in Latin America was fertile soil for social concerns from a biblical perspective."[5]

Doing Theology Along the Road

From 1963 to 1965, René Padilla had done doctoral studies in New Testament under F. F. Bruce at Manchester University in England. He says that the questions posed by Marxism in his high school student days were probably what took him to the topic of his doctoral dissertation: *Church and World: A Study of the Relation Between the Church and the World in the Teaching of Paul the Apostle.*[6] In his teaching in IFES circles after his return from Manchester, René made us all aware that Pauline eschatology was a key to our understanding of God's action in history and a Christian view of history that would make sense in the dramatic context that surrounded us in Latin America. On the other hand, Pedro

---

[4]I have summarized the process from Berlin 1966 to Lausanne 1974 in *The New Global Mission* (Downers Grove, Ill.: InterVarsity Press, 2003), pp. 24-27.

[5]C. René Padilla, "My Theological Pilgrimage," *Journal of Latin American Theology* 2 (2009): 103.

[6]C. René Padilla, *Church and World: A Study of the Relation Between the Church and the World in the Teaching of Paul the Apostle* (Manchester: Manchester University Press, 1965).

Arana's master's thesis at the Free College of Edinburgh (1967-1969) had the title *Providencia y revolución* (Providence and Revolution). From a Reformed perspective that he contextualized, he also dealt with the Christian view of history prompted by the questions posed by the development of a revolutionary movement in Latin America.

As I reflect about what vaccinated us against the intellectual virus of Marxism, especially its attractive dynamic view of history, one important factor was the thought of John A. Mackay, a Scottish theologian who had been a missionary in Latin America before becoming the president of Princeton Seminary in 1936. In his book *A Preface to Christian Theology*, written during World War II (1941), he presented a Christian view of history nurtured in part by the thought of Danish theologian Søren Kierkegaard, Russian post-Marxist thinker Nikolai Berdyaev and Spanish philosopher Miguel de Unamuno. These writers nurtured my own efforts to articulate my faith as I spoke in campuses all over Latin America. Several colleagues of my generation have agreed about how powerfully we were touched by two symbols that Mackay used in his book: the balcony and the road.

Writing about the search for God and ultimate things, Mackay insisted on the importance of our attitude in a spiritual search. He says:

> The first precondition necessary for achieving insight into God and man is that the seeker place himself in the appropriate perspective for this, the greatest of all quests. For the apprehension of truth is, to a very large extent, a question of perspective.[7]

He then describes two different attitudes that he calls first "the Balcony" and then "the Road." The balcony is a symbol for that attitude in which the seeker is a spectator "for whom life and the universe are permanent objects of study and contemplation." Then Mackay continues,

> By the Road I mean the place where life is tensely lived, where thought has its birth in conflict and concern, where choices are made and decisions are carried out. It is the place of action, of pilgrimage, of crusade, where concern is never absent from the wayfarer's heart.[8]

---

[7]John A. Mackay, *A Preface to Christian Theology* (New York: Macmillan, 1941), p. 27.
[8]Ibid., pp. 29-30.

Therefore, as Latin American thinkers we chose to do our theology not contemplating Christ from the comfortable distance of the balcony, a secure and easily received orthodoxy, but following him on the troubled roads of our Latin American lands. As Argentine Methodist theologian José Míguez Bonino wrote, "Mackay helped us to construct a new Latin American spiritual history without rejecting our cultural roots, and start a 'dialogue of love' with our culture without departing from the biblical roots of our faith."[9]

A LATIN AMERICAN THEOLOGY
Evangelical and Contextual in a Global Dialogue

The growing awareness of the lack of an evangelical theology that would respond to the dramatic changes affecting Latin American societies developed in different and varied places, and the process culminated in 1970 when twenty-five evangelical thinkers founded the Latin American Theological Fraternity (LATF) in Cochabamba, Bolivia.[10] The first steps in the initial consultation of 1970 were to establish a biblical foundation for theology and an agenda in which an important point was to make a distinction between the biblical content and the Anglo-Saxon trappings that we had received from missionaries and previous generations of Protestant thinkers. We engaged in the development of a contextual theology that aimed to be "forged in the heat of Evangelical reality in Latin America, in faithfulness to the Word of God."[11] We perceived that this kind of theology could not limit itself to being "an adaptation of an existing theology of universal validity to a particular situation . . . aided by benevolent missionary paternalism."[12] Its aim was to offer "a new open-ended reading of Scripture with a hermeneutic in which the biblical text and the historical situation become mutually

---

[9]José Míguez Bonino, quoted in John Sinclair, prologue to *Un escocés con alma latina* (Mexico: CUP, 1990), p. 15.

[10]Later on the name was changed to Latin American Theological Fellowship.

[11]Samuel Escobar, "Biblical Content and Anglo-Saxon Trappings in Latin American Theology," *Occasional Bulletin*, Latin American Theological Fraternity, no. 3 (October 1972): 2.

[12]C. René Padilla, "Biblical Foundations: A Latin American Study," *Evangelical Review of Theology* 7 (1983): 86.

engaged in a dialogue whose purpose is to place the Church under the Lordship of Jesus Christ in its particular context."[13]

In July 1972 the LATF organized a consultation on evangelical social ethics. There were three parts in the program: first, an analysis of the Latin American situation, with papers by Charles Denton, Orlando Costas and myself. This was followed by an evaluation of responses from the postconciliar movement in the Catholic Church by José Míguez Bonino and from the movement Church and Society related to the World Council of Churches by René Padilla. The third was the presentation of theological responses with papers from Justo L. González, Pedro Arana and Juan Carlos Ortiz.[14] Later that year, for the second assembly of the LATF (December 1972), the theme was "The Kingdom of God and Latin America." Four of the five papers that were published show a serious and patient work with the biblical text as the authors dealt with the church and the kingdom, the kingdom and history and the kingdom as a hermeneutical key for understanding the whole biblical message. The fifth paper was an effort to interpret the meaning of the Protestant presence in Latin America under the light of the doctrine of the kingdom. It dealt with a Christian perspective about history and the dynamic promise of the Protestant presence.[15]

These consultations are the first time we find in the LATF a reference to liberation theologies. As Gustavo Gutiérrez has stated, the birth of liberation theology took place in Chimbote, Peru, in 1968, a few months before the meeting of the Latin American Catholic Bishops in Medellin, Colombia. His book *Teología de la liberaciòn: Perspectivas* was published first in Spanish in 1971.[16] So liberation theologies started to be an interlocutor for the LATF when the development of a contextual

---

[13]Ibid.

[14]C. René Padilla, ed., *Fe cristiana y Latinoamérica hoy* (Buenos Aires: Certeza, 1974).

[15]Papers about the kingdom and the church were presented by René Padilla and Emilio Antonio Núñez. José Míguez Bonino explored the kingdom and history, John Howard Yoder dealt with the kingdom as a hermeneutical key, and I dealt with the kingdom, eschatology and social and political ethics in Latin America. See C. René Padilla, ed., *El reino de Dios y América Latina* (El Paso, Tex.: Casa Bautista de Publicaciones, 1975). Some of the papers were published in English in the LATF *Theological Bulletin*.

[16]*Teología de la liberaciòn: Perspectivas* was translated by Sister Caridad Inda and John Eagleson as *A Theology of Liberation* (Maryknoll, N.Y.: Orbis, 1973).

evangelical theology had already been going on for more than a decade. This evangelical reflection had a strong missiological component in which the evangelization of Latin America was a key element of the identity of the churches that saw Latin America as a mission field. To the degree that evangelical theology remained close to the life of these growing churches, it took a unique missiological and holistic thrust.

And then came Lausanne in 1974. As I have pointed out elsewhere, after the Berlin Congress of 1966 there were several regional congresses: in Singapore for Asia (1968), Minneapolis for the United States (1969), Bogotá for Latin America (1969), Ottawa for Canada (1970), Amsterdam for Europe (1971), and Madrid for Spain (1974). These were steps in a developing process that culminated in Lausanne. In a way, René Padilla's now famous paper "Evangelism and the World," which impacted the International Congress on World Evangelization (Lausanne 1974), was a summary of his doctoral dissertation.[17] Thus Lausanne was not a missiological and theological monologue of European or North American evangelicals, but a global dialogue, not an easy one, but dialogue anyway. In it theological work was done, searching for biblical answers to issues such as the need for a renewed awareness of the social dimensions of the gospel, the development of contextual ways of expressing the faith in order to communicate it in different cultures, and the critical revision and evaluation of missionary methodologies that were a contradiction to the missionary style modeled by Jesus himself.[18]

The Lausanne Covenant expresses well the growing theological awareness of evangelicals from all over the world that were doing theology along the road, as they walked in obedience to Christ. The contributions of Latin Americans such as René Padilla, Orlando Costas and myself to the Lausanne Covenant in 1974 came from theological convictions that had been developing in the previous decade of the 1960s. You will find them, for instance, in paragraph two on the authority and power of the Bible, five on Christian social responsibility, ten on evan-

---

[17]Samuel Escobar, "Evangelical Missiology: Peering into the Future at the Turn of the Century," in *Global Missiology for the 21st Century*, ed. William D. Taylor (Grand Rapids: Baker, 2000), pp. 101-22.

[18]J. D. Douglas, ed., *Let the Earth Hear His Voice: International Congress on World Evangelization, Lausanne, Switzerland* (Minneapolis: World Wide Publications, 1975).

gelism and culture, and eleven on education and leadership. There is evidence of the beginning of a global theological dialogue that followed after Lausanne in a book that was organized and edited by René Padilla, to which fifteen evangelists and theologians contributed chapters commenting on the Lausanne Covenant. Its title, *The New Face of Evangelicalism*, expresses well the reality that a renewing theological movement was afoot.[19]

Padilla has provided us with a careful summary of his own contribution to the follow-up conferences that developed in the 1970s and 1980s from Lausanne. For instance, he wrote key papers for the consultations on the homogeneous unit principle for the missionary action of the church (Pasadena 1977), on gospel and culture (Willowbank, Bermuda 1978), simple lifestyle (London 1980), and evangelism and social concern (Grand Rapids 1983). The resulting documents of these consultations incorporated sections and passages from René's papers, and all of them, as well as his famous presentation in Lausanne 1974, were included in his book *Mission Between the Times*.[20] A new revised and updated edition of this book was published for the third Lausanne conference in Cape Town, October 2010.[21] For any attentive reader of these papers from René it becomes evident that he was developing a theological criticism of some forms of current American missiologies that were reductionist in their understanding of the gospel.

As an example of this critical approach on the basis of biblical exegesis of the New Testament material, Padilla strongly opposed some tenets of the church growth missiology, such as the concept of homogeneous units. "Its advocates," he says, "have taken as their starting point a sociological observation and developed a missionary strategy; only then, a posteriori, have they made the attempt to find biblical support."[22] What he envisions is a different missiology: "The missiology that the church needs today ought to be perceiving the people of God not as a quotation that

---

[19]C. René Padilla, ed., *The New Face of Evangelicalism: An International Symposium on the Lausanne Covenant* (Downers Grove, Ill.: InterVarsity Press, 1976).

[20]C. René Padilla, *Mission Between the Times* (Grand Rapids: Eerdmans, 1985).

[21]C. René Padilla, *Mission Between the Times*, rev. ed. (Carlisle, Cumbria: Langham Monographs, 2010).

[22]Padilla, *Mission Between the Times*, p. 168.

simply reflects the society of which it is a part but as 'an embodied question mark' that challenges the values of the world."[23] Initial criticism of the church growth theory developed into a critical evaluation of what I have called "managerial missiology."[24]

A new possibility had been opened for a creative reading of Scripture as a dialogical and communal exercise involving the multicultural and international fellowship of believers around the planet. Part of the Latin American contribution to the discussions about "Gospel and Culture" in Willowbank 1978 was a clear conviction that it had become necessary to develop a fresh reading of the Bible as a dynamic interplay between the text and the interpreters.[25] This contribution was incorporated in the *Willowbank Report*, which sets the agenda for an evangelical theology that is aware of its missiological context. Protestantism can only be enriched and revitalized by it, being ready to accept the consequences of this new dialogical situation:

> Today's readers cannot come to the text in a personal vacuum, and should not try to. Instead, they should come with an awareness of concerns stemming from their cultural background, personal situation, and responsibility to others. These concerns will influence the questions which are put to the Scriptures. What is received back, however, will not be answers only, but more questions. As we address Scripture, Scripture addresses us. We find that our culturally conditioned presuppositions are being challenged and our questions corrected. In fact, we are compelled to reformulate our previous questions and to ask fresh ones. So the living interaction proceeds.[26]

The Challenge of Liberation Theologies

Evangelical theology in Latin America had a definite missiological thrust. After all, the initial step for the existence of the LATF had been taken

[23]Ibid., p. 169.
[24]See "Managerial Missiology," in John Corrie, ed., *Dictionary of Mission Theology: Evangelical Foundations* (Downers Grove, Ill.: InterVarsity Press, 2007), pp. 216-18.
[25]See especially C. René Padilla, "Hermeneutics and Culture," in *Down to Earth*, ed. John R. W. Stott and Robert Coote (Grand Rapids: Eerdmans, 1980), pp. 63-78; Orlando Costas, "Conversion as a Complex Experience: A Personal Case Study," in *Down to Earth*, ed. John R. W. Stott and Robert Coote (Grand Rapids: Eerdmans, 1980), pp. 173-92.
[26]Stott and Coote, *Down to Earth*, p. 317.

during a Congress on Evangelism. Later on, the milestones of our theological march were the following Congresses of Evangelism (CLADE for their initials in Spanish) that our fellowship organized starting with the CLADE II in Lima 1979, then CLADE III in Quito 1992, and CLADE IV in Quito 2000. This missiological thrust was also an expression of the strong evangelistic vocation of evangelical churches in Latin America, and it coincided with the renewed awareness of the missionary nature of the church that had been taking place in Europe as a response to the fact of a de-Christianization process, following the crisis of Christendom which is still going on in the continent. As Brazilian Lutheran Valdir Steuernagel has said: "Missiological reflection had to struggle with issues such as poverty and justice, working with the assumption that evangelization and quality of life are not strangers to each other. Both are branches of the Gospel tree and should not be separated from each other."[27]

By the mid 1970s, liberation theologies had advanced significantly in Latin America and inspired similar theologies in other parts of the world. Since the publication of Gustavo Gutiérrez's classic *A Theology of Liberation* in 1973, this new way of doing theology caught the attention of theologians and religious leaders in the English-speaking world.[28] Though there had been antecedents of this theology in the Protestant circles of Church and Society in Latin America (ISAL), it was basically a Roman Catholic phenomenon. During the 1960s the winds of reform had been blowing in the Roman Catholic Church, especially from the Second Vatican Council with its biblical and liturgical innovations, which were the result of trends that had been developing for decades and were brought to light by the courageous reforming spirit of Pope John XXIII. After Vatican II, Scripture had become the source of renewal for the theological task and liberation theologians made abundant use of Scripture and proposed new hermeneutical keys. This prompted a response from evangelical theologians in Latin America.

First came a book by Andrew Kirk, a British Anglican who, as a mis-

---

[27]Valdir Steuernagel, "An Evangelical Assessment of Mission: A Two-Thirds World Perspective," in Vinay Samuel and Chris Sugden, eds., *A.D. and Beyond: A Mission Agenda* (Oxford: Regnum Books, 1991), p. 3.

[28]Gustavo Gutiérrez, *A Theology of Liberation: History, Politics, and Salvation*, rev. ed. (Maryknoll, N.Y.: Orbis, 1988).

sionary in Argentina, had participated actively in the birth and growth of the LATF. His work presented a careful evaluation of the hermeneutics of liberation theologians. The title, *Liberation Theology: An Evangelical View from the Third World,* describes well the intention of the author.[29] Later on in 1986, Emilio Antonio Núñez, a respected church leader and theologian in Guatemala, published his book *Liberation Theology,* which described with masterstrokes the Latin American situation. His volume used a systematic theology approach that at the same time evaluated liberation theologies and stated an evangelical alternative.[30] My own book *La fe evangélica y las teologías de la liberación* had a missiological approach, and placed an exposition of the new theological trend within the continuum of the relationship between Protestants and Catholics in Latin America.[31] As its title indicates, I also clarified the fact that there were at least three different lines among liberation theologians: a pastoral line, an academic line and a radical revolutionary line.

The challenge of liberation theology may be summarized in the three new perspectives it proposed. First, it offered a new and critical reading of the history of the Catholic Church in Latin America within the perspective of a critical reading of the history of Spanish colonialism and American and European neocolonialism. Protestants had always been critical of the Catholic Church and agreed with this critical reading. Second, liberation theology also offered a new reading of Scripture, a fresh reading through the perspective of the poor, a vision from the underside. This was the most engaging aspect of liberation theology for evangelicals. It uncovered the abundant biblical material about God's special preference for the poor and the prophetic criticism of social injustice. Evangelicals had not paid enough attention to it.

The third proposal of liberation theology was a new vision of what

---

[29]J. Andrew Kirk, *Liberation Theology: An Evangelical View from the Third World* (London: Marshall, Morgan & Scott, 1979).

[30]Emilio Antonio Núñez, *Teología de la liberación: una perspective evangélica* (San José, Costa Rica: Caribe, 1986); trans. Paul E. Sywulka as *Liberation Theology* (Chicago: Moody Press, 1986).

[31]Samuel Escobar, *La fe evangélica y las teologías de la liberación* (El Paso: Casa Bautista de Publicaciones, 1987). There is no English translation, but my main critical evaluation points appear in *Liberation Themes in Reformational Perspective* (Sioux Center, Iowa: Dordt College Press, 1989).

Christian practice of the faith should be in Latin America. They were asking the hierarchies to take sides with the poor and not with the rich, as they used to do in order to keep their privileges and political power. It is important to acknowledge that after World War II, a new generation of Catholic missionaries from Canada, the United States, Belgium and France went to serve among the poorest of the poor in Latin America. They painfully discovered that the traditional alliance of the Catholic hierarchies with the landowners, the army and the rich was one of the factors that preserved the unjust structures. From that practice of service to the poor came the theological request for "a preferential option for the poor." When the bishops of Latin America gathered for their continental conference in Medellín 1968, the winds of renewal from Vatican II were blowing and they decided to take that preferential option for the poor which liberation theologians such as Uruguayan Juan Luis Segundo and Peruvian Gustavo Gutiérrez were asking for.[32]

Taking into account this background, it is possible to understand and take seriously the definition of theology proposed by Gustavo Gutiérrez:

> The theology of liberation offers us not so much a new theme for reflection as a new way to do theology. Theology as critical reflection on historical praxis is a liberating theology, a theology of the liberating transformation of the history of mankind and also therefore that part of mankind—gathered into *ecclesia*—which openly confesses Christ.[33]

Here Gutiérrez also criticizes the traditional rationalistic theology of Catholic scholasticism. We could agree with him up to a certain point. I have described the way that evangelical theologians came to see theology as an activity that takes place on the road of obedience to Christ and not simply as an intellectual contemplation from a distant balcony. This is what René Padilla expresses when he says:

> Liberation theology is undoubtedly correct in criticizing this rationalistic

---

[32]In their introductions to liberation theology, Míguez Bonino and Núñez offer helpful historical backgrounds of the origin and development of the movement. For my own missiological perspective, see chapters 3-6 of my book *Changing Tides: Latin America and World Mission Today* (Maryknoll, N.Y.: Orbis, 2002).

[33]Gutiérrez, *Theology of Liberation*, p. 15.

tendency in theology. From a biblical perspective, God's *logos* became a historical person. The knowledge of this *logos* is therefore not merely an intellectual knowledge of ideas, rather it involves commitment, fellowship, and participation in a new way of life. Gospel truth is always truth to be lived out, not merely truth to be intellectually known.[34]

On the other hand, for the most radical liberation theologians the best that Christians could have done in Latin America in those decades of the 1960s and 1970s was to join the liberation movements that proposed a radical social revolution. Since they attributed a scientific status to the Marxist analysis of society, this was the only way out for them. The traditional Christian virtue of helping the poor was of no use because it only postponed the more urgent task of changing society radically. René Padilla's criticism is loud and clear:

> When liberation theology finds in Marxism a political strategy to establish the Kingdom of God, it has clearly fallen prey to a humanist illusion that is in agreement with neither the historical facts nor biblical revelation. Such an action amounts to a sociological kidnapping of theology.[35]

There was also a different approach to liberation theologies in the work of theologians that would define themselves as evangelicals but would accept and use creatively but critically more insights from liberation theology. Argentine José Míguez Bonino wrote a comprehensive introduction to the movement with the title *Doing Theology in a Revolutionary Situation*.[36] The use of liberation approaches and categories is also evident in two books from the late Puerto Rican theologian Orlando Costas. The first, *Christ Outside the Gate,* reflects the missiological pilgrimage of this Hispanic, who during his first pastorate in an American city became aware of the oppressive structures and prejudices that affected the Hispanic minority, and the need for the churches to become aware of the social dimensions of their presence and testimony.[37] This awareness marked

---

[34]C. René Padilla, "Liberation Theology II," *The Reformed Journal* 33 (1983): 15. This material was published later on as a chapter in Daniel Schipani, ed., *Freedom and Discipleship* (Maryknoll, N.Y.: Orbis, 1989), pp. 34-50.
[35]Ibid., p. 17.
[36]José Míguez Bonino, *Doing Theology in a Revolutionary Situation* (Philadelphia: Fortress Press, 1975).
[37]Orlando E. Costas, *Christ Outside the Gate* (Maryknoll, N.Y.: Orbis, 1982).

his missionary work in Latin America and then his return to the Hispanic
periphery in U.S. society. The second, *Liberating News*, is an effort to
develop a theology of evangelization from the perspective of Hispanics in
the United States and the unique contribution they can make to evangelical theology.[38] Cuban American Justo L. González offers us a systematic
theological exposition of classical theological themes from the perspective
of the Hispanic minority in the United States. Most appropriately the title
of his book is *Mañana*.[39]

Thus evangelical theology in Latin America carried on a critical assessment of both managerial missiology and of liberation theologies. On the
other hand, evangelical theologians carried on a constructive task in their
effort to articulate a contextual evangelical theology. In this phase the
thrust of theological reflection has been Christological. It is in Christology that we have had the most creative contributions from evangelical
reflection, and the most acute debates, though we do not have one global
systematic exposition. I have described the process as "the search for a
Missiological Christology."[40]

Theology as Reflection on Evangelical Practice

During the last decade of the twentieth century, Latin American societies went through a transitional period that saw the end of revolutionary utopias. The collapse of "real socialism," symbolized by the fall of
the Berlin wall in 1989, left the liberationist rhetoric without concrete
points of reference in history. A process of relative democratization extended through the continent. Instead of lawyers, generals or novelists,
pragmatic economists and engineers now lead these countries through
the hard road of accommodation for survival within the strictures of
global market economies in a unipolar world. In some countries the
ideological terror of the guerrillas and the armed forces has been replaced by a daily hyper dose of virtual violence through American TV,

---

[38]Orlando E. Costas, *Liberating News* (Grand Rapids: Eerdmans, 1989).
[39]Justo L. González, *Mañana: Christian Theology from a Hispanic Perspective* (Nashville: Abingdon, 1990).
[40]This is the title of my contribution to William A. Dyrness, ed., *Emerging Voices in Global Theology* (Grand Rapids: Zondervan, 1994). See also chap. 10 of my book *Changing Tides*.

Internet and videogames, and the actual violence of drug traffickers and common criminals.

Within Catholicism, with the rise of John Paul II, a strongly anti-communist Polish pope, a reactionary movement to undo Vatican II displaced liberation theologies to a marginal position in the Catholic Church. Theologians who had been consultants in Medellin 1968 were not even allowed to participate in the Third Conference of the Latin American Bishops in Puebla 1979. Hundreds of priests and nuns, even bishops like Monsignor Romero in El Salvador that had taken an "option for the poor," became martyrs during the 1970s and 1980s, victims of the military or of gangs working for rich landowners or ambitious entrepreneurs. However, power in the local hierarchies of most countries has gone back to the hands of the traditional conservative sectors.

Against this background there was in this period an explosion of religious activity that took social scientists, Christian leaders and theologians by surprise. In almost every city you find old theaters converted into evangelical worship places, Catholic priests from Spain or the United States imitating the open air preaching techniques or the healing services of Pentecostal pastors, and the United Bible Societies publishing a study Bible with notes written by an interconfessional working group. Another part of the picture, however, is the coming of a wider religious pluralism. Academic foundations sponsor the revival of pre-Hispanic witchcraft, while both Catholics and evangelicals have to compete with Afro-Brazilian spiritists and New Age militants to get airtime on TV. Some theological categories developed by liberation theologies or evangelical missiologies are quickly becoming obsolete and outdated for those that are searching for pastoral discernment in order to understand what is going on.

The new generations of evangelical theologians in Latin America are now in the process of evaluating the work of the initial generation and carrying on their theological work as an effort to reflect on evangelical praxis in the light of the Word of God. I will limit myself to only a few names and outline from my perspective the theological agenda they are engaged in. Two comprehensive studies of evangelical theology in Latin

America have been published recently. Sharon E. Heaney, a young Irish scholar, carried on a careful research process in Latin America and Spain for her doctoral thesis, "Contextual Theology for Latin America: Liberating Themes in Evangelical Perspective." Her work was published in England.[41] Next Daniel Salinas from Colombia published his doctoral thesis, *Latin American Evangelical Theology in the 1970's: The Golden Decade*.[42]

Today, we perplexed theologians, not only in Latin America but in many other parts of the world, are invited to look at the facts of an emerging "Third Church."[43] It is the emerging church of the poor with its oral theology, narrative preaching, dreams and visions, signs and wonders, and transformative spiritual power, which at given points does far more for the poor than the elaborate social agendas of traditional denominations. Maybe in the North and South the time has come for theologians to do at a global scale what Richard Mouw calls "consulting the faithful," that is, intellectuals learning from popular religion.[44]

The question is still missiological but the setting has changed. In the 1970s the frame of liberation discourse was the fact that the Roman Catholic Church had officially made an "option for the poor," avowedly placing itself besides the masses and away from the dominant elites. That was a challenge not only for Catholics but also for Protestants of every kind. What became evident in the 1980s and 1990s was that the poor masses in Latin America were opting for the evangelical and Pentecostal churches that had been growing at a significant pace and becoming more visible actors in society. Posing it in its simplest form, the theological question becomes a search for discernment: Are these new facts the work of the Holy Spirit? The question can be opened up in a threefold manner. First, is the emergence of these new forms of popular Protestantism a sign of God's Spirit moving within the social realities of our times? Is this the new wine of the Spirit reviving his church from

---

[41]Sharon E. Heaney, *Contextual Theology for Latin America* (Carlisle, U.K.: Paternoster, 2008).

[42]Daniel Salinas, *Latin American Evangelical Theology in the 1970's: The Golden Decade* (Leiden: Brill, 2009).

[43]The expression was coined by missiologist Walbert Bühlman to describe the new global church, contrasting it with the dominant Eastern church of the first thousand years of our era and the dominant Western church of the second millennium that ended with the twentieth century.

[44]Richard Mouw, *Consulting the Faithful* (Grand Rapids: Eerdmans, 1994).

below? This would be the pneumatological question. Second, are the new structures of mission, new forms of worship and new ways of communication typical of this popular Protestantism the new wineskins that the Spirit will use in the twenty-first century? This would be the ecclesiological question. Third, is this religious revival going to bring transformation so that the evil forces that are disintegrating postmodern societies will be controlled and human life preserved? This is the eschatological question.

Evangelical theology in Latin America is now exploring in a systematic way the doctrine of the Holy Spirit in relation to the existence and mission of the Protestant churches there. I ask myself, why is it that as evangelical theologians in Latin America we did not place the Holy Spirit earlier in our agenda? Could it be that evangelical dialogue at a global scale imposed a "modern" agenda on us so that the role of the Holy Spirit is mainly to help us to arrive at correct propositional truth? The only references to the Holy Spirit in the "Declaration of Cochabamba," the foundational document of the LATF in 1970, are references to the role of the Spirit in illuminating the Word in order to help us interpret Scripture. That is very "evangelical" indeed. However, we have not even one sentence about the Spirit empowering his church for mission and mobilizing all church members for a true priesthood of all believers.[45] In other words, there is no reflection about that living dimension of our own reality. While the Holy Spirit was driving the rank-and-file of popular Protestant churches to mission so that they grew in a spectacular way, evangelical theologians were unaware of the importance of reflection on their own practice as a way of doing theology.

The pneumatological question connects with Christology as we work in identifying and evaluating the final fruit of this popular Protestantism. Pentecostal theologians such as Norberto Saracco in Argentina, Ricardo Gondim in Brazil, Darío López in Perú and Eldin Villafañe in the Hispanic churches of the United States have contributed to this exploration. To begin with, work in the ecclesiological question involves

---

[45]More attention should be paid at this point to the missiological reflection of Kenneth Strachan and the "Evangelism in Depth" movement. See his book *The Inescapable Calling* (Grand Rapids: Eerdmans, 1968).

the task of writing a critical and systematic history of Protestantism in Latin America and the sociological analysis of life in the Protestant communities. Mexican Carlos Mondragón, Peruvian Juan Fonseca and Colombian Pablo Moreno have been working in setting the historical record straight. Paul Freston from Brazil is carrying on exhaustive work of social analysis of the Pentecostal participation in politics in Latin America. This kind of study provides the raw material for theological work in what I have called the eschatological question.

The relationship between Word and Spirit was the subject of the Fourth Latin American Congress of Evangelization (CLADE IV in Quito, Ecuador, September 2000). During that event there were Bible expositions and position papers on the book of Acts from a Latin American perspective. René Padilla edited and published them in book form as *La fuerza del Espíritu en la evangelización*.[46] Some of the most challenging chapters in this volume are contributions from women theologians: Lilia Solano from Colombia, dealing with utopias as a challenge to evangelical faith; Angelit Guzmán from Peru, dealing with new wine in old wineskins; Rebeca Montemayor from Mexico, dealing with the community of the Spirit as a new humanity; and Rachel Perobelli from Brazil, dealing with witness to the ends of the earth in the power of the Spirit.

Let me end by paying a tribute to my colleague of pilgrimage René Padilla. Without visionary publishers, it is impossible to sustain an international theological dialogue in our time. René Padilla is appreciated all over Latin America for his untiring labors not only as a theologian but also as a publisher. He has served as an enthusiastic and hardworking editor of several collective volumes. Additionally, he has been the publisher that has stimulated and encouraged some authors to complete manuscripts and with evangelical and literary discernment has selected from manuscripts that were available. René, as you are a Wheaton alumnus, it is a special joy to express to you my deepest gratitude at the Wheaton Theology Conference. For your part in the development of a Latin American evangelical theology, thank you.

---

[46]C. René Padilla, ed., *La fuerza del Espíritu en la evangelización* (Buenos Aires: Kairos, 2006).

For Further Reading

Bonino, José Míguez. *Faces of Latin American Protestantism*. Grand Rapids: Eerdmans, 1997.

Escobar, Samuel. *Changing Tides: Latin America and World Mission Today* Maryknoll, N.Y.: Orbis, 2002.

Heaney, Sharon E. *Contextual Theology for Latin America*. Carlisle, U.K.: Paternoster, 2008.

Journal of Latin American Theology, published twice a year.

Padilla, C. René. *Mission Between the Times*. Rev. ed. Carlisle, Cumbria: Langham Monographs, 2010.

Yamamori, Tetsunao, and C. René Padilla, eds. *The Local Church, Agent of Transformation: An Ecclesiology for Integral Mission*. Buenos Aires: Kairós, 2004.

5

SONGS OF HOPE
OUT OF A CRYING LAND

AN OVERVIEW OF CONTEMPORARY
LATIN AMERICAN THEOLOGY

Ruth Padilla DeBorst

. . .

INTRODUCTION
A Tango of Hope During Dark Days

The days were dark. Persecution raged. People were being pried from
home and land. Some were thrown in prison. Others simply "disappeared." The land, as in the day of Cain and Abel, was crying out. Yet,
against all natural expectations, from within the pain, loss and uncertainty, a song of hope rang forth and carried people forward.

> Christ Jesus, . . .
> being in very nature God,
> > did not consider equality with God as something to be grasped
> but made himself nothing,
> > taking the very nature of a servant,
> > being made in human likeness.
> And being found in appearance as a man
> > he humbled himself
> > and became obedient to death—
> > > even death on a cross!
> Therefore God exalted him . . .
> > every knee should bow. (Phil 2:6-10)

The good news for Jesus' early followers is that God was not distant, dead or indifferent to their condition but rather *with* and *among* them, in the midst of the pulls and tugs of Roman imperial expansion, of temple power and of the incomprehension of their Jewish and Greek ancestors alike.

Fast forward several centuries and spin your way around the globe. Meet my people in Argentina, under the military dictatorship of the mid and late 1970s. The days were dark. Persecution raged. People were being pried from home and land. Some were thrown in prison. Others simply "disappeared." The land, as in the day of Cain and Abel, was crying. Yet, again, against all natural expectations, from within the pain, loss and uncertainty, a song of hope rang forth and carried people forward. The words of Methodist bishop Federico Pagura were arranged into a tango by Uruguayan musician Perera. Titled *Tenemos Esperanza* ("We Have Hope"), the song celebrates Emmanuel, God with us, incarnate in our land and among our people.

> Because God entered the world and history;
> Because God broke silence and agony;
> Because God filled the Earth with God's glory;
> Because God was light in our cold night.
> Because God was born in a lowly manger;
> Because God sowed love and life;
> Because God broke the hardened hearts
> and raised up the humble hearted.
>
> CHORUS
> That is why we now have hope
> That is why we do not give up the fight,
> That is why we look to the future with confidence.
> In this, my land.

This hymn rings out: a hopeful testimony of the good news from my native Colombia; from Argentina, where I grew up; from Ecuador, where three of my children were born; from El Salvador, where I served for several years; and from Costa Rica, where I currently live with my husband and several of our kids. A deeply theological affirmation that there is no sociopolitical, economic, ecologic or religious context in which God's gracious presence, in Word and Spirit, does not take on flesh and walk among God's people for the sake of God's good purposes. A song of hope, bursting forth in our language, with the rhythms of our heart and the music of our people.

Laying out an overview of contemporary Latin American theology is a monumental task. Almost as challenging as attempting to serve a plate of Latin American cuisine! And no, we do *not* all eat tacos and enchiladas! *Asados* and *rodizzios*, *pupusas* and *arepas*, *chirmol* and *puchero*, *patacones* and *casamiento*, the list could go on forever. I must, obviously, set a more modest horizon. I will not attempt here to initiate you in the richly variegated intricacies of the multiple theological strands present in our vast continent. Instead, and at the risk of oversimplification, I will only set out to posit one core characteristic of authentically Latin American theology, of the multitonal array of songs with diverse rhythms born out of the interaction of God's people with God's Word in a crying land. Rather than a systematic, academic discipline reserved for intellectual elites, authentically Latin American theologies, in their liberationist, holistic evangelical and Pentecostal strands, are communal practices of hope and indigenous praxis that resist being defined by categories imposed from the outside.

I will first paint an oversimplified portrait of Christianity in Latin America, noting particularly that hopeful contextual engagement is the common thread shared by the various theological strands. Then I will hone in on a movement of which I am a part, the Latin American Theological Fellowship, and flesh out our identity. I will end with a call for respectful intercontextual theological praxis that overcomes the imposition of categories and contestations from one part of the global church on the rest and allows us to compose hopeful songs out of our crying lands.

CHRISTIANS IN LATIN AMERICA
A Broad-Stroke Portrait

Undeniable today is the fact that the religious map of Latin America has been redrawn. In a continent identified so intrinsically with Roman

Catholicism that the organizers of the Edinburgh 1910 Missionary Conference considered it off limits for Protestant mission and did not even include Latin American delegates, by the 1970s and 1980s, Protestant churches were springing up at an accelerated rate. Growth was so dramatic that theologian Guillermo Cook would not be accused of negligent scholarship when in 1994 he affirmed that "'the new face of the church in Latin America' is largely a Protestant story."[1] He cites Mike Berg and Paul Pretiz's example: "in Brazil, on any given Sunday, more Christians attend [Protestant] worship than attend worship at Roman Catholic churches."[2]

But to whom in Latin America might we appropriately assign the term *Protestant* or *evangelical*? To the theologian who was stoned as a boy in Colombia for not praying the Hail Mary in his public school? To the tailor-suited, joke-cracking, mega-evangelist who fills Buenos Aires's stadiums? To the young woman who tutors children in a Lima slum? To the Guatemalan so-called apostle, in his late-model BMW? To the rural community of believers massacred by the army in El Mozote, El Salvador? To the students on campus who, after their Bible study, meet with protestors in order to influence their tactics? To the preacher on the La Paz park corner? To the thousands gathered for hours of worship through song and dance, challenging city noise ordinances?

From the sword-brandishing, cross-bearing *conquistadores* to the prophetic calls of Bartolomé de las Casas in favor of the indigenous people; from the torture-blessing priests in many modern dictatorships to the martyr priests who denounced injustice; from the adherents to Catholic Christendom to the followers of "the other Spanish Christ";[3] in spite of its unified formal structure, it would be misleading to conceive of the Roman Catholic Church in Latin America as a cohesive and homogeneous front. Although in a prevailingly Roman Catholic environment, *evangélico* has loosely been applied to all non-Roman Catholic Christians in Latin America and those Latin Americans who

[1]Guillermo Cook, *New Face of the Church in Latin America: Between Tradition and Change*, American Society of Missiology Series 18 (Maryknoll, N.Y.: Orbis, 1994), p. xiii.
[2]Ibid., p. ix.
[3]John Alexander Mackay, *The Other Spanish Christ: A Study in the Spiritual History of Spain and South America* (New York: Macmillan, 1933).

see themselves as inheritors of the sixteenth-century Protestant Reformation,[4] the previous snapshots point to a broad diversity. Thanks, however, to this association with the Reformation, the terms *evangelical* and *Protestant* are often used interchangeably within Latin America and in scholarly writing.[5] In recent years, and especially with the upsurge of neo-Pentecostal movements and the desire to differentiate from them, many traditional Pentecostal and charismatic churches also comfortably apply the same term, *evangelical*, to themselves. Argentine theologian and ethicist José Míguez Bonino portrays the multiple faces, or expressions, of Latin American Protestantism in its liberal, evangelical, Pentecostal and ethnic strands.[6] And when it comes to defining himself, this Methodist minister's statement is revealing:

> I have been variously tagged a conservative, a revolutionary, a Barthian, a liberal, a catholic, a "moderate," and a liberationist. Probably there is truth in all of these. It is not for me to decide. However, when I do attempt to define myself in my innermost being, what "comes from within" is that I am *evangélico*.[7]

Although we must be wary of attempts to homogenize Latin American evangelicals into one set prototype that will only result in caricatures, we can safely use Peruvian missiologist Samuel Escobar's working definition: "to be evangelical means doctrinal firmness, evangelistic passion, personal piety, a different lifestyle from the rest of the world, and also social conscience."[8] Word and world, piety and social ethics, this back and forth movement of mutually informing missional engagement is present with greater or lesser intensity in many strands of Latin American Christianity, from liberation theologies to evangelical and *integral mission* movements. According to Paraguayan Titus Guenther, both the more "conservative" and the more

---

[4]Emilio Antonio Nuñez, "Herederos de la Reforma," in *América Latina y la Evangelización en los Años 80: Un Congreso Auspiciado Por la Fraternidad Teológica Latinoamericana* (Lima: CLADE-II, 1979).
[5]Anne Motley Hallum, "Taking Stock and Building Bridges: Feminism, Women's Movements, and Pentecostalism in Latin America," *Latin American Research Review* 38, no. 1 (2003): 172.
[6]José Míguez Bonino, *Faces of Latin American Protestantism* (Grand Rapids: Eerdmans, 1997).
[7]Ibid., pp. vii-viii.
[8]Samuel Escobar, "¿Qué Significa Ser Evangélico Hoy?" *Misión* 1 (1982): 18.

"progressive" families of churches have much more in common than differentiating them when it comes to their presence and Christian witness within Latin America.[9] As the book *Pentecostalism and Social Transformation* records, even Pentecostals, often stereotyped as alienated and otherworldly, are increasingly demonstrating commitment to the transformation of their context in light of the gospel.[10] Along these lines, and in relation to women, Hallum explains: "Religion and politics observers repeatedly note that Pentecostal religion provides positive social and economic benefits for many poor women in Latin America, and more importantly, involves them in large communities of women."[11] Church becomes for women the place to pool meager resources, to find mutual support, childcare and health.[12] Yet further, church helps women gain strength to resist machismo: "Latin American women's movements seemed to be inventing a new kind of feminism, which was at the same time maternal and community-based."[13] Not only are the lives of women transformed by their involvement in the church, but "with family values a high priority in Pentecostalism, men change their behavior—they stop drinking and smoking, stop cheating on their wives." A certain "reformation of machismo" takes place.[14] As women gain empowerment in the church, formally or informally, male and female roles are slowly transformed and underlying gender inequalities are overcome. Worth citing is the testimony of a pastor in El Salvador, who after studying at the Center of Interdisciplinary Theological Education expressed: "I'm determined to give my wife the place she deserves in our home and in God's mission." Other graduates of the same program have engaged in antiviolence campaigns, recycling and literacy projects as concrete expressions of a renewed vision of God's kingdom on earth.

At the same time, "Pentecostal involvement in social change does

---

[9]Luis Scott and Titus Guenther, *Del Sur al Norte: Aportes Teológicos desde la Periferia* (Buenos Aires: Ediciones Kairós, 2003).

[10]Dario Lopez, *Pentecostalismo y transformacion social* (Buenos Aires: Kairos Ediciones, 2000).

[11]Hallum, "Taking Stock and Building Bridges," p. 171.

[12]Ibid., p. 176.

[13]Ibid., p. 181.

[14]Sarah Cline, "Competition and Fluidity in Latin American Christianity," *Latin American Research Review* 35, no. 2 (2000): 245.

not stop at providing aid for suffering people. There is an increasing awareness among Pentecostal leaders of the structural nature of evil and involvement at the grassroots."[15] As in the United States today, it simply does not hold true that all evangelicals in Latin America are socially and politically conservative. Although chastened by the shameful performance of political leaders identified as evangelicals who also head the list of human rights abusers, a small but growing number of evangelicals is stepping into the public sphere, contributing to constitutional and legislative processes, and advocating for human rights in relation to land, indigenous communities and labor.

Before moving on, mention must sadly be made to another contrasting face. For large sectors of the Latin American church, under the motto "The more the merrier and most is a must," the race is on for the biggest building, the longest-reaching radio and the record number of members. There is power in numbers, they say, so the growth of evangelicals is cause for celebration. Power is also derived from association. And under the motto "We are children of the King," many mover-and-shaker, up-and-coming Christians scramble to mix in with the local governing elites and establish international business or "ministry" connections that will favor their interests. Power is also projected through images and public relations. So under the motto "God has put you as head and not as foot," the "gospel" is marketed and campaigns are cast wide through mass media and mass music. Christian conferences are held in posh resorts and contemporary "apostles" wear, drive and exude the symbols of success. Massive growth, allegiance with state and financial leaders, and the impact of positive images crowd out any need for suffering. The days of being persecuted or excluded for our faith,

---

[15]Cook, *New Face of the Church in Latin America*, p. 273. Also Paul Freston, Byker Chair Professor of Sociology at Calvin College, has written extensively about the political involvement of evangelicals in Brazil. See Paul Freston, *Evangelicals and Politics in Asia, Africa, and Latin America* (Cambridge: Cambridge University Press, 2001); *Protestant Political Parties: A Global Survey* (Burlington, Vt.: Ashgate, 2004); *Evangelical Christianity and Democracy in Latin America* (New York: Oxford University Press, 2008); "The Transnationalization of Brazilian Pentecostalism: the Universal Church of the Kingdom of God," in *Between Babel and Pentecost: Transnational Pentecostalism in Africa and Latin America*, ed. André Corton and Ruth Marshall-Fratani (Bloomington: Indiana University Press, 2001), pp. 196-215; "The Universal Church of the Kingdom of God: A Brazilian Church Finds Success in South Africa," *Journal of Religion in Africa* 35, no. 1 (2005): 33-65.

when we were a minority with no say in the makings of our countries, are buried in the past. "Today we are powerful," many boast. Attitudes, lifestyles and theologies like these paint the background for Míguez Bonino's caution in light of the growth of evangelicals in the region: "It is no more a question of what will happen with Christianity in Latin America but of what will Christianity do here. This question does not so much demand an analysis as a confession and commitment."[16] The issue at stake here is not one of conceptual assent to a set of doctrines or of the use of appropriate evangelical jargon. The issue here is a matter of identity, mission and ethics.

IDENTITY SHAPED BY BELONGING
The Latin American Theological Fellowship

When North Americans are asked for names evoked by the words *theology* and *Latin America*, the people most mentioned are Gustavo Gutiérrez, Archbishop Oscar Romero, the Boff brothers and the like. Indeed, liberation theology, in its Catholic and Protestant forms, has certainly been a prolific and globally influential movement. Yet have you heard of such a thing as Latin American *evangelical* theology? Colombian theologian Daniel Salinas helps us respond:

> The literature . . . fails to point out that simultaneously with liberation theologies there was an evangelical Christian group of Latin American theologians that was also producing theology from Latin America. With few exceptions, the historiography of Latin America theology has either ignored or misrepresented them.[17]

He continues:

> In the mid 1980s, the Swiss historian Jean-Pierrre [*sic*] Bastian described them as "a biblical-conservative reformist sector of intellectuals" that intends to "develop a Latin American theological thought." In 1990 David Stoll referred to this group as "distinctively Latin American as

---

[16]Míguez Bonino, "The Condition and Prospects of Christianity in Latin America," in Cook, *New Face of the Church in Latin America*, p. 266.
[17]Daniel Salinas, *Latin American Evangelical Theology in the 1970's: The Golden Decade* (Leiden: Brill, 2009), p. 13.

well as distinctively evangelical" theologians who "wanted to pursue social issues without abandoning evangelism, deal with oppressive structures without endorsing violence, and bring left-and right-wing Protestants back together again."[18]

Although, as I shall explain, Latin American evangelical thinking has encountered and impacted global Christianity, it is not until recently that its influence is being recognized at scholarly levels in the North. No overview of Latin American Christianity, however, is complete without a presentation of the Latin American Theological Fellowship (known alternately as Fraternity or FTL), a movement that sees its mission as promoting theological reflection, serving as a platform for dialogue and strengthening the church and its mission in Latin America in light of the reality of God's kingdom and God's justice.

Let me provide a brief historic overview. The Primer Congreso Latinoamericano de Evangelización (CLADE I), held in Colombia in 1969, was sponsored by the Billy Graham Evangelistic Association and owed its program, objectives and participants to its U.S. conveners. But the time was ripe for other voices and other concerns from *inside* Latin America to come to the forefront. Samuel Escobar's paper on "The Social Responsibility of the Church," along with the questions raised by many of the Latin Americans present made it clear that Christian engagement with things political, economic and social was not restricted to Roman Catholic liberationist thinkers.[19]

A year later, a core group of leading Latin American evangelicals, unsatisfied with the lack of openness to their concerns on the part of the CLADE I organizers and committed to hone together a truly Latin American *and* biblical response to the multilayered crisis in Latin America, convened a meeting in Cochabamba, Bolivia. The participants, most of whom were active in the national university student movements affiliated with the International Fellowship of Evangelical

---

[18]Ibid., p. 15.

[19]For a condensed English version, see Samuel Escobar, "The Social Responsibility of the Church," *Latin America Evangelist*, March-April 1970. The text was edited and published in English under the title "The Social Impact of the Gospel," as a chapter of *Is Revolution Change?* ed. Brian Griffiths (London: Inter-Varsity Press, 1972), pp. 84-105.

Students (CIEE-IFES), also shared a deep-seated commitment to the church and its transformational mission in their context. There they constituted the FTL. Cook defines the FTL as follows: "It is not an association of theologians, but a fraternity of Evangelical Christians, pastors, teachers, doctors, lawyers, social scientists, who meet in local chapters to reflect biblically on their faith and practice."[20]

The International Congress on World Evangelization (ICOWE), held at Lausanne, Switzerland, in July of 1974, became the world-reaching platform for this budding Latin American evangelical theology. Latin Americans' calls to forgo "cultural Christianity," the identification of Christianity with a culture or a cultural expression and particularly applied by René Padilla to the "American way of life," resonated with Christians from around the Majority World. Although such expressions, along with outspoken pleas for consideration of the social, political and economic implications of the gospel, struck fear in many Western delegates, the final draft of the Lausanne Covenant includes these as essential dimensions of evangelism. With this step toward a renewed vision of the mission of the church in the world, the Latin American Theological Fraternity became somewhat of a catalyst for the coming together of leaders from Asia, Africa and Eastern Europe who shared such integral interpretations of the gospel and eventually gathered in the International Fellowship of Evangelical Mission Theologians (INFEMIT).

Rather than deriving identity from tightly bounded denominational, theological or ideological constraints, or narrowly defined creeds or methodologies, the FTL draws its identity from three core belongings: it situates itself within the transforming and all-encompassing action of God, within a trifold reading of Word, person and context in constant redefinition, and within a multifaceted community of followers of Jesus Christ.

First, the FTL situates itself within the transforming and all-encompassing action of God and is committed to continue deriving its

---

[20]Guillermo Cook, "Protestant Presence and Social Change in Latin America: Contrasting Visions," in *Coming of Age: Protestantism in Contemporary Latin America*, Calvin Center Series, ed. Daniel R. Miller (Lanham, Md.: University Press of America, 1994), p. 136.

mission from this belonging. The acknowledgement of God's all-encompassing rule spills over into an all-encompassing, holistic under-standing of the evangelizing mission of the people of God. No area of human experience is out of bounds. Hence FTL consultation topics range from the kingdom of God to economics, from higher education to the participation of Christians in politics, from youth and violence to art and liturgy, from peace-building to indigenous spirituality and in-tegral mission. Underlying the vision and work of the FTL is the con-viction that all God's people are called to "theologize," that is, to wres-tle communally in thought and action with Word and world in a constant search for understanding, and to faithful and just living in our context. Hence, continent-wide Congresses held in 1979 (CLADE II, Perú), in 1992 (CLADE III: "The Whole Gospel for All Peoples from Latin America") and in 2000 (CLADE IV: "Word, Spirit and Mis-sion") were not closed events, attended only by elite, academic or "pro-fessional theologians," or religious workers. The FTL is made up of pastors, lawyers, artists, teachers, historians, biologists, administrators, community leaders, students and musicians. No occupation is more holy than another, and every profession can be practiced as Christian ministry. Neither have these gatherings been restricted to one or two denominations. Guillermo Cook illustrates:

> CLADE III Congress demonstrated that a holistic approach to mission and evangelization is on the rise in Latin America. Surprisingly, witness to the entire needs of persons and of society is being practiced and es-poused by theologically conservative churches. Some of the most out-spoken critics of structural injustice are Pentecostals.[21]

A prolific publication program has accompanied and engendered theological and ethical discussion, engaging Latin American laity in active reflection and service, and leading the church in a constant evalu-ation of its contribution to the broader society. Authors include those already cited, such as Escobar, Padilla and Míguez Bonino, as well as historians, psychologists, philosophers and missiologists such as Justo González, Elsie Powell, Orlando Costas, Nancy Bedford, Harold Se-

---

[21]Cook, *New Face of the Church in Latin America*, p. 54.

gura, Darío López, Esly Carvalho, Ricardo Barbosa, and many others.

Second, the FTL situates itself within a trifold reading of Word, person and context in constant redefinition. In the FTL we are convinced that we read and are read by the Word of God in light of our contextual realities, which ask questions of the Word and are in turn questioned by the Word. There is a coming and going between person, context and Word, a hermeneutical flow that permits neither independent propositional abstraction nor nonreflective pragmatic action. In the words of Valdir Steuernagel, taken from the title of his theological jewel, our task is to *"hacer teología junto a María"* (do theology alongside with Mary), in the full simplicity of the common people.

> Shouldn't theology be a simple matter? Something of the people, of God's people, something composed of rhythm and rhyme, something of a fast beating heart and a womb heavy with God's concerns, a sweaty thing, a thing of the soul, with the smell of obedience and the taste of commitment.[22]

Is our theologizing going to grow out of and transform our reality? Then it must sing with the rhythm and rhyme of our people! Possibly some may enjoy inherited German operas and bar songs, and British and American hymns. But we dance to our own salsas and sambas, we love through our boleros, we lament through our tangos, and we protest through our home grown *"nueva trova."*

The FTL's stated objectives are to

> promote reflection on the gospel and on its significance for human beings within Latin American society, to stimulate the development of an evangelical thinking that is attentive to the questions of life within a Latin American context. The FTL recognizes the normative character of the Bible as the written Word of God and seeks to listen, under the Holy Spirit's direction, to the biblical message in relation to the relativities of our concrete situations.[23]

---

[22]Valdir Steuernagel, *Hacer teología junto a María* (Buenos Aires: Ediciones Kairos, 2006), p. 48, my translation.

[23]"Visión—Misión—Objetivos," *Fraternidad Teológica Latinoamericana*, www.ftl-al.org/index .php?option=com_content&view=article&id=4&Itemid=11.

I believe we are showing signs of adulthood in this hermeneutical commitment. One such sign was the disappointment of our delegates to the Third Lausanne Congress on Global Evangelization held in Cape Town when some of the sessions were reduced to affirmations of doctrinal presuppositions and "propositional truths" with no reference to the historical and sociopolitical context of the text and no links between the text itself and our own context, as if those constructs were the very Word of God.

Finally, the FTL situates itself within a multifaceted community of followers of Jesus Christ. From its beginnings the FTL has valued the Christian community as the locus, the initiator and the incarnator of theological reflection engaged with both Word and context. We do not attempt to raise up Lone Ranger scholars or superwomen academicians. Our ideal is not the supersoloist performing for awed crowds. We would rather aim for communal creation, for music nights we hold once a month in our Casa Adobe, in which everyone brings along their instruments and voices and we create music together. Nor do we aspire to create a grand institutional structure. We are a fellowship, part of the church we desire to nourish. We have identified ourselves as an evangelical movement. At the same time, from our infancy we have encouraged broadly open spaces of dialogue and reflection, attempting to "create a framework for dialogue among people who confess Jesus Christ as Lord and Savior and who are willing to reflect biblically in order to communicate the gospel within Latin American cultures."[24] Our practice of theology is community business.

Composing Songs of Hope as a Global Church

It is true: death and oppression, abuse and injustice, corruption and violence are rampant in Latin America. No other continent boasts such extreme inequality between rich and poor. Our forests and jungles have been plundered, along with their indigenous inhabitants. Fair trade agreements with the most powerful nation of the world are not proving

---

[24]Ibid.

as fair to local producers as they were billed to be. Six out of every ten children in our continent live, and die, in poverty.

In light of this reality we must ask: Are there any grounds for hope? Can Christians engage in a theological praxis that will ring out in hopeful songs out of our crying lands? Along with Federico Pagura I have full confidence that we do have grounds for hope. So I issue three invitations or challenges for Christians from North and South of the border:

1. Can we walk together in our ongoing theological praxis of belonging to God's integral mission? Perhaps this will mean that in an ecclesial context in which we are told that the priorities of evangelization are limited to strategies for reaching, recruiting and adding up the numbers of converts among unreached people groups, followers of Christ from North and South of the border will need to fearlessly denounce such a posture as reductionistic and unfaithful to the gospel. Perhaps in a world that has lost all sense of direction, including ethical expectations, where the market or those who benefit from its current order rule and the vast majority are excluded, responsible Christians from North and South can no longer be satisfied with leading discussions, raising questions and superficially interacting in our conferences and publications with the multiple disciplines of social, economic and pastoral knowledge and practice. Perhaps a missiological vocation consistent with the gospel demands that we infuse these disciplines and their methodologies, objectives and practices with the values of God's kingdom. Perhaps we need to seek a fresh movement of the Spirit so that we may flesh out new communitarian church models rooted in local contexts for the sake of mutual transformation. Perhaps we need to live out the whole gospel and perhaps that practice will turn our theologizing into hopeful song.

2. Will you walk with us, admitting our need for ongoing reformation as Word, person and context interact? Perhaps Christians from North and South need to acknowledge that we are all forming our identities in a process of constant reaccommodation with our changing environment. In other words, our task of forming bridges and situating ourselves within this trifold reading of Word, person and context is never finished. We never master the perfect articulation, the determinative theological formulation, the final composition, let alone the automatically and universally applicable category.

An enduring struggle for Latin Americans in all dimensions of existence is that of honing an autochthonous identity. Freedom from the Spanish Empire was earned two hundred years ago. But years of oppression of our native people still yield deep scars. And the imprint of U.S. hegemony in the entire region continues to mark our political, economic, social and religious identity to this very day. Beyond the scope of this paper is an explanation of the historical ins and outs, ups and downs of U.S.-Latin American relationships. Suffice it here to apply to the church scene the popular phrase often used in describing the condition of our entire continent south of the Rio Grande: Latin America is "too close to the United States and too far from God." Battles, political, ideological and theological, fought in the North have often and sadly been transplanted and bred in Latin American soil. Consequently, denominationalism and polarizations between more ecumenical and more evangelical wings of the church have bred suspicion, created competing institutions and made collaboration difficult. Our proximity also makes us vulnerable to the uncritical transfer or imposition of categories honed north of the border.

Paul Freston, a British-Brazilian theologian recently warned: "It is important to understand that Latin American Christianity cannot be understood in terms of North American Christianity—that goes for both Catholicism and Protestantism."[25] So please do not tell us that we must all line up with your constructs! Can the hundreds of churches in our lands pastored by women benefit from their gifted ministry without the burden of determining if they are complementarian or egalitarian, terms that most of them have never even heard? Can we walk together in search of increasing faithfulness in changing times, admitting that we all wear blinders and need one another in order to see until Christ is fully revealed among us and God's will is done on earth as it is in heaven?

---

[25]Paul Freston, "Christianity and Conflict in Latin America," transcript of symposium on "Religion, Conflict and the Global War on Terrorism in Latin America," April 6, 2006, *Pew Forum on Religion and Public Life*, http://pewforum.org/Government/Christianity-and-Conflict-in-Latin-America.aspx.

3. Would you walk with us as we continue to discover what it means to belong to a community of theologian practitioners? In a political and religious atmosphere in which the powerful sow polarization and antagonism, border conflicts and atrophying nationalism, can Christians from North and South seek to promote encounter and mutual strengthening among immigrant brothers and sisters from neighboring countries, from abandoned regions, from distant lands? Can we recognize the face of Christ in that of the stranger and the alien? When some in the religious camps, like a few of the powerful voices at Lausanne III, try to establish strict and polarizing categories of who is in and who is out, the FTL is attempting to walk humbly, following the complex and at times disconcerting way of the wide embrace and the open table.

In Latin America as in North America the challenge to all who identify as Christians is the incarnation of a socially committed spirituality that draws deeply from the wells of faith, hope and love, and engages in the deeply complex and painful realities of its context with the hopeful proclamation of a different reality. This presence demands awareness not only of the biblical visions of justice and peace but also of the issues and demands of our day, including the place and responsibility all nations and people have in the world scene. God's reign of justice transcends national interests and borders. No realm is outside the bounds of Christian endeavor: Christians are called to hone skills and expertise in all fields of knowledge and science, and to collaborate, interdisciplinarily, interdenominationally and internationally, in local and global responses for the promotion of full life for all people so that we may all be drawn closer to God and God's good purposes for God's world.

May God grant us hope in Latin America and beyond so that we may sing, imagine and together create ways forward! May we live and sing together as citizens of God's kingdom, in full confidence that one day it will be fully here!

> Because a dawn witnessed God's victory
> over death and fear and all untruth.
> No one can now stop God's story
> Nor hinder the arrival of God's eternal kingdom. Amen.

6

CHRISTIAN CHINESE THEOLOGY

THEOLOGICAL ETHICS OF
BECOMING HUMAN AND HOLY

Khiok-Khng Yeo

• • •

Concerns and Orientation

This chapter is committed to "Christian Chinese theology" (CCT), rather than "Chinese Christian theology." Both terms pay attention to the dynamic relationship between theology and Chineseness (culture, phi-losophy, text, ways of life and so on), but the latter seeks to express Christian theology *culturally*, while the former also commits to that task but ultimately reads cultures *biblically* and *Christianly*. Allow me to make three remarks on the orientation of this chapter regarding CCT.

The relationship between local and global. It is an honor but humbling to present "Christian Chinese theology," and I am aware that my scope is rather selective and my purpose limited. Nevertheless I hope an inter-scriptural approach will guide our understanding of CCT. Both the evangelical Christians and the Confucianists treasure their respective scriptures as authoritative rules of life. But for Christian Chinese who are familiar with both texts, CCT will seek to fulfill the Chinese text with the Bible. By grounding our discussion scripturally (even for non-Chinese Christians or Christians who do not know Confucian classics), the canonical texts (rather than speaking of Chinese culture in general) will provide a more stable hermeneutical tool to help us construct a CCT that is helpful not only to itself but also to the Christian global theologies.

I hope the proposed thesis of "theological ethics" in CCT will benefit both parties: on the one hand, the Chinese culture that awaits its fulfillment from the Christian theology (see "Theological Ethics"), and on the other hand, a global theology that is often dominated by a Eurocentric mindset and thus such "normative" theology is in need of critiques from global theologies. A truly CCT will maintain a Chinese *cultural* identity and a Christian *theological* identity *concomitantly*, without capitulating to some other cultural models of Christian theologies.

The biblical paradigm of crosscultural interpretation. Since CCT is a young development and none have a crystal ball, CCT can best be constructed as we discern the paradigm of Christian theologies in the West, particularly that of the Protestant trajectory with which we are familiar—from the biblical source of the Old and New Testaments to the patristic period and to the Reformation. History seldom repeats itself; historical events often rhyme, however, and these events grant wisdom to those who live faithfully with the Lord of the history as he guides and consummates in Christ. I am convinced that "crosscultural biblical interpretation" is practiced by the biblical writers, the church fathers and many theologians in the West. The biblical text that is interpreted does not exist on its own; it exists in a cultural discourse and uses a language embedded in the world of culture. In the biblical paradigm we observe that Hellenization influences the translation of the Hebrew Scripture. Greek philosophical thoughts are readily expressed through the New Testament (for example, *logos* in the Gospel of John) and patristic writings (for example, Augustine's use of neo-Platonic categories). So my envy of theologians in the West has in turn challenged me to read the Bible crossculturally.[1]

The relationship between revelation and language, that is, the nature and

---

[1]See Khiok-Khng Yeo, *Rhetorical Interaction in 1 Corinthians 8 and 10: A Formal Analysis With Preliminary Suggestions for a Chinese, Cross-Cultural Hermeneutic* (Leiden: Brill, 1997); *What Has Jerusalem to Do with Beijing? Biblical Interpretation from a Chinese Perspective* (Harrisburg: Trinity Press International, 1998); *Ancestor Worship: Rhetorical and Cross-Cultural Hermeneutical Response* (Hong Kong: Chinese Christian Literature Council, 1996), in Chinese; Khiok-Khng Yeo, ed., *Navigating Romans Through Cultures: Challenging Readings by Charting a New Course* (Edinburgh: T & T Clark, 2004); Yeo, *Eve, Gaia and God* (Shanghai: Huadong Shifan Daxue, 2008), in Chinese; Yeo, *Musing with Confucius and Paul: Toward a Chinese Christian Theology* (Eugene, Ore.: Cascade Books, 2008).

process of sacred texts. Christianity has no sacred language, and the gospel of the church is neither culture nor language specific. As Lamin Sanneh writes, Christianity from its beginning till now has been *"a translated religion without a revealed language."*[2] The biblical message is always proclaimed "in-carnationally," that is, in its own culture "in-linguistically." We should take our cue from the Pentecost event, where the gospel is presented in the local tongues of the people (Acts 2:1-13). Yet it is precisely this point of the biblical paradigm that warrants us to take "local language" seriously, for we have seen in Chinese church history that when theology is not translated into local tongues, neither does it transform (or fulfill) culture nor does Scripture maintain its sacred force to transform lives.

Christianity is not a religion bound by border, confined in building, privileged to any single race. Christian theology "breaks into" cultures and seeks the process of a homegrown faith. Because of the force of globalization (which in most cases is another form of Westernization) today, Chinese biblical commentaries and theological writings present themselves as "culturally neutral," which turns out to be *tacitly Western* (European and North American).[3] The result is that either traditional historical-grammatical exegesis or radical postcolonial interpretation dominates the Chinese theological landscape. The former pays little if any attention to the language and culture-specific situation of the Chinese readers. Of course, an increasing number of Chinese Christians prefer to know more about English (Bible) and less about Mandarin (Union Version), and are becoming more knowledgeable about Aristotle and less about Confucius. Any radical interpretation that seeks to deconstruct the Bible and Western culture in the interest of promoting "purely" Chinese culture is also not helpful to CCT.

Based on these three concerns, the recent development of CCT is not that bleak,[4] but more can be done. So in this paper, I want to offer

---

[2]Lamin Sanneh, *Whose Religion Is Christianity?* (Grand Rapids: Eerdmans, 2003), p. 97 (italics added).

[3]Looking at various biblical commentaries and series of the last twenty years, one will be surprised to see how rarely Chinese authors deal with the biblical text in terms of Chinese culture.

[4]See the following Chinese works of Liu Xiaofeng (in both Hong Kong and China), the Insti-

three suggestions to rejuvenate CCT and global theologies:

1. CCT is part of the biblical-theological development that began in the canonical formation of the Bible, and will continue till the end times when "every tribe and language and people and nation" glorify God (Rev 5:9; see also Rev 7:9; 14:6).

2. CCT is part of the indigenous theology that needs to be shaped globally. Rather than giving a broad survey of CCT, I will focus on a small but most important segment of CCT, namely, the theological ethics of "becoming human is to be holy," undertaken from the perspective of interscriptural reading.[5]

3. CCT's methodology will need to include that of a crosscultural hermeneutic of the Bible, for it will in turn validate the sacredness of the biblical text, that is, to have the power to speak across space and time, and to transform the cultures which the biblical text engages.

Crosscultural Interpretation and Sacred Texts

Text and crosscultural interpretation. What is Christian Chinese theology? That raises the further questions: What is Chinese culture? And what is Chinese cultural interpretation? Every culture changes over time. No culture has a homogeneous, unchanging identity. Keeping this in mind, it is also important to be clear about basic definitions, in this case, what one means by *Chinese*, and at the same time to be cautious and not claim too much for one's definition. In our time, an emerging modern (largely Western) global culture—through trade, travel, technology and so on—threatens traditional cultural identities and values. Despite all that, I believe the perennial Chinese characteristic is found in the Chinese cosmology of *Dao De*, "the Way of Morality." Even among those Chinese who intentionally want to reject the

---

tute of Sino-Christian Studies (Hong Kong), and the Biblical Library series published by Shanghai VI Horae Press.

[5]If interested, see Khiok-Khng Yeo, "Paul's Ethic of Holiness and Chinese Morality of *Renren*," in *Cross-Cultural Paul: Journeys to Others, Journeys to Ourselves*, ed. Khiok-Khng Yeo, Charles Cosgrove, and Herold Weiss (Grand Rapids: Eerdmans, 2005), pp. 104-40. On a brief review of history and models of Chinese theology, see ibid., pp. 104-20.

Confucianist ideal, the Confucian ethic often still plays a significant role in their thinking and way of life.[6] So the DNA of "Chineseness" is *Dao De*; its basic role will remain and continue despite its nuances through translation and transmutation across space and time.

The Chinese DNA is not just in me, being a Chinese interpreter, it is also in the Chinese Bible. The nature of the biblical text as written in the original languages and translated into various versions of the Chinese language contribute to the richly textured meaning of the Bible. However, I, as an interpreter, do not simply have the Chinese DNA, I also have a Christian DNA. Thus as a Christian Chinese interpreter, I come to the Bible and the Chinese classics not as a detached, "objective" observer but as a subjectively engaged and interested interpreter, one who has been shaped by the Bible and by the Chinese tradition. One can imagine that my theological interpretation as a Christian Chinese is bound up in this tricky, yet exciting, hermeneutical negotiation between the biblical text and the Chinese culture.

The Holy Scripture exerts its sacred life force through the interpretive and communicative process, since Scripture assumes that the Holy Writer of the texts wills the sacred Word to speak over time and space—and here we approach the issue of "crosscultural interpretation."[7] Biblical or theological interpretation is a redemptive process, especially for the readers. The interpreter reads the text in order to understand the meaning of the text, and the text reads the interpreter in order to inscribe a meaningful narrative and to transform the world of the interpreter. All theological expression or interpretation is *cross*cultural to the degree that theology and culture are not identical, though they need each other and share some common tasks. If the cultures of the Bible and those of the interpreters are identical, crosscultural interpretation

---

[6]For example, the Confucian ethic of knowledge and action is found in Maoism. Despite Mao's rejection of the Confucianist ideal of how to be fully human, he in fact also held to Confucian political ethics. On Mao, see Khiok-Khng Yeo, *Chairman Mao Meets the Apostle Paul* (Grand Rapids: Brazos, 2002), pp. 123-26.

[7]"Crosscultural interpretation" descriptively refers to either (1) the use of cultural resources (such as the myths, philosophy or concepts of the Sumerian, the Egyptian, the Jewish or the Greco-Roman world) by biblical authors to express their understanding of God, or (2) the use of contemporary, cultural resources (such as indigenous texts or cultural frameworks) by biblical interpreters as hermeneutical tools to read the Scripture.

will not be necessary, but if they do not have anything in common, interpretation will not be possible.

Scriptures in Christian and Chinese classics. Every religion, in the East or West, has sacred scriptures that form the foundation of its cultural ideals. The orientation of these religions may be different, but each canonical, sacred text embodies the spirit of the people group. Scriptures are sacred texts that contain communal wisdom, have stood the test of time and continue to sustain the community. Our work in CCT assumes the scriptures of the Confucian classics as the ideal text of the Chinese culture.[8] The intertextual reading that is inherent in the Confucian classics and biblical canon via a Christian Chinese approach extends itself into the interscriptural reading between these two texts, with the hope that the Bible will be expressed using Confucian language, and the Confucian ethics will be fulfilled by the gospel.

Theological Ethics of CCT

Chinese understanding of ethics. The key concept in Confucius's ethics can be seen in his usage of *dao* (the *Analects*). *Analects* 4:8 reads, "Knowing *dao* in the morning, one can die in the evening."[9] The point here is that one ought to know *dao* before one's death, and that the purpose of being human is to live in a harmonious relationship with *dao*. But what is this *dao* Confucius is talking about?

Dao is the way or the vision of life to be practiced. It is referred to as *tiandao*, "the Way of heaven," in *Analects* 5:13 or *rendao*, "the Way of humanity," in *Analects* 15:29.

1. *Tiandao* occurs in the *Analects* only in 5:13, which speaks of the way of *tian* as the divine paradigm for culture (*wen*). Building a cultural ethos is not merely a secular, humanistic task. It is foremost obedience

---

[8]The Confucian classics are called the Four Books (*Sishu*)—the *Great Learning* (*Daxue*), the *Doctrine of the Mean* (*Zhongyong*), the *Analects* (*Lunyu*), and *Mencius* (*Mengzi*). They contain a comprehensive understanding of the moral, philosophical and political worlds of human endeavor in China. Besides proverbial sayings, the Four Books also contain history, oracles, poetic texts, dialogues and debates.
[9]See Chen Shihchuan, *Lunyu Duxun Jiegu* [Confucian Analects. A Revised Text and New Commentary] in Chinese (Hong Kong: Sanlan, 1972), p. 50.

to or the implementation of the will or way of *tian*. A Confucian culture has spiritual force.

2. *Rendao* in *Analects* 15:29 can be translated as "'a way of becoming consummately and authoritatively human.' As 15.29 tells us: 'It is the person who is able to broaden the way, and not the way that broadens the person.'"[10] *Dao* is not speculative truth. While *dao* in Chinese refers to one's relationship with the cosmos, *de* denotes the actualization of the self in wholeness within the social and ethical realms. Because of the unity between *dao* and *de*, Confucianists seek to follow the pattern of heaven and earth, and hope that they will be led by the rightness of the heavens and the benefits of the earth so that all under heaven might be in harmony.

The word *dao* connotes the universal way or cosmic moral principle. Just like *tian*, *dao* is eternal in its existence and creative in its power. *Dao* is self-generative; it is the metamorphosis of a self-contained universe. "*Dao* is a wholly spontaneous principle, without any trace of personality."[11] It is interesting to note that the word *dao* corresponds to *logos*, "word," "reason," "thing" and so on in Greek. In both classical cultures (Chinese and Greek) *dao*, *tianli*, "cosmic order" and *logos* were used to designate the creative principle or wisdom that generates that way of life which is harmonious and fulsome.

Christian understanding of "the Way." The Chinese understanding of *dao* as the Way that originates in the ultimately timeless and unknown is different from Paul's theology that God has been made known in Christ. Paul believed he lived at the end of time—such beliefs are called, collectively, eschatology. He also believed that the end of time had been inaugurated by the crucifixion and resurrection of Jesus Christ, an event that came totally unexpected in history, as out of the future, by revelation—that is, apocalyptically (Gal 1:4). These conceptual elements are called apocalyptic eschatology, and together they provide the background for understanding Paul's Christology and so-

---

[10]Roger T. Ames and Henry Rosemont Jr., *The Analects of Confucius: A Philosophical Translation* (New York: Random House, 1998), pp. 45-46.
[11]Derk Bodde, "Harmony and Conflict in Chinese Philosophy," in *Studies in Chinese Thought*, ed. Arthur F. Wright (Chicago: University of Chicago Press, 1953), p. 23.

teriology (doctrine of salvation) as well as his understanding of freedom and the ethical life.

Paul's apocalyptic eschatology is grounded in Christ. Christ reveals (*apocalypse*) the mystery and the pattern of the cosmos, and Christ defines the end, the *telos*, the goal and purpose of the cosmos. The issue here is not disclosing God's acts of salvation that were hidden in the past. Rather, the issue is the inbreaking of God into the cosmos and the present age in a way that is redeeming for all. In Paul's words, "when the time had fully come, God sent his Son. . . . [T]he Spirit of his Son into our hearts" (Gal 4:4, 6). Before God's breaking into the present evil *aeon*, "age," human beings were in bondage; after the revelation of Christ, human beings can live in freedom.

Intertextual and interscriptural reading: Christian Chinese reading. Framed within the eschatological motif of current Jewish expectation, Paul's theology of resurrection points to the new openness of the human condition and the clarity of the future. As an aspect of Paul's eschatological theology, the concept of resurrection is a challenge to Confucius's cyclical, ahistorical understanding of *dao*. So, are Confucius and Paul worlds apart? Is CCT possible at all?

Confucianist cosmology does acknowledge the open-endedness of the Way (*dao*). The goal (*telos*) of Confucius's moral world is harmony between heaven (*tian*) and humanity/humaneness (*ren*). According to Confucius, it is the ethical life that actualizes the creativity and goodness of heaven (*tian*). Confucius sees being human as loving others (*renren* or *airen*), and that loving others fulfills the mandate of heaven (*tianming*). From the perspective of *dao*, "Way," freedom exists only within the order of things. Whether in an individual or in a community, freedom results from following the right course and being in tune with how things are as ordered by *dao*, "the cosmic Way." Paul's ethic of freedom is rooted in God's act of forgiving love in Jesus Christ that liberates, through faith, those enslaved by the power of sin and death. While Confucius explains the moral life as the way of *dao*, Paul places hope for the human predicament of sin, evil and death in the imminent coming of the kingdom of God. It is the resurrection of Jesus that points humanity toward God's future. It is humanity's destiny to be saved because the *telos* "goal" of history, proleptically revealed in Jesus' resurrection from the dead, is salvation, not destruction.

Despite the differences between Confucius and Paul (thus Chinese culture and Christian theology), they are not antagonistic to the point of being irreconcilable. In fact, creative dialogue is necessary, as Confucius's moral world can be illuminated by the theology of Paul, and Paul's understanding of faith can be articulated more succinctly in the language of communal ethic. I hope to show in the following discussion that several concepts central to the thought of Confucius and Paul are mutually complementary, and even if they are conflicting in appearance, it is actually healthy to hold them in tension.

1. Both the Chinese and the Pauline traditions have some similarity with the Hebraic notion of *dabar* as dynamic and auditory. In Confucius's cosmology the understanding of *dao*, "Way," is akin to the Hebrew concept of *dabar*, "word." Although Scripture is encoded with the infinite divine *logos*, the loci and existence of meaning do not evolve until speech breaks the silence of the text.[12] In the interaction and communion of the divine text (Scripture) and the human "text" (narrative) comes the possibility of meaning for human existence.

2. Paul's discussion of divine self-revelation and of the divine-human relation, found in Romans 1:18-32, is comparable to the Confucian understanding of *dao*, "Way," and *tian*, "heaven," as well as to the dialectical relationship between the transcendent and immanent *tian*, "heaven," and thus between *dao*, "Way," and *de*, "ethics." In Romans 1 Paul explains that his gospel of Jesus Christ contains the power of God for salvation, based not on works but on faith. Paul argues that despite the revelation of God's (invisible) nature and the moral obligation of humanity arising from it, all people sin against him and fall short of his glory. According to Confucius, *tian*, "heaven," is both transcendent and immanent: creative *dao*, "Way," is transcendent, an elusive aspect of *tian*; immanent *tian* is the all-pervading life force that expresses itself in virtue.[13] For Confucius, transcendence is best known in its imma-

[12]Michael Fishbane, *The Garments of Torah: Essays in Biblical Hermeneutics* (Bloomington: Indiana University Press, 1989), p. 125.
[13]Mou Zongsan, *Zhongguo Zhexue De Tezhi* [The Special Features of Chinese Philosophy] (Tai-

nence; it is the virtue that reveals one's relationship with *tian*. The mandate of *tian* is to be moral selves, the free expression of oneness with *tian*.

While the cultural contexts (the Confucian ethic in response to political chaos and Paul's theology in Romans in response to the belief and mission of early Christians in Roman Empire), and the emphasis (the Confucian privileging of ethics over religion and Paul's grounding of Christian ethics on Christology) addressed are different in Confucius and Paul, their arguments are similar. They include (1) the ethical quality of the eternal power and divine nature of God, (2) the ethical demand implicit in the self-revelation of God's righteousness (3) the universality and clarity of God's self-revelation in creation (for which reason humanity is "without excuse" [Rom 1: 20]).

Theological ethics—ethics and theology. Though the Confucian classics are ideal cultural texts of the Chinese and the Bible is the canonical text for Christians, the shared concern of the Confucianist and the Christian texts for Christian Chinese lies in their concern for the formation of a community rule that leads to freedom and integrity. As a Christian Chinese I find that Confucius's ethical teaching can be enriched by Paul's understanding of God's Spirit—as that which gives birth to and enables the ethical life. But I also find the ethical reading of Paul's letter to be helpful; too often in Western scholarship, for example, Romans and Galatians are read as theology without ethics. Here, I see the intertwined relationship between theology and ethics in both texts—this relationship is what I call the "theological ethics" of CCT. I use the Confucian notion of *de*, "morality" or "virtue," in reading Paul's understanding of God's Spirit; I use Paul's understanding of the Spirit as the initiator of ethics when reading Confucian *de*.

Both Confucius and Paul believe that the good life is governed not by violence but by virtue. Both understand the power dynamic behind all human relationships, be they rulers or common citizens, Jews or Gentiles. The notion of ruling with virtue is paradoxical. The virtue of the ruler or a dominant group is seen to be such a persuasive force that

pei: Xuesheng, 1998), pp. 30-31, writes of *tian* as both immanent and transcendent reality.

subjects or minority groups are expected to be obedient. "Theological ethics" of CCT reveals that subjects obey not because of physical force but because of the superior virtue of the leader. Likewise, in the case of the Galatian controversy, the rhetorical question states the behavior of a Christian community: Could Jewish Christians have expected Gentile Christians to submit to Jewish propriety because the former understood the law to be the means of virtue formation in their own lives and in the lives of the Gentiles?

To be holy is through becoming human. There are subtle differences between the ethics of Confucius and Paul, but the end result of CCT may be the same. According to Confucius, to be human is to be a holy ("religious" or "pious") person.[14] According to Paul, to be holy is to be human. Confucius approaches anthropology from a cosmological and sociopolitical perspective; Paul approaches anthropology from a theological, or rather Christological, perspective. Paul's anthropology is Christologically defined (in Gal 3:28) and is subsumed under divine grace, whereas Confucius understands being human as the endowment of heaven (*tian*).

Paul believes the power of God's Spirit is essential for believers to live a life of holiness, a life pleasing to God. Compared with Confucian ethics, Paul would *appear* to put less emphasis on the ethical responsibility of the believer. Yet with a closer reading one may be surprised to see that Paul does not view the life pleasing to God as simply something poured into human beings from a transcendent source; there are *explicit imperatives* Christians must carry out (Rom 12–16; Gal 5–6). For Paul, the life of holiness (sanctification) is based on justification. Justification is a gift of God received by faith. Justification does not stop at restoring our status as acceptable to God. It calls for a response, for obedient living and living in a trusting relationship.

Sanctification is not a succession of human works. The new life of sanctification has its ground exclusively in the death and resurrection of Christ. Sanctification is a process in which the indicative ("you are a new creation") and imperatives ("act like a new creation") are harmo-

---

[14]Qian Mu, *Gongzi Yu Lunyu* [Confucius and the Analects] (Taipei: Liangjing, 1976), pp. 194-95.

niously embraced. The fact of "being in Christ" moves toward "becoming like Christ." This understanding of ethics is, of course, distinctively Christian, or rather Pauline, though to my Chinese ears the language sounds Confucianist with respect to a life of holiness as a *process of obedience*.

In their ethical systems Confucius and Paul share the following views, and thus the theological ethics, of CCT. First, both systems emphasize the ethical life as relational, a consequence of belonging to God the Holy One or to transcendent *tian* (heaven). Paul argues that the term *holiness* has the meaning of belonging to the Holy One, the Lord. Because one belongs to the Lord, one is expected to be ethically just and morally good. Similarly, Confucius argues that it is the transcendent *tian* that gives the mandate for human beings to be morally good, so that what is immanent (ethics) reflects what is transcendent (*tian*).

Second, both Pauline and Confucian ethics understand that the process of sanctification is aimed toward loving one's neighbor. For Paul, growth in the process of sanctification is directed toward the ultimate goal of realizing the image of God in human beings. The process is initiated in the life of faith through grace. It is a life of love toward one's neighbor as an expression of a life of faith and love toward God. Similarly, for Confucius, ethics is the way to become human, and to be human is to love others. Sanctification is a process of human moral perfection achieved by means of fulfilling *daode*, "the Way of virtue/ morality," *tiandao*, "the Way of heaven," *rendao*, "the Way of humanity," and *tianming*, "the mandate of heaven." In CCT we can state that the will of heaven for any community is to practice the law of life, that is, the law of love. Such reading is "redemptive" to the Confucianist and the Christian cultures that can too easily fall or drift from their own canonical texts—such as loving one's family members only or loving with a limit and conditions.

Paul speaks most clearly of sacrificial love, yet not even he explicitly commands his readers to follow Jesus' teaching of "loving your enemies." For the New Testament, to be human is to be bound to God, and to be bound to God is to be bound to loving one's neighbor (Mt 19:19; Mk 12:31; Lk 10:27; Rom 13:10; Gal 5:14; Jas 2:8). The test of piety comes when one's neighbors become one's enemies (Mt 5:43-44). Although enemies sometimes turn out to be good neighbors, cruciform love continues even when the neighbor is the enemy (Lk 10:36). This test is especially important in Confucianist and Christian societies where family, clan and church interests often marginalize outsiders.

Paul's way of highlighting cruciform love enriches Confucius's understanding of *ren* (*agapē* in Greek New Testament; *ren-ai* in Union Version of the Chinese Bible) in that the reality of God in Christ shows that divine grace is the spiritual force of ethics. Confucius sees morality (*de*) as the expression of heaven, *ren* as the essence of being human. The apostle Paul teaches that divine grace is the foundation of ethics; cruciform love is the way God redeems the world. For Chinese Christians (thus CCT) who seek to engage Confucian ethics with Pauline theology, cruciform love is the way to become fully human and holy. The cruciform love of Paul's theology and Confucius's ethics of *ren-ai* both believe that to be human is to reach out in love. Both believe that no human being is alone. The other's welfare is a part of one's well-being; Christ's passion is the peace of all, and divine love (*agapē* or *ren-ai*) the mandate for all to become fully human.

Toward Global Christian Chinese Interpretation

As we have seen, Confucian classics and the Bible are fairly close at certain points while differing radically from each other at others. Holding on to their incommensurability in tension is a challenging interpretive move of CCT that will fulfill each other's blind spots.

I believe that Christ completes or extends what is merely implicit or absent (theology, transcendence, spirit) in Confucius; without Christ, the Confucian ethic too quickly (even in early Chinese history) degenerates into a system of ritualistic behavior. But the Confucian ethic amplifies various elements of Christian theologies (for example, community, virtues) that are underplayed in Western Christianity. The Christ of God (in the Bible) can bring Chinese classics and cultures (such as Confucian ethics) to their fulfillment while protecting the universal church from the aberrations of Chinese history, and while protecting China against the aberrations of Christian history and inter-pretation in the West. CCT has something to say to the universal church that needs to be heard. CCT will discover its *global* mission if it can be allowed to find its own biblical interpretation.

CCT is geared toward a global Christian theology whose theological ethics is that of "loving one's neighbor." This is a virtue of humility and an ethic of shared responsibility, since any cultural interpretation, whether Chinese or English, needs the theology of eschatological cri-tique.[15] That is, Christ, who is truly divine and truly human, discloses the eschatological dawning of God's truth and also signals the limita-tion of interpreters' present knowledge. While every indigenous theol-ogy may be valid in its context, every theology is partial and therefore its limitation overcome through crosscultural (global) interpretations. The purpose of this paper is to demonstrate the potential for a theo-logical ethics of "loving one's neighbor" in global theologies.

For Further Reading

Chiu, Milton M. *The Tao of Chinese Religion*. Lanham, Md.: University Press of America, 1984.

England, John C., and Archie C. C. Lee, eds. *Doing Theology with Asian Re-sources: Ten Years in the Formation of Living Theology in Asia*. The Pro-gramme for Theology and Culture in Asia 1983-1993. Auckland: Pace, 1993.

Yeo, Khiok-Khng. *What Has Jerusalem to Do with Beijing? Biblical Interpreta-tion from a Chinese Perspective*. Harrisburg: Trinity Press International, 1998.

Zhang Longxi. *The Tao and the Logos: Literary Hermeneutics, East and West*. Durham, N.C., and London: Duke University Press, 1992.

---

[15]Khiok-Khng Yeo, "Culture and Intersubjectivity as Criteria for Negotiating Meanings in Cross-Cultural Interpretations," in *The Meaning We Choose*, ed. Charles Cosgrove (Edinburgh: Sheffield; T & T Clark, 2004), pp. 81, 99.

7

SOME INSIGHTS INTO
INDIAN CHRISTIAN THEOLOGY

Ken Gnanakan

• • •

There has been a search for Indian Christian theology over the past century, with some very brilliant minds creatively engaged in varied approaches. Some are penetrating innovative and indigenous studies related to Indian religions, and others have attempted to preserve the biblical doctrines untainted by local influences. On the other hand, we find some more recent theologies attempting to address sociopolitical issues. In this chapter we will consider a few well-known theologians (mainly so-called liberal thinkers) both from academic and religious contexts as well as from socially oriented theologies. However, the main thrust is to provide some foundational themes to help grapple with the Indian context more effectively.

A. J. Appasamy

Several surveys of Indian theologies go back to Bishop A. J. Appasamy (1891-1975), an eminent Indian Christian who became bishop in the Church of South India and author of some seminal theological writings. Appasamy was personally stirred by the Bhakti tradition and its similarities with Christianity. He wrote his doctoral thesis, titled *The Mysticism of Hindu Bhakti Literature Especially in Its Relation to the Mysticism of the Fourth Gospel*, in 1922 at Oxford University and followed up with more popular writings.

Appasamy utilized a number of terms from the Hindu scriptures in order to develop his theology for the Indian context. The word *avatara* was used for Jesus' incarnation, yet making it clear that this was not the same as the Hindu concept, which had its limitations. Christ's incarnation was not an illusion or an appearance, but real. The three-fold source of authority in Hinduism—Scripture (*sruti*), reason (*yukti*) and experience (*anubhava*) was employed, but with the addition of church (*sabha*).[1]

Although criticized by some for an overemphasis on Hindu categories, Appasamy was deeply religious, speaking freely of the communion between God and human beings through Jesus Christ. But his weakness in not emphasizing the whole work of Christ and the gravity of human sin needs to be mentioned.

Rethinking Christianity

Appasamy found likeminded thinkers and inspired a number of Indian theologies such as the influential "Rethinking Group." The group featured the noted P. Chenchiah (1886-1959) and V. Chakkarai (1880-1958), who gained prominence for their insights into a theology for the Indian context. Flourishing in the middle of the 1900s, Chakkarai made a deeper study into the concept of *avatara* by blending Western and Indian thought and developing some seminal ideas in his book *The Cross and Indian Thought*.[2]

Writing during the time of the debate over the Christ of faith and the Jesus of history, Chakkarai emphasized that Christ is Emmanuel—God with us, and experienced now. The Jesus of history, he said, is to us the *avatara* of God, not just a static entity but dynamic. He freely utilized Hindu thought to depict Jesus as the *satpurusha*—the true man, and like his contemporaries, viewed Hinduism as the preparation for Jesus' coming.

The Madras group, as Appasamy, Chenchiah and Chakkarai were

---

[1] Aiyadurai Jesudasen Appasamy, *Christianity as Bhakti Marga* (London: Macmillan, 1927).

[2] Vengal Chakkarai, *The Cross and Indian Thought* (Madras: Christian Literary Society for India, 1932).

popularly called, published their book *Rethinking Christianity in India*, which anticipated the International Missionary Conference held in Tambaram in 1939.[3] The Rethinking Group openly questioned numerous aspects of the agenda of the conference and continued to develop what they felt was the Indianization of theology.

These theologians were definitely ahead of their time, as it is only now that we have begun to appreciate their insights. Much of Christian theology in India, particularly among evangelicals, continues to be a repetition of Western thoughts and categories. The fear of most evangelicals was that because Christianity is distinct from Hinduism, it had to be treated distinctly. That is no problem. But to say that as Christianity gets embedded into India it should maintain Western forms would be depriving the gospel of its dynamic power. The gospel that came into a Jewish setting has continued to adapt itself wherever it is making inroads.

Raymundo Panikkar and the Unknown Christ of Hinduism

Within this climate it is not surprising that Raymundo Panikkar (1918-2010) wrote *The Unknown Christ of Hinduism*, arguing that Christ is universal and that his presence and reality must be articulated in Hindu categories.[4] Panikkar originally wrote this as a doctoral thesis on Shankara—an influential Hindu philosopher and teacher who established the Advaita or nondualistic Vedanta school of Hinduism.

Shankara's philosophical theories were intended to combat the influence of Buddhism in India, which were seen as heretical. The Advaita system of philosophy taught that we are all part of one unchanging, monistic reality known as Brahman—the ground of being. Shankara is often considered India's greatest philosopher, and his influence on Indian thought, religion and culture cannot be underestimated.

---

[3]D. M. Devasahayam and A. N. Sudarisanam, eds., *Rethinking Christianity in India* (Madras: A. N. Sudarisanam, 1938).

[4]Raimon Panikkar, *The Unknown Christ of Hinduism: Towards an Ecumenical Christophany* (Maryknoll, N.Y.: Orbis, 1981).

Panikkar was born to a Hindu father and a Catholic mother, and clearly reflected this marriage in his theology. He argued that Christ is the meeting place for Hinduism and Christianity. Christ is present in Hinduism, but not yet recognized. Although developing much more Hindu emphases later, Panikkar at this stage claimed that Hinduism was a kind of Christianity in potential and had to be explored within Indian theology.

Jesus the Fulfillment

The previously mentioned theologians were reacting against those who thought that Western theologies were adequate and had to be left untouched. The search for an Indian theology was thought to be an objectionable exercise because it diluted the purity of the gospel and biblical theology. Basic to such arguments was the fact there was discontinuity between Christianity and the religions of India. To them, it was abhorrent even to talk about a cultural identity because it contradicted a distinct Christian culture that existed, invariably assumed to be Western Christian culture.

The radical theologies were challenging this assumption, claiming that there was continuity between all religions and Jesus Christ. J. N. Farquhar (1861-1929), who had a great influence on Appasamy, Chenchiah and Panikkar, proposed that Jesus Christ was the "Crown of Hinduism," as the title of his influential book suggested.[5] It is a sincere attempt to relate the ultimate revelation of God in Christ to all that he thought was commendable in Hinduism. The fact of *continuity* was being explored by those like Farquhar, considering Hinduism as *praeparatio evangelica* and Christianity as the fulfillment of Hinduism.

While Farquhar popularized this idea of fulfillment, it was the "Vedic Theology" of K. M. Banerjee (1813-1881) who first pointed to such an approach. Banerjee, a committed Indian Christian who was equally at home with the Bible as with the Hindu scriptures—the

---

[5]J. N. Farquhar, *The Crown of Hinduism* (London: Oxford University Press, 1913).

Vedas—wrote his book *The Arian Witness* in 1875. Basically, his approach was to seek to prove the common origins of both the Aryan and the Jewish race by pointing out a number of parallels, including creation, the Fall and the flood.[6] What is commendable in Banerjee is the more positive evangelistic intention, employing Hindu terms to effectively communicate Christ without confrontation.

Devanandan's Theology of Religions

Another influential Indian theologian was Paul Devanandan (1901-1962), who underlined that Jesus is the revelation of God for people of all faiths. Yet he did not hesitate to recognize that some truth was to be found outside. He emphasized the view that it is possible, though difficult, to distinguish between cultural and religious Hinduism.

Devanandan understood religion or faith as a series of concentric circles—creed, cultus and culture—a system of doctrinal beliefs, the religious rites and ceremonies, and the worldview and lifestyle respectively. The innermost circle is a creed. Invariably, when a religion interacts with its environment, the impact is first felt in the outer circle, area of culture, only later upon the cultus, and still later, if at all, on the creedal core itself.

Devanandan believed that at that time in Hinduism there was a renascent movement taking place. The new values of person, society and history were definitely foreign to the age-old Hinduism with its caste system and *karma sansara*. So, he asked, from where does Hinduism absorb these new elements? His thesis is that new Hinduism is directly the result of the Christian message. It is in the interaction with the gospel of Jesus Christ that Hinduism has been shaped with new values through the creative activity of the Holy Spirit. Therefore, there was need to enter into dialogue with people of other faiths and discover the hidden Christ.[7]

While commending Devanandan, we must add that today's India

---

[6]Krishna Mohan Bannerjee, *The Arian Witness* (Calcutta: Thacker, Spink, 1875), p. 103.
[7]Paul David Devanandan, *Christian Concern in Hinduism* (Bangalore: Christian Institute for the Study of Religion and Society, 1961).

is definitely different. There is certainly a revival taking place with the emergence of fundamentalist tendencies that attack any such assumptions. Yet the impact of Christianity on the Indian religion cannot be denied.

M. M. Thomas and a Christ-Centered Syncretism

M. M. Thomas (1916-1996) developed his distinctive "Christ-centered syncretism," with an emphasis on conversion not of individual but of whole religious systems to Christ—ultimately all religions and ideologies will be found in Christ. This prolific Indian writer and theologian from his vast experience in the ecumenical movement affirms the work of Jesus Christ as one that transforms all religions and ideologies from within. Although the abolition of religion will only be realized fully in the end, in the eschaton, the path is available even now both through secular and religious movements. A partial realization of the eschaton is seen right now. He traces some significant movements and the individuals behind them to demonstrate the transforming effects of Christ.[8]

Thomas strengthens his claim with facts that show the "Christian" influence within secular and religious movements. It will not be disputed that apart from preaching and converting men and women openly to Jesus Christ, missionaries have had a significant part to play in the development of nations through education, health and agriculture, and have even seen religious, political, social and economic transformations. But Thomas does not talk about the centrality of Christ in terms of a commitment to the historic Jesus Christ, nor even any open acknowledgment of Christ in these movements. It is a cosmic Christ who remains a nebulous entity—an anonymous Christ.

However, the stress on the cosmic and universal lordship, the centrality of Jesus Christ to all of creation and history, has biblical backing, as long as it becomes an integral part of human history. Although in the interest of open dialogue this is commendable, Devanandan and

---

[8]M. M. Thomas, *Man and the Universe of Faiths* (Madras: Christian Literature Society, 1975).

Thomas need to define how this faith can be the same as the faith toward salvation through Jesus Christ. But the "cosmic" impact is to be accepted—religions are reforming, and there is definitely a noticeable influence of Christianity on society. Raja Ram Mohan Roy (1772-1833) brought a reformation to Hinduism in his time as he encountered the message of Jesus Christ. God is at work in the world even apart from saving men and women. He is also shaping history and all that is in it.

Samartha and Plural Ways

Pluralism has had its influence on Indian theologians, particularly writing from a country with so many major religions. An eminent Indian theologian, Stanley Samartha (1920-2001), a pluralist, affirms, "The question . . . is not whether there *may* be plural ways of salvation. In multireligious situations the fact is that there *are* plural ways of salvation, experienced and articulated in different ways."[9] He, like other pluralists, pleads for Christians to be open to recognize the validity of other experiences of salvation.

Samartha's aversion to exclusive claims has a questionably noble desire—peace and harmony in society as the ultimate goal of Christian message. The pluralistic answer, while sounding generous, however, must be recognized as a fundamental problem, which is not so obvious outside. Every religion defines its notion of salvation in relation to its understanding of this world and the reality beyond. To accept that we could bring about harmony while each one increases his commitment to his own distinctive belief and provokes conflicting attitudes could be suicidal.

Samartha's reminder for us to recognize the validity of other ways must also allow us the privilege of looking seriously at our own. Men and women in the New Testament encountered Jesus himself, not merely his salvation. Pluralists seem to be caught up in merely the human manifestation of salvation rather than the fundamental relationship that provides this privilege.

---

[9]Stanley J. Samartha, "The Cross and the Rainbow: Christ in a Multireligious Culture," in *The Myth of Christian Uniqueness*, ed. John Hick and Paul F. Knitter (Maryknoll, N.Y.: Orbis, 1987), p. 77.

The Human Agenda

Most of the theologies that we have surveyed have dealt with the Indian religious context and not so much with the socioeconomic realities. We return to M. M. Thomas, who became an ardent proponent of humanization, a popular concept in World Council of Churches circles. Thomas saw this secular goal of humanization and its fulfillment as being critical to the understanding of the "kingdom." The result of this obsession for a human agenda is that there was no difference between the goal of Christian mission and the secular goals of humankind.[10]

The concept of humanization clearly became central to Thomas with a "theology of humanization" taking root in the ecumenical soil and evangelism seen as relevant only if humanization was its goal. He began stressing evangelism as service. Since for Thomas redemption is only one aspect—the spiritual—of the total goal of humanization, evangelism was only one part of the Christian mission. These are indeed penetrating insights that assist evangelicals in their own search for more meaningful engagement in the world and its struggles today.

Dalit Theology

The emergence of Dalit theologies are beginning to echo humanization in reaching to an oppressed and downtrodden people. A major proponent of Dalit theology is Arvind P. Nirmal (1936-1995), a Dalit Christian in the Church of North India. Criticizing the Brahminic dominance of Christian theology in India, Nirmal believes that Indian theology should reflect the struggle of Dalits, who make up about 70 percent of Christians in India. Nirmal drew on the concept of the suffering servant in Isaiah 53 to identify Jesus himself as a Dalit.[11]

Dalit theology emerges out of their attempt to seek a new identity for themselves rather than the Hindu label that has suppressed them. In their struggle against historical as well as present domination, Dalits want their own identity as people, and not as outcasts in relation to

---

[10]M. M. Thomas, *Salvation and Humanisation* (Madras: Christian Literature Society, 1971).

[11]Arvind P. Nirmal and V. Devasahayam, eds., *A Reader in Dalit Theology* (Madras: Gurukul Lutheran Theological College, 1990).

Hinduism. They have been socially and culturally, economically and politically subjugated and marginalized through three thousand years of our history owing to the caste-based social structure of India. There have been increasing media depictions of Dalits as the most degraded, downtrodden and exploited in our society.

Dalit theologies are partly inspired by Latin American liberation thinking, although the socioeconomic realities of India are different. The Latin American liberation theologians are primarily struggling against socioeconomic and political oppression, while the Indian version is fighting religious caste oppression. Hence, some Dalit theologians claim that the use of the Marxist analysis of socioeconomic realities of liberation theology is inadequate in India.

Some Theological Themes

The approaches to Indian theologies we have surveyed are more concerned with religion and perhaps cater more to the higher Brahminical ideologies. These sometimes purely academic approaches do not get down to the core where the masses in India are hurting. Rather than continuing further in socioeconomic themes, I see the need for an integrated approach. When religious attitudes change, social life, economic conditions, political values and other interrelated areas must be transformed. Some integrating themes must be considered and these are addressed briefly.

A theology of spirituality. Living amid a people who are religious and following various (sometimes controversial) spiritual paths, Christian theology will need to address the theme of spirituality. In fact, this should be central to all other themes. Roman Catholics and later the Protestants (Puritan, Anglican and others) have been working in different ways through church history to write about and practice spirituality. Some of these possess very deep spiritual disciplines that have undergirded theology.

Unfortunately, there has been a tendency in the West, as well as in the Hindu background, to consider spirituality only as a personal (sometimes private) practice divorced from the world. If we look back at the Old Testament prophets we see some very concrete expressions of their spirituality affecting society around them. Such reminders of corporate spirituality have been heard recently and are influencing the Indian church.

A strong, holistic spiritual foundation will find expression in various practical dimensions. For instance, there is the kind of spirituality that must find its expressions even in ecological dimensions. With reminders of God's creation and our relationship to the created order, we need holy attitudes that are much wider than inner, personal experiences. Our spirituality must carefully nurture positive attitudes to the world.

A theology of suffering. Basing our theology on creation as well as redemption gives us a realistic attitude toward suffering. The experience of physical and mental pain is an inevitable part of life and needs a balanced theology amid various distortions of popular preaching. Undoubtedly, suffering is the consequence of the Fall. Paul writes about creation awaiting its liberation from its bondage to destruction, groaning as in the pangs of childbirth (Rom 8:19-22). Human beings are prone to suffering not only because of this flawed nature of creation but also because of their own sinfulness.

This being the future reality, we need to develop a theology that will address human suffering here and now. Some theologies of prosperity will need to be rejected. There is adequate biblical teaching to show the continuing pain and suffering in the present. Theology must holistically address the recent natural disasters that have caused thousands to suffer and die in pain. Why should our theology be silent on these issues? People are hurting and cry out to the church for answers. It was such suffering that led Kazoh Kitamori (1916-1998) to develop his *The Theology of the Pain of God*—the pain of God that heals our pains.[12]

A Theology of Health and Wellness

Related to suffering is the need for a theology of health and wellness. In a day when Indian gurus with their holistic approaches to health are

---

[12]Kazoh Kitamori, *The Theology of the Pain of God* (London: SCM Press, 1966).

gaining popularity all over the world, a theology of health and wellness will serve to correct wrong notions.

The Judeo-Christian tradition is clearly holistic in its understanding of health and disease. Diseases today need to be considered from various perspectives and not just from Western medical systems, tacitly accepted as Christian. The current growing interest in alternative medicine questions the conventional approach to medicine. The Indian ayurvedic and the Chinese systems are appealing to the masses. Christians are being challenged amid such trends. The underlying philosophy of holistic medicine is the balance between physical, psychological and spiritual, emotional, and social forces. Some will also consider the influences of natural energies and environmental elements. If God is Creator, then should all such approaches be totally dismissed as being demonic? A theology of health and wellness must address the increasing pressures on the church from such holistic influences.

A theology of creation. I have been making frequent reference to our Creator God, and this leads us to a major area that needs to be theologized in addressing all the aspects of human life. Whether we speak of a common ground for religions or of a concern for socioeconomic and political issues, one of the first things we face is to recover a positive attitude toward creation. We need to develop a theology of creation. Our concentration has been on theological themes relating to redemption, and that is not totally wrong. But that is not all that the Bible says about God's dealings with human beings. When we start with the powerful truth that God is Creator, we affirm that there is an ongoing relationship between God and all creation. This God is the initiator and sustainer, and therefore continues to graciously relate to all creation of which we are only a part. Themes such as ecology, culture, religion, humanization, HIV and AIDS, bribery/corruption, wealth and economics, and so on will all find their place.

The church has not sufficiently interpreted the glorious fact of creation. That is why the concepts of "image of God" and "dominion" have caused endless debate within discussions of environmental exploitation. We often assert that humans are the climax of creation, implying that we are most special to God and all else is secondary.

Lynn White Jr., in his seminal article, "The Historical Roots of the Ecological Crisis," laid the blame squarely on the biblical doctrine of creation for breeding an anthropocentric and arrogant approach to creation which has led to exploitation and consequently the environmental disaster.[13]

We may not agree with these criticisms, but we need to bring some correctives. Possessing God's image and exercising dominion, rather than being seen in authoritative or hierarchical terms or even a privileged position, needs to indicate godly attitudes and gracious action toward nature and to all human beings. This is where we underline commonality and continuity with all people. We need to hold our theology of redemption close together with a theology of creation. A proper understanding of the meaning of the image of God in us should help us move into this kind of involvement in our world today. The New Testament reference to the image portrays Jesus Christ as the perfection of the image (Jn 1:14-18; 2 Cor 4:4; Col 1:15; Heb 1:3). The model of Christ underlines our serving in love, and this must be underlined even more. If God's image was perfect in Jesus Christ, then this image is worthy of emulation. Jesus came to heal and not to harm. He came to carry out God's desires, not to satisfy his own cravings. When we consider such aspects of the image of God, the concept becomes a powerful tool in bringing environmental care through Christians into our world today.

A theology of religions. Our multifaith context today frequently confronts us with the question, Is the God of the Christian, the Muslim and the Hindu the same? Even more specifically, one is often asked, Is the God of the Christian, Muslim and the Jew the same, as they all draw from the Old Testament?

Lesslie Newbigin, the well-known British missionary to India, speaking from his own rich experience among Hindus, provides some insights into an understanding of God in encounters between non-Christian religions and the gospel. Every missionary knows that it is impossible to communicate the gospel without acknowledging in prac-

---

[13]Lynn White Jr., "The Historical Roots of the Ecological Crisis," *Science* 155 (1967): 1203-7.

tice that there is "some continuity between the gospel and the experience of the hearer outside the Christian Church." He elaborates:

> One cannot preach the gospel without using the word "God." If one is talking to a person of a non-Christian religion, one is bound to use one of the words in her language which is used to denote God. But the content of that word has necessarily been formed by his experience outside the Church. By using the word, the preacher is taking the non-Christian experience of the hearer as the starting point. Without this there is no way of communicating.[14]

Newbigin reminds us that this fact by itself does not refute the position we are considering, but it makes it "impossible to affirm a total discontinuity between Christian faith and the religions."[15] For him, anyone who has had intimate friendship with a devout Hindu or Muslim would find it impossible to believe that the experience of God his friend speaks about is simply illusion or fraud. Those interacting with devout men and women in India will need to humbly accept this fact.

In communicating the gospel we are bound to use some common language, common concepts and even address one another as worshipers of God. That is precisely what the theologians we have briefly considered were attempting to do, and evangelicals have not fully accepted it. But we will recognize that there are biblical parallels. For instance, Paul's oft-quoted message on Mars Hill starts with a very positive introduction: "I perceive that in every way you are very religious" (Acts 17:22 ESV). He referred to the altar to "the unknown God." There is a continuity that Paul establishes rather than a condemnation of their religious beliefs. Similar to the way Jesus was able to positively commend the "faith" in the life of the Gentile centurion, Paul is able to commend their worship, even though this is to an unknown God rather than some known manifestation.

Paul's commendation comes even though he has earlier been "greatly distressed." Christians in India, meeting men and women who truly desire to worship the true God, but who still linger within idolatry, face

---

[14]Lesslie Newbigin, *The Gospel in a Pluralistic Society* (Grand Rapids: Eerdmans, 1989), p. 173.
[15]Ibid., p. 174.

this situation. We are distressed by some practices but discern a longing for God. The understanding of God and salvation are different, but the desire is the same. Paul has no problem accepting the Athenian sincerity and building on their understanding of God, or lack thereof, in order to present the reality of Jesus Christ. We should not be surprised to find common elements. Missionaries who have worked with primitive peoples, sometimes with even more developed religions, have discerned parallels that are striking.

Drawing from the apostle Paul (although some argue against it), we can conclude that there is no justification for any outright condemnation of the religious leanings of human beings and their limited understanding of God and related concepts. Even amid all the perversion that is externally apparent, there is a sincere search deep within for the true God, a search that God himself can utilize for his glory. Just like these Greeks, there are many Hindus who search for the unknown beyond the known, the truth beyond all the falsehood, the light beyond the darkness. Rather than defining the differences, it is best to build on commonalities.

Our religious context in ferment calls for action. We need to look afresh at the biblical texts for such commonness, such that will bring us back to a real relationship to our world that the incarnated Jesus himself identified with. Merely distancing ourselves through our exclusive attitudes will take us no further than where we are. Is there an underlying fundamental factor that lies behind the reality of religion? Wilfred Cantwell Smith spoke of "religiousness," but the emphasis was on external attributes. We look for deeper common characteristics expressing a concrete commonality that is even deeper than religiousness.[16]

The term I prefer is *religionness*, as this could more precisely describe the deeper factor. It is not merely the feeling or the expression, but that deeper something which makes men and women feel and express their outward religion. It is the factor that is inescapably part of humankind in their being essentially and inextricably a part of God's creation. If *religion* is not the acceptable term, then we should not be speaking of

---

[16]Wilfred Cantwell Smith, *The Meaning and End of Religions* (New York: New American Library, 1962).

religion-ness but perhaps *god*-ness or even *creation*-ness.

Paul stated that "since the creation of the world God's invisible qualities—his eternal power and divine nature—have been clearly seen, being understood from what has been made" (Rom 1:20). The emphasis is on that which is known about God himself. This preparatory revelation made available to the whole world must essentially link us with all men and women rather than separate us from a world to which we integrally belong. The fact that people are made in the image of God must invest them with a capacity to know God, although their sin hinders them from fully recognizing him and receiving the redemptive benefits of this knowledge. There is very little ground for us to say that sin completely eliminates the knowledge of God. Religious traditions, even religions themselves, may be filled with error and human and demonic influences, but there is an essential core behind with a direction toward the divine. That is the common element that we need to discover.

As a theologian wanting to base conclusions on the facts revealed in the Bible, I therefore find no problem in accepting that there is some commonness in all religions. Take, for instance, prayer and meditation. Are these not characteristic of all religions? With our Western orientation, we sometimes dismiss meditation as Hindu or Buddhist. Awe and worship are natural responses to the pressure of the divine among all human beings. Sacrifice has not been purely a Jewish religious act. There are even supernatural manifestations like healing, prophesying and other gifts that are found in various religious practices. Perhaps these acts are wrongly directed, perverted at times, even demonic, but their prevailing presence tells us something. If we are committed to the fact that God is Creator, we will need to accept a grounding from which many of the religious, social and cultural manifestations find their root.

Even more importantly, there ought to be some commonality in our understanding of God himself. The apostle Paul seemed to have no problem with this fact as I noted earlier. Once we place this underlying principle within a proper biblical framework that takes into account the reality of sin, the influence of Satan and the fact of the redemptive work of Christ, we would be on the way to a theology of religion that is much needed within our growing multireligious context.

Some Propositions for a Theology of Religions

In summary, we may consider seven propositions that will assist us in writing a theology of religion appropriate to our context, yet true to the biblical claims.[17]

1. A theology of religions will need to begin with a commitment to God as Creator of heaven and earth. This commitment will consider the widest circle of God's dealings with humankind, accepting all men and women as made in the image of God. There is therefore an inherent spirituality in all humankind.

2. Although all humankind is the creation of God and therefore belongs to God, the Bible clearly underlines the influence of Satan and his forces within all creation. Hence, all spiritual activity is not necessarily of God. There is sufficient evidence, directly and indirectly, to reveal the work of Satan drawing men and women away from God.

3. The Bible depicts men and women as sinful and fallen. Subsequently, they have been distanced from God. Yet, because of their being made in the image of God, there is within them a direction toward God. There is within every human being this inherent "religionness" that gifts them with the capacity to know God. It is this religionness that leads to religion. In this sense, religion is a necessity, being a pre-Fall reality. I do not mean that religion is necessarily good. Being created by God, the pressure of the divine impels all humanity to get back to the Creator. However, men and women, being made in the image of God, are also capable of setting their own direction.

4. Since religion is a consequence of the religionness of humankind directing them toward God, God has revealed himself in a limited way in all religions. Whether this is to be seen as "general" or "pre-

[17]Ken Gnanakan, *Proclaiming Christ in a Pluralistic Context* (Bangalore: Theological Book Trust, 2000).

paratory" revelation, God is active even in religions, not in order to transform them but to convict and draw men and women into a true relationship with himself. The Holy Spirit is active, convicting men and women of their sin and revealing the truth and grace of the Lord Jesus Christ.

5. Although we may speak of God revealing himself to religious people even outside of Jesus Christ, this revelation does not directly bring salvation. It points toward, even leads toward, salvation. It has pre-salvific significance, preparing people to accept the grace and truth of God. A person or a community may genuinely experience the revelation of God outside of Jesus Christ, but the test of its genuineness is that the Holy Spirit will lead the individual or the community to an encounter with the Lord Jesus Christ, through whom alone salvation is available for all who believe.

6. There is therefore continuity between the religionness of humankind and the revelation of God in Jesus Christ. This is not the same continuity as in the case of Israel's history and its fulfillment in Jesus Christ. It is purely the continuity based on our creationality, from which people can be drawn further toward an experience of new creationality in Christ. Evangelism and dialogue based on this continuity will bring a more positive involvement in the lives of men and women searching for God in many different directions.

7. There is only one decisive revelation of God available to all the world, and that is his revelation through the Lord Jesus Christ. Although this final revelation has already been made known to us in the historic event of Jesus' life, death and resurrection, the world is yet to fully come face to face with God's grace and justice in his ultimate triumph at the climax of history.

For Further Reading

Boyd, Robin. *An Introduction to Indian Christian Theology.* Madras: Christian Literary Society, 1975.
Gnanakan, Ken. *Proclaiming Christ in a Pluralistic Context.* Bangalore: Theological Book Trust, 2002.

Prabhakar, M. E., ed. *Towards a Dalit Theology.* Delhi: ISPCK, 1990.

Sumithra, Sunand. *Christian Theologies from an Indian Perspective.* Bangalore: Theological Book Trust, 1990.

Thomas, M. M. *Secular Ideologies of India and the Secular Meaning of Christ.* Bangalore: Christian Literature Society, 1976.

8

AFRICAN THEOLOGY

James Kombo

• • •

AFRICAN THEOLOGY
Scope

While this paper is an exposition of African theology, its primary focus is the factors that have shaped the past, the present and the future of biblical interpretation and theological engagement in Africa. For one, African theology plays a role like Hermes the Greek god, who was entrusted with the singular responsibility of transmitting the deliberations of the gods at Mount Olympus not only to the citizens but also to the ethnic peoples across the borders of the Roman world. In playing a hermeneutical role, African theology appreciates Africa and its dynamics as well as the yawning gap between the continent and the Bible in its historical and cultural setting.

African theology has attempted to bridge this gap by engaging in what I see as four dominant patterns of conversation: (1) discussions about God—this was the earliest form of African theology, and it concerned itself primarily with the area of continuity between God in the Bible and God in the African primordial narratives—*Ngai, Nkulukulu, Nyasaye, Nyambe*; (2) debate about the rationale for the translation agenda, transposing the Bible into respective contemporary indigenous language; (3) reflections about depicting Christianity as essentially an African religion; (4) exploration of contextual theologies—insisting on contextualized African theological expressions. These hermeneutical rubrics have not only determined the nature of theological debates in Africa, but they also represent the major theological divides or paradigms within African theology, namely, identity theology, incarnation theology, African/world Christianity theology and contextualization theologies.

1. Identity Theology

Theologia Africana championed by Bolaji Idowu, John S. Mbiti, Gabriel M. Setiloane and Charles Nyamiti in the 1960s and the 1970s was really identity theology. These scholars expressed their theological views in the context of identity discourses and, more specifically, the debate on whether the pre-Christian Africa had a sense of God. In order to ground the message of God that had struck a chord with so many Africans, these early African theologians were convinced that it was absolutely necessary to affirm that God, who was the source of the message of the Christian faith, was not imported into Africa through the missionary enterprise. In other words, these early discussants based their position on their understanding of cultural continuity, revelation, studies on the relationship between Yahweh and the religions of the Near Eastern world, and their grasp of the African primal religions and the African philosophy. They concluded that the God of the Bible was the same God known to Africa by various names, and as such he could not have been foreign or a mere figment of imagination but was always part of the African reality.

Today, these God discussions appear to have been rejuvenated and widened under the rubric of studies on identity, referentiality or theological language. The first African Anglican bishop, Ajayi Crowther, appears to have set the pattern when instructing his clergy. He insisted:

> When we first introduce the Gospel to any people we should take advantage of any principles which they themselves admit. Thus, though the heathen in this part of Africa possess no written legends, yet wherever we turn our eyes, we find among them, in their animal sacrifices, a text which is the mainspring of the Christian faith: "Without shedding of blood there is no remission." Therefore we may with propriety say: "That which ye ignorantly practise, declare we unto you. 'The blood of Jesus Christ the Son of God cleanseth from all sin.'"[1]

---

[1] Ajayi Crowther, quoted in Jesse Page, *The Black Bishop* (London: Simpkin, 1910), p. 282.

In a sense Bishop Crowther was concerned with what the Ghanian theologian Kwame Bediako has discussed as identity and the Christianization of the African past. This idea, which forms a good part of Bediako's theological pillars, would serve the valuable purpose of providing Africa with "cultural continuity" within which the referentiality of theological language will be meaningful.[2] When Greek and other European languages, for instance, gave the Christian faith their own god names, they were, in their own way, "Christianizing" their indigenous concept of the divine. Christianity took the god names from the cultures and filled them with new content. In other words, by Christianizing the divine, they were able to identify the reality referenced. This referentiality, as in the case of the African names for God such as *Nyame*, *Modimo* and *Nyasaye*, allows for a crescendo of the highest degree in the theological language—Jesus is *Nyame*; he is *Modimo*; he is *Nyasaye*.

2. Incarnation/Translation Theology

The incarnation paradigm of African theology accepts a common intellectual crystallizing point for Africa, represented in a singular cosmology and focuses on the "Africanization" agenda, which, in a sense, is the equivalent of the Hellenization of the Christian faith from the second to the fourth centuries of the church.[3] Like in Hellenization, Christianity in this case gets incarnated into the African metaphysics, and the African narratives, in turn, are also changed by the gospel.

This dynamic interaction between African intellectual culture and

---

[2] Kwame Bediako, (*Theology and Identity* [Oxford: Regnum, 1992], pp. 9-10) like Mbiti, is of the conviction that the African traditional past is part of the *praeparatio evangelica*. Some African scholars such as Okot p'Bitek, Ali Mazrui, Setiloane, Christian Gaba and Samwel Kibicho argue that to view the African traditional religions as *praeparatio evangelica* amounts to refusal to look at the latter on its own terms. Okot p'Bitek called this kind of scholarship "intellectual smuggling" (O. p'Bitek, *African Religions in Western Scholarship* [Kampala: East African Literature Bureau, 1970], p. 88).
[3] T. S. Maluleke argues that positing Africanization as the new task of African inculturation theology, as Bediako does, may not be as groundbreaking as it may seem. He reasons that the proposal is based on juxtaposing Christianization and Africanization (T. S. Maluleke, "Half Century of African Christian Theology," *Journal of Theology for Southern Africa* 99 [1997]: 4-23).

CATEGORY 1
God The only one with the "divine force." The ultimate explanation of the origin and sustenance of both humankind and all things.
CATEGORY 2
Spirits Every spirit distinguished by the nature of its "force." Some spirits are weaker than the others.
CATEGORY 3
Ancestors Superhuman beings and the spirits of those who died a long time ago but are still active in determining the affairs of the living. Each of the ancestors distinguished by their respective "life force."
CATEGORY 4
Man Human beings who are alive and who are about to be born. Each human being distinguished by respective "life force."
CATEGORY 5
Animals and Plants Remainder of biological life. Each of these distinguished by respective "life force."
CATEGORY 6
Phenomena and objects without biological life Rocks, space, time, beauty. Each is distinguished by respective force.

Figure 8.1. African cosmology

the gospel gives a new agenda and shape to African Christianity. Interaction of this kind has always interested and characterized Christianity. Indeed its basic logic helps explain conversion. Distinguishing a convert from a proselyte, Andrew Walls writes:

> To become a convert . . . is to turn, and turning involves not a change of substance but a change of direction. Conversion, in other words, means to *turn what is already there in a new direction*. It is not a matter of substituting something new for something old—that is proselytizing, a method that the early church could have adopted but deliberately chose to jettison. Nor is conversion a matter of adding something new to something old, as a supplement or in synthesis. Rather, Christian con-

version involves redirecting what is already there, turning it in the direction of Christ.[4]

The interest of incarnation theologians is in identifying and employing
in the theological process those African primordial narratives or categories
of reality already available. This is the approach of Placide Tempels, Alexis
Kagame and John S. Mbiti. Translation theologians such as Kwame Bediako, Lamin Sanneh and Andrew Walls have also done much by way of
highlighting the connection between the gospel and native intellectual
tools within the larger conversation. Figure 8.1 is a representation, in broad
strokes, of African cosmology within which the faith is to incarnate.

Not much real *theologia* has taken advantage of this primordial narrative. The debates of the 1960s and 1970s on contextualization still
appear to be attracting some attention. If Christianity's incarnation
into the African nomenclature is to succeed then, as the translation
paradigm of African theology argues, our theologizing process must
recognize African cosmology and engage in theological discourse along
the lines of African categories of existence.

3. African/World Christianity Theology

World Christianity and its local expression, African Christianity, are
other formidable theological hermeneutics that have emerged recently.
Lamin Sanneh has defined World Christianity as

> The movement of Christianity as it takes form and shape in societies
> that previously were not Christian, societies that had no bureaucratic
> tradition with which to domesticate the gospel. In these societies Chris-
> tianity was received and expressed through the cultures, customs, and
> traditions of the people affected. World Christianity is not one thing,
> but a variety of indigenous responses through more or less effective local
> idioms, but in any case without necessarily the European Enlighten-
> ment frame.[5]

---

[4]Andrew Walls, "Old Athens and New Jerusalem: Some Signposts for Christian Scholarship in
the early history of Mission Studies," *International Bulletin of Missionary Research* (October
1997): 148.
[5]Lamin Sanneh, *Whose Religion Is Christianity: The Gospel Beyond the West* (Grand Rapids: Eerdmans, 2003), p. 22.

The thrust of this paradigm is its acceptance of Christianity as an African religion. It also underscores the essential difference of African Christianity as well as its growth patterns in relation to the rest of the world. For this theological paradigm the success of Christianity in Africa, and indeed elsewhere, has to do with both its essential difference and the connection between Christianity and Africa's primal religions. Philip Jenkins comments on this as follows: "individuals came to believe the message offered, and found this the best means of explaining the world around them."[6] Sanneh echoes the same idea:

> Africans embraced Christianity because it resonated so well with the values of the old religions. . . . People sensed in their hearts that Jesus did not mock their respect for the sacred or their clamor for an invincible Savior, so they beat their sacred drums for him until the stars skipped and danced in the skies. After that dance the stars weren't little anymore. Christianity helped Africans to become renewed Africans, not remade Europeans.[7]

Statistically, Christianity globally started out in the past century 81 percent white, and ended at 45 percent, with Africa enjoying the largest share of the shift. Christians in Africa grew from 8 million in 1900 to 360 million in 2000. This trend is not going to stop any time soon. Indeed this is a huge change ethnically and in terms of the essence of Christianity. Sanneh has expressed similar sentiments: "Africa has become, or is becoming, a Christian continent in cultural as well as numerical terms, while on the same scale the West has become, or is rapidly becoming, a post-Christian society."[8] For Bediako, these numbers mean that African Christianity has attained the status of what he calls "representative Christianity."[9] Sanneh puts it more graphically. For him, this is an "irruption of Christian forces in contemporary Africa

---

[6]Philip Jenkins, *The Next Christendom: The Coming of Global Christianity* (Oxford: Oxford University Press, 2002), p. 44.

[7]Sanneh, *Whose Religion Is Christianity?* pp. 42-43.

[8]Ibid., p. 36.

[9]Kwame Bediako, "African Theology as a Challenge for Western Theology," unpublished paper delivered at Utrecht, October 2002.

[which] is without parallel in the history of the church."[10]

The significance of this paradigm for global theology lies in its vindication and creative treatment of Africa's primordial narrative. It also confronts global Christianity with the stark reality of both the numerical and the ethnic shift of Christianity to the global South and to Africa in particular. This shift does not only give particular prominence to African theology, but in a more fundamental way it creates space for African theology in the global arena and declares its essential difference. In other words, this model raises the question, At what point does a contextual theology move from the periphery to the center?

4. Contextual Theologies

The contextualization agenda has dominated theological discourse since the 1970s. Indeed varieties of contextual theologies in Africa appear to indicate deliberate, structured and pragmatic efforts through which the message may be more deeply experienced, secured, shared and born out of the need to obey God. Among the major contextual theologies in Africa are African inculturation theology, African black theology, African liberation theology and African women theology. In all cases, something from outside (the *magisterium* in the case of the Catholics and the gospel for evangelicals) is preserved as the new reality and is brought into the African context.

The African inculturation theology. African inculturation theology is perhaps the oldest form of contextual theology in Africa. It was initially a response to cultural oppression. The earliest manifestations of this strand of contextual theology were the African Independent Churches (AIC). In Catholic circles, the early seeds of inculturation theology were sown in the adaptation and later inculturation discourses. Whereas African inculturation theology seeks to deal with the relationship between culture and theology, it has not sorted out neatly the nature of this relationship. Roughly four distinct approaches have been maintained. The first approach says that African traditional religions had no

---

[10]Lamin Sanneh, *Translating the Message: The Missionary Impact on Culture* (Maryknoll, N.Y.: Orbis, 1989), p. 188.

or only distorted revelation and no salvation. This position is articulated mainly by Byang Kato and Tukunboh Adeyemo.[11] The second approach allows for revelation but rejects any possibility for salvation. John S. Mbiti, Charles Nyamiti and Kwame Bediako are the major proponents of this view.[12] The third group argues for both revelation and salvation in African traditional religion, *but* they also insist that the highest revelation and salvation are only in the Christian faith. The proponents of this are Patrick Kalilombe and Laurenti Magesa.[13] The final group argues that there is indeed revelation and salvation in African traditional religions. For this position, all religions are unique and relative ways of salvation. Among the proponents of this view are Samuel Kibicho, Anatole Byaruhanga-Akiiki and Okot p'Bitek.[14]

African black theology. This model of theology was historically confined to apartheid-era South Africa and received its inspiration from American black theology. The best of reflections on African black theology are in the works of Beyers Naude, Trevor Huddleston, Manas Buthelezi, Desmond Tutu, Alan Boesak, Frank Chikane and Albert

[11]Byang Kato, *Biblical Christianity in Africa* (Achimota, Ghana: Africa Christian Press, 1985), p. 11; see also his *Theological Pitfalls* (Kisumu, Kenya: Evangel Publishing House, 1975), p. 16; Tokunboh Adeyemo, *Salvation in An African Tradition* (Nairobi: Evangel Publishing House, 1979), p. 96; see also his "The Salvation Debate and Evangelical Response," *East African Journal of Evangelical Theology* 2 (1984): 4-19.

[12]Charles Nyamiti, *African Tradition and the Christian God* (Eldoret: Gaba Publications, 1979); see also his *The Way to Christian Theology for Africa* (Eldoret: Gaba Publications, 1978). On John S. Mbiti's line of thought see his "ὁ σωτὴρ ἡμῶν as an African Experience," in *Christ and Spirit in the New Testament*, ed. Barnabas Lindars and Stephen S. Smalley (Cambridge: Cambridge University Press, 1973), pp. 397-414; and his other work "Some Reflections on the African Experience of Salvation Today," in *Living Faiths and Ultimate Goals: A Continuing Dialogue*, ed. S. J. Samartha (Geneva: WCC, 1974), pp. 108-19.

[13]Patrick Kalilombe, "Evangelization and the Holy Spirit," *African Ecclesial Review* 18 (1976): 8-18; see also his article "The Salvific Value of the African Religions," *African Ecclesial Review* 21 (1979): 143-56. See also Laurenti Magesa, "Evangelisation," *African Ecclesial Review* 24 (1982): 354-362; and also "Who Are 'the People of God'?" *African Ecclesial Review* 26 (1984): 204-12.

[14]Samuel Kibicho, "The Teaching of African Religion in our Schools and Colleges and the Christian Attitude Towards This Religion," *Africa Theological Journal* 10 (1981): 29-37; see also his "Revelation in African Religion," *Africa Theological Journal* 12 (1983): 166-77; A. Byaruhanga-Akiiki, *Spirituality in African Traditions*, BOLESWA Occasional Papers on Theology and Religion 1 (University of Botswana, Lesotho and Swaziland, 1988); see also his work "African Traditional Values for Human Development," *Church Contributions to Integral Development* (Eldoret: Gaba Publications, 1989), pp. 45-62. See also Okot p'Bitek, *African Religions in Western Scholarship* (Nairobi: Kenya Literature Bureau, 1970).

Nolan. For these men, as indeed for the many who chose this approach
to doing theology in Africa, Christianity and the gospel had a political
dimension and could only be relevant to the extent that it centered on
justice, liberation and a preferential option for the poor. Other mile-
stone developments within African black theology included the 1982
election of Alan Boesak as the chair of the World Alliance of Reformed
Churches, the subsequent suspension of the membership of the Afri-
kaner Reformed Churches and the declaration of apartheid as a heresy,
thereby declaring also a *status confessionis*. Boesak's church, the Neder-
duitse Gereformeerde Sendingkerk (NGSK), responded to the *status
confessionis* by drafting the Belhar Confession,[15] which won approval in
1986. Whereas the NGSK's response gave rise to the Belhar Confession, the Ecumenical Institute for Contextual Theology drafted the
Kairos Document, which proposed a "prophetic theology."[16] It is important to note that whereas Alan Boesak carried out his contextualization
task in the context of World Alliance of Reformed Churches, the others raised their voices in their capacities as secretary general of the
South African Council of Churches (SACC): Desmond Tutu (1978-
1985), Beyers Naude (1985-1988) and Frank Chikane (1988-1995).
The ideals of the South African black theology enshrined in the Belhar
Confession and the Kairos Document informed the South African
Truth and Reconciliation Commission, which met between February
1996 and October 1998 under the chairmanship of Desmond Tutu and

---

[15]The message of Belhar Confession is simply as follows: "Because the secular gospel of apartheid fundamentally threatens the reconciliation in Christ as well as the unity of the church of
Jesus Christ, the NGSK in South Africa declares that for the church of Jesus Christ a *status
confessionis* exists." The Belhar Confession affirmed the unity of the church (against the separate churches under apartheid), the centrality of reconciliation to the gospel message, and the
principles of justice and peace as basic to the nature of God.
[16]"The Kairos Document, 1985," *South African History Online*, www.sahistory.org.za/article/
kairos-document-1985-0. The Kairos Document criticized the "state theology" found mainly
among the Afrikaners and which was developed with the express purpose of defending apartheid on biblical grounds. The document also criticized the "church theology" mainly found
among the English-speaking Christians, which went for a cheap form of reconciliation, justice
and nonviolence, that did not require reconciliation to go with repentance, that did not see
justice of reform as insufficient in South Africa and that did not reckon the fact that state violence makes individual nonviolence impossible in South Africa. The "prophetic theology" proposed by the Kairos Document required justice against tyranny and appealed to the oppressed
majority to embrace hope as opposed to supporting the powerful in their quest to bring about
radical reform to an unjust system.

provided the pillars upon which post-apartheid South Africa stands.

African liberation theology. The foundations of African liberation theology were laid at the first Pan African Conference of Third World Theologians held in Accra, Ghana, in December 1977. At this meeting there was a deliberate effort to transform African theology into a liberation theology. The trend would gain momentum in the 1980s, at which time its proponents reached a consensus that there was no single common "African culture" and that whatever was left of the individual cultures had undergone such significant erosion that culture as such was no longer a critical factor in any theologizing process. For this group of theological thinkers the issue for Africa was multifaceted pauperization manifested mainly in grinding poverty, political oppression, disease and ignorance. Thus the African liberation theologians saw their project not only as declaring the inculturation paradigm defunct but also as clarifying the basis of such change made necessary by the African realities of the time. Jean-Marc Éla, for instance, came to the conclusion that if theology is to be at the cutting edge, it must not be encumbered by Africa's past. For him, a model for theologizing must evolve that would have the inbuilt capacity to expose and correct the causes of poverty, political oppression, disease and ignorance. Other theologians who have found this model relevant are Bénézet Bujo, Fabien Eboussi-Boulaga, Mercy Amba Oduyoye, Laurenti Magesa, J. N. K. Mugambi and David Gitari.

African women theology. African women theology shares many features of African liberation theology. The theology does not seek to add a new theological treatise to those already existing; instead it sees itself as a new hermeneutic of the Christian faith and thus a new way of understanding Christianity as a whole and also a new way of living the faith.[17] By embracing this contextual theology, African women theologians are convinced that they will affect the basic constitution of theology in such areas as Christology, and forms of church life such as constitutions of churches, liturgies, catechesis and moral options. They

---

[17]Teresa Okure, "Women in the Bible: African Women's Perspective," in *Third World Women Doing Theology: Papers from the Intercontinental Women's Conference, Oaxtepec, Mexico, December 1-6, 1986*, ed. Virginia Fabella and Dolorita Martinez (Port Harcourt, Nigeria: Ecumenical Association of Third World Theologians, 1997), pp. 149-59.

will also usher in a new universality in which the women's issues are paramount and classical church divisions are rendered irrelevant.[18] Among prominent theologians from this paradigm are Nyambura J. Njoroge, Isabel Phiri, Mercy Amba Oduyoye, Yvette Aklé, Mia Brandel-Syrier and Anne Nasimiyu-Wasike.

5. African Evangelical Theology: Which Way Forward?

African evangelical theology as a distinct expression of African theology has existed since the early 1970s. It sought to distinguish itself from other contextual theologies by accenting the Bible and the preaching of the good news of Jesus Christ. Historically, it was the project of the Association of Evangelicals in Africa (AEA), which is an affiliate of the World Evangelical Alliance.

Unfortunately, only a small portion of the African church has membership in the Association of Evangelicals in Africa, with a big bulk either being Catholics, members of the All Africa Conference of Churches (AACC) or the Organization of African Instituted Churches (OAIC). Moreover, the church in Africa, regardless of its denominational divides and confessional complexities, sees itself as largely evangelical. In East Africa for instance, the words *watu wa injili*, "the people of evangel," are found among the independent churches, the Catholics, mainline Protestants, Anglicans and Pentecostals. The categories used to define the boundaries of evangelicals as seen in the West and adopted by the Association of Evangelicals in Africa (AEA) appear separatist and not desirable.

---

[18]Amoah and Oduyoye, in the article "The Christ for African Women," seek to deal with what women say about Christology and whether traditional statements of Christology take into account women's experience. For these women theologians, Christology is so dominated by male chauvinism that in its present form it lacks any pretense to be of serious consequence to the African woman (see Elizabeth Amoah and Mercy Amba Oduyoye, "The Christ for African Women," in *With Passion and Compassion: Third World Women Doing Theology*, ed. Virginia Fabella and Mercy Amba Oduyoye [Maryknoll, N.Y.: Orbis, 1988], pp. 35-46). Similar sentiments are expressed in Teresia M. Hinga, "Jesus Christ and the Liberation of Women in Africa," in *Will to Arise*, ed. Mercy Amba Oduyoye and Musimbi Kanyoro (Maryknoll, N.Y.: Orbis, 1992), pp. 183-94; and M. Morny, "Christ Restores Life," in *Talitha, Qumi! Proceedings of the Convocation of African Women Theologians*, ed. Mercy Amba Oduyoye and Musimbi Kanyoro (Ibadan, Nigeria: Daystar Press, 1990), pp. 149-54.

The other challenge for African evangelical theology is the rise of the World Christian paradigm that actively appeals for engaging the primordial narratives within each context. African evangelical theology has in the past been criticized for ignoring African worldviews in its theological process. Mercy Oduyoye once responded to the African evangelicals as follows: "The rejection [of the] African worldview by an African shows how successful the Christian missions were in alienating Africans from their 'Africanness.'"[19] John Parrat has also evaluated Byang Kato, "the founding father of modern African evangelical theology," rather harshly.[20] According to Parrat, Byang Kato failed "to make allowance for the fact that throughout its history Christianity has had to come to terms with the cultures in which it has been implanted."[21]

Today more than any time in the history of African Christianity, the church is united in the supremacy of preaching the gospel of Jesus Christ, "Christ died for our sins according to the Scriptures" (1 Cor 15:3). Nothing can be added to the perfect achievement wrought by Christ, and sinners are invited to turn to Christ in faith. Much emphasis on the significance of the Bible and its confessional interpretation is based on the understanding that the gospel claims are traceable to one solid source, the Bible.[22] Archbishop Peter Akinola of the Anglican Church of Nigeria, articulating a typical evangelical reaction in mood and logic in his assessment of same-sex marriages in the Episcopal churches of America, said, "I didn't write the Bible, it's part of our Christian heritage. It tells us what to do. If the word of God says homosexuality is an abomination, then so be it."[23] This hallmark of the African church, as Jenkins argues, is an important stepping-stone

[19]Mercy Amba Oduyoye, *Hearing and Knowing: Theological Reflections on Christianity in Africa* (Maryknoll, N.Y.: Orbis, 1986), p. 62.

[20]Mark Shaw, *The Kingdom of God in Africa: A Short History of African Christianity* (Grand Rapids: Baker, 1996), p. 278.

[21]John Parratt, *Reinventing Christianity: African Christian Theology Today* (Grand Rapids: Eerdmans, 1995), p. 63.

[22]See Tokunboh Adeyemo, ed., *Africa Bible Commentary* (Nairobi: WordAlive; Grand Rapids: Zondervan, 2006).

[23]"The Church of Nigeria (Anglican Communion) and the Homosexuality Issue," *Church of Nigeria Anglican Communion*, www.anglican-nig.org/hobstatementaug.htm.

that African evangelical theology must use.[24]

Over thirty-five years ago, Byang Kato stated that it is undeniable that we "have a unique contribution to make to theological debates."[25] At that time Kato felt sad that the evangelical fraternity was, in fact, finding "itself in the situation of trying to exist without a theology."[26] There has not been a drastic alteration to this observation. Where there is change, the temptation has been to quench the curiosity of the parched palates of the myriads who have said yes to Christ with secondary theology often couched in local expressions of some grand global agenda. African evangelical theology must acquaint itself with the works of the world's leading evangelical theologians. But it must be familiar with the reflections of its own luminaries such as Byang Kato and Tokunboh Adeyemo. However, if this is all the African evangelical theology does, then it remains a mere secondary theology that concerns itself with reinterpretation and adaptation of either the *magisterium* or other peoples' previous discourses.

African evangelical theology cannot afford this luxury. Rather it must determine to reserve a significant place for primary theology by ensuring four things: (1) actively engaging the African primordial narratives in direct theological discourses. From here we get to identify not only the questions Africa is asking but also the logic and manner of presentation; (2) encouraging the use of vernaculars as languages of change and empowerment in worship and reflections; (3) maintaining candid and vibrant conversations between the good news of Jesus Christ and Africa's current multidimensional challenges and opportunities. Note that evangelicals have been seen to be aloof, preferring to carry only the message of the good news; (4) encouraging and preparing leadership enabled to answer questions emerging from the African grassroots. This we can do with God's help.

---

[24]Philip Jenkins, *The New Faces of Christianity: Believing the Bible in the Global South* (Oxford: Oxford University Press, 2006).
[25]Byang Kato, "Theological Anemia in Africa," in *Biblical Christianity in Africa* (Achimota, Ghana: Africa Christian Press, 1985), p. 11.
[26]John S. Mbiti, quoted in ibid., p. 11.

For Further Reading

Adeyemo, Tokunboh. *Salvation in African Tradition*. Nairobi, Kenya: Evangel
Publishing House, 1979.

Adeyemo, Tokunboh, ed. *Africa Bible Commentary*. Nairobi, Kenya:
WordAlive; Grand Rapids: Zondervan, 2006.

Bediako, Kwame. *Theology and Identity: The Impact of Culture upon Christian
Thought in the Second Century and in Modern Africa*. Oxford: Regnum
Books, 1992.

———. *Christianity in Africa: The Renewal of a Non-Western Religion*. Edinburgh: Edinburgh University Press; Maryknoll, N.Y.: Orbis, 1995.

Kato, Byang H. *Theological Pitfalls in Africa*. Kisumu, Kenya: Evangelical
Publishing House, 1975.

———. *Biblical Christianity in Africa: A collection of papers and addresses*.
Achimota, Ghana, West Africa: Africa Christian Press, 1985.

9

MIDDLE EASTERN THEOLOGY IN EVANGELICAL PERSPECTIVE

Martin Accad

• • •

When we think of the contemporary Middle East, geographically we are looking at the region stretching from Turkey to Yemen, and from the eastern Mediterranean coast, including Egypt on the eastern edges of North Africa, to Iran on the western edges of Central Asia. The present chapter, however, will focus only on the Arab Middle East, and specifically on theological resources published in the Arabic language. No reference will be made to Turkish or Persian theological writing and thinking, nor to Messianic Jewish theological writing and thinking coming out of Israel and written in Hebrew. Strictly speaking, these may be seen as significant gaps in the present survey. However, neither time and space nor linguistic accessibilities have allowed me to include such resources. Perhaps the present contribution will begin to shape an Arab platform from which new ties may be created with the other Middle Eastern traditions that have been left out, and perhaps one day this will become the catalyst for the emergence of a more comprehensive contemporary Middle Eastern theological tradition in the proper sense of the term. But for now, it is important to point out that what this chapter looks at is actually "Arab Middle Eastern Theology," rather than "Middle Eastern Theology" in evangelical perspective.

The present article will convey a sense that the Middle Eastern Christian theological tradition is quite poor, which may sound rather strange, seeing as the Christian tradition altogether emerged originally in the Middle East. Indeed, the words and deeds of Jesus recorded in the Gospels, as well as the further theologizing discourses of the apostle Paul and others in the New Testament, are the starting point and the essence of the Middle Eastern Christian theological tradition. However, this article looks at the contemporary period, and specifically at the last sixty years or so. Finally, at times the study will feel more like an assessment of the Arabic language publishing business than a proper assessment of the Arab Middle Eastern theological tradition.

Survey of Arab Christian Writings in the Middle East Through the Twentieth and Twenty-First Centuries

Sources of information about Arab Christian publications. For a survey of what Christians of the Middle East have written in the Arabic language through the twentieth century, we are fortunate to have in our possession the fruit of a vast project undertaken by the Middle East Council of Churches (MECC) in collaboration with the Catholic Press (now called *Dār al-Mashriq*, "Orient Publishers"): *Dalīl al-Kitāb al-Masīhī* (Catalog of Christian Books). This project of surveying and inventorying all Middle Eastern Christian publications written in Arabic was launched in December of 1978, following a consultation between Orthodox, Catholic and Protestant publishing houses of the region hosted by the Middle East Council of Churches.[1] A first volume was published in 1980, covering publications from 1950 to January 1, 1980, which includes about 1,867 titles. A second volume was then published in 1993, covering the decade between 1980 and 1990, which ended up comprising about 960 titles.[2] Both volumes are written in Arabic. The sheer statistical increase in the number of publications between the two periods (1,867 titles in thirty years, compared to 960 titles in just ten years) was indicative of a significant trend beginning to emerge in the Christian Arab Middle Eastern world. The publishers pointed out

---

[1]See the Introduction to vol. 1 of *Dalīl al-Kitāb al-Masīhī* (Beirut: Catholic Press & MECC, 1980).

[2]These figures result from my own count. According to the introduction to volume 2, the first volume contained about sixteen hundred titles and the second contained about one thousand titles (ibid., p. 5).

three main observable trends that are worth summarizing:

1. A significant number of publications in the Arabic language between 1950 and 1980 are translated from Western languages rather than written originally in Arabic by Arab writers. And a large number of these works are translations of primarily devotional Christian material. Even the writings of the Eastern church fathers, notably those who wrote in Syriac and in Arabic, are easier to find translated into Western languages than translated and edited into Arabic. This realization led the project facilitators to point out the crucial need for training in writing skills, with a view toward encouraging Arab Christians to address contemporary regional social, political and religious issues directly in the Arabic language.

2. About fifty percent of the publications from those first thirty years are devotional and ascetic in nature, failing to address contemporary issues, except in an exhortative and moralistic style. These primarily include sermon collections, biographies and hagiographies, educational materials, and Christian ethics.

3. The project participants also pointed out the significant lack of literature in Arabic pertaining to issues of ecumenical and interfaith relations. On the other hand, a significant number of publications deal with the text of the Bible, including various Arabic translations and editions, studies, introductions and so on.

This project of inventorying and cataloging Arab Christian publications was picked up and will continue to be updated through the so-called database project of the Arab Baptist Theological Seminary. I was fortunate to be given access to the unpublished preliminary data, which I have used for the present essay to trace all publications since 1990. As far as the three trends mentioned are concerned, which were identified by the initial project facilitators, the *translation* trend over the past two decades seems to have dropped down to about 30 or 40 percent of the sum total of Arabic Christian publications, with the Protestant publishing houses majoring in that area. The publication of academic works and of books more specialized in specific subject areas is clearly on the rise as well. The Arab Baptist Theological Seminary alone now has a dedicated department for the production of academic works in Arabic, with a focus on textbook-level materials. It focuses both on the translation of high-quality evangelical works from the West as well as sponsoring Arab theologians from the region to compose textbook-level works in Arabic. Finally, the efforts of organizations such as the MECC seem to have borne some fruit in encouraging publishers to produce more in the area of ecumenical and interfaith issues.

Some of the main figures in three traditions. Many priests, monks, pastors and teachers have contributed to the Arabic-language library and the religious imagination and psyche of the Arab Christian Middle-Easterner over the past century. The reader of Christian books in Arabic, however, will be struck by the massive contribution of a few key authors who have played a major part in the significant increase of Christian literature in Arabic over the past twenty years. Among these, three authors stand tall above all others. Incidentally, each is from one of the three traditions covered in the present study.

Maronite priest Būlus (Paul) al-Feghālī in Lebanon has around two hundred titles published between 1990 and 2010, and none before the 1990s according to the MECC catalog. The writings bearing his name belong almost entirely to the field of biblical studies, including introductions and commentaries on the whole Bible as well as on the various books of the Old and New Testaments. His Bible commentaries combine patristic material, mainly from the Syriac tradition, with contemporary exegesis, primarily from European sources. As might be expected, the sheer volume of his production has meant that his commentaries are more cumulative than innovative. Some of his work also belongs to the field of biblical theology.

Feghālī has also initiated and led a Hebrew-Arabic interlinear translation of the Old Testament and a Greek-Arabic interlinear translation of the New Testament. Not least, Feghālī was extensively involved in the final stages of translation and revision of the ecumenical version of the Arabic Bible. In addition to biblical studies Feghālī has devoted a good part of his writing to the editing and translation of patristic texts from the Syriac tradition, including many of the writings of Aphrāhāṭ, Ephrem, Jacob of Serug, Narsai, Theodore of Mopsuestia, Bar Hebraeus and others. Coptic Orthodox monk Matta al-Maskīn, in Egypt, is

another Bible scholar that stands out among other Arab Christian writers. His writings, which are in excess of 150 titles over the past twenty
years, as well as four others in the decade of the 1980s, are a mix of
Bible commentaries, Bible introductions, biblical and systematic theology, editions of patristic monastic writings, liturgy and spirituality.
Matta al-Maskīn's approach to biblical exegesis and theology is mystical
and patristic, traditional and pastoral in nature. His writings clearly
convey the concerns and interests of the Coptic Orthodox Church.

On the Protestant side, Egyptian pastor and theologian Makram
Najīb has been the most prolific, with over one hundred titles bearing
his name. Beginning with *Introduction to the Minor Prophets* in 1980, he
has gone on to address various life issues and social challenges facing
the Arab Middle Eastern Church, often by bringing in a strong biblical
perspective, or even casting his topic entirely in the framework of a
study of a certain book of the Bible. He deals with sociological and
political issues such as freedom, civility, power, the state of Israel, progress and pluralism, presenting a biblical perspective. But he also addresses other issues more specific to the life of the church, such as baptism, the gifts of the Holy Spirit, evangelism, conversion and
eschatology. Of these three giants, it is ironic that it is the Catholic and
Orthodox who have invested the bulk of their work in biblical exegesis.
Of the three, however, it is Makram Najīb who seems most in touch with
the contemporary challenges facing the church of the Middle East, and
his approach to these topics is strongly biblical. His writings are obviously addressed to the lay church person rather than to the scholar, as
can be seen even in the size of his publications. About a third of his
productions are under one hundred pages, and only about 20 percent
exceed two hundred pages. His writing style is popular but not shallow.
On the other hand, at least 75 percent of Fr. Feghālī's books and commentaries exceed two hundred pages, and over a quarter are greater
than five hundred pages. As for Matta al-Maskīn, about half of his production, namely the ones dealing with various issues of Coptic church
life, are under two hundred pages and obviously addressed primarily to
the common Coptic Christian. The other half are much more volumi-
nous, comprising primarily his commentaries on the Bible.

Of course one might question whether the sheer mass of authorship is itself a reflection of significance and influence. When one thinks of the literary production of contemporary Arab Christian authors, no particular title stands out. In the Middle East, it is the volume rather than the groundbreaking innovation and creativity that has thus far left its mark on the reading public and the church. The three authors singled out here have been the main Arabic-writing shapers of theological thinking and Bible reading. "Arabic-writing shapers" needs to be specified, for it might well be argued that the translated works of popular Western authors and television personalities are actually the main shapers of the Arab Middle Eastern Christian mind today, particularly among the youth.

Principal overall features of each of the three traditions. If Protestant publishers can claim the larger portion of the pie in the area of Bible and theology, it should be pointed out that quantity does not necessarily reflect quality. In retrospect, if the translation of popular Christian literature from the West turns out to have been an obstacle to the emergence of new, creative and context-relevant theological thinking, then the Protestant tradition would also be the one most guilty of that offense.

When it comes to scholarly works written directly in Arabic, with a few exceptions, these seem to be largely the publication of class notes by seminary professors, often not even through professional publishers. It must be said, however, that this is beginning to change. It is perhaps due to the fact that several regional Protestant seminaries have now been around for several decades that a number of Arab Protestant scholars are beginning to publish the fruit of their life's labor, and some of it is of high quality.

Catholics, on the other hand, seem to have been better at producing scholarly theological works in the Arabic language. Catholic publishers are one step ahead of their Protestant counterparts in that a large portion of what they publish is directly written in Arabic. However, one notices that a large portion of what is written is cumulative rather than analytic and innovative. The major influencers are European theologians rather than Americans; the sources are in French, German and Italian rather than English language. But they are more like a good-quality masters-level paper than a Ph.D.-level dissertation. This is nevertheless one step beyond translation and, it would seem, a crucial step in the growth and development of original creative thinking.

When we come to the Orthodox, they seem to be the trailblazers of theological writing in Arabic during the modern period. There seems to be much less influence from the West on their writings. One might reproach many of them, however, for their somewhat esoteric rather than critical academic approach to theological thinking. Many of their writings are steeped in the patristic tradition, an accumulation of centuries of traditional theological thinking, rather than in the thinking of contemporary theologians from the West.

If one were to offer a general assessment of the three traditions, it would seem that though each has some exceptional authors, the bulk of the Arab Middle Eastern theological production often misses the crucial element of the contemporary rhetorical context. The result is a Protestant theological discourse that is largely a mental translation of Western, and particularly American, thinking; Catholic theology that often feels like a paraphrase of European thinking; and Orthodox theology so steeped in the patristic tradition that it often misses the most influential factors of contemporary Arab culture.

Toward a Middle Eastern Evangelical Theology

From translation movement to theological "tradition." When thinking about Arab Christian theology, it may be wise to not too quickly deplore the abundance of translated Western Christian books into Arabic. History indicates that a very significant philosophical tradition can actually emerge out of a translation movement. The journey of Greek philosophy and science from its original Greek language to Arabic via Syriac, and then into Latin and finally into modern European languages is a fascinating and well-documented one.[3] One could argue

---

[3]See for example the accounts of F. E. Peters, *Aristotle and the Arabs: The Aristotelian Tradition in Islam* (New York: New York University Press, 1968); Dimitri Gutas, *Greek Thought, Arabic Culture: The Graeco-Arabic Translation Movement in Baghdad and Early Abbāsid Society (2nd-4th / 8th-10th centuries)* (New York: Routledge, 1998); Richard C. Taylor and Peter Adamson, eds., *The Cambridge Companion to Arabic Philosophy* (Cambridge: Cambridge University Press, 2007).

that no creative and innovative Arab Middle Eastern theological tradition will emerge in a vacuum, but that a massive translation movement might need to precede it.

The intense interaction that was triggered by this crosscultural and cross-linguistic exchange, one could argue, was also at the root of the emergence of an Arab Christian tradition in the context of Islam. At the dawn of Islam, Christians of the East expressed their worship, theology and exegesis in Greek, Syriac, Coptic, Armenian and other local languages. After political control of the region changed hands from Greek Byzantium and Persian Sassanians as early as the first few decades of the Arab Muslim conquests, Eastern Christians continued to use their "religious" languages for quite a while. It is the cultural exchange described earlier that stimulated these Greek, Syriac and Coptic Christians gradually to adopt Arabic as their ecclesiastical and theological language. Despite the fact that there were Arabic-speaking Christian tribes in northern Arabia long before Islam made its appearance (such as the Ghassanids in northwest Arabia and the Lakhmids in the northeast), their liturgical language had nevertheless been primarily Syriac. Only after Middle East Christians adopted Arabic as their language of religious expression can we begin to speak of an Arab Christian "tradition."

There is, however, a flip side to that phenomenon. Very soon Christians in the Middle East had to try to explain their understanding of God, Christ and other complex theological concepts to their new Arab masters, using the *lingua franca* of the conquering empire. This new Arab neighbor came from a far more pragmatic tribal culture with little intellectual sophistication. It would take a while until the emerging Middle Eastern society would develop a certain level of cultural homogeneity, and until then, as I have shown elsewhere, the sort of Christian discourse that developed in Arabic tended to be apologetic and defensive in nature rather than constructive and assertive.[4] The hermeneutical context in which Arab Christian theological discourse had to develop in its early days was perceived as mostly hostile to the complex

---

[4]Martin Accad, "Did the Later Syriac Fathers Take into Consideration Their Islamic Context When Reinterpreting the New Testament?" *Parole de l'orient* (USEK) 23 (1998): 13-32.

jargon that had developed in the church's language about God and Christ over the past few centuries. It is almost as though the emerging Arabic-speaking church had been thrown four hundred years back, before the Chalcedonian developments, to the era of the Arian and Ebionite controversies, and the new linguistic tools available to Arab Christians were far from adequate at that stage to perform the job.

To a large extent, these powers are still at play today in the Middle East. But instead of the defensive and reactionary discourse about God developed in the early stages, an important segment in that church seems to have opted for escapism. Some have adopted a Western-style theological discourse, others have escaped into an esoteric and traditionalist discourse, and yet others have embraced a self-help agenda that follows the latest popular trends of the Western church. These are safer routes than the reactionary discourse, but they are out of touch with the realities on the ground.

To conclude this section, let us focus a little bit on the Protestant segment of the Arab church and adopt a constructive approach. Due to the lack of sufficient literary resources to study theology at a higher level in the Arabic language, most Protestant theological programs at a masters level in the Middle East—and these are not many—are taught in English. Even a number of the undergraduate programs are in English. As a result, Arab theology students often graduate having acquired a limited theological vocabulary in the Arabic language. These limitations are transferred to the local church, and the ability of believers to engage their Arab Muslim culture sensitively and fluently is limited as well. When some graduates choose to pursue a doctoral degree, their main options are to go to the West. After they return to teach at seminaries in the Middle East, they are likely to transfer back that same handicap to their students.

What is needed is a movement of translation of high-quality evangelical theological works into Arabic, which will become the foundation of graduate-level theological formation. At that point emerging leaders will become much more capable of engaging their society and culture competently and creatively. Gradually, new generations of writers will emerge whose Arabic theological idiom is natural and fluent, and who are able to address their context in a relevant manner, providing tools and resources for the church to face its ever-changing challenges. These are the necessary ingredients if we are to witness the emergence of a truly Arab evangelical tradition in the Middle East, rather than simply continue to express an Arabized version of Western theological ideas.

What would make our theology more Middle Eastern? A further point to be made, in light of the previous argument, is that for Arabic-speaking theology to be truly Middle Eastern, it needs to be deeply connected with its cultural context. No demonstration is needed to the effect that Middle Eastern culture at this point of the region's history is primarily a Muslim culture. One might argue that the Arab church has been in touch with its Islamic context through its history, as witnessed by the vast amount of apologetic and polemical literature that has been written to address Muslim challenges to Christianity and to challenge Muslim theological claims. However, what is needed is a move from a reactionary to a constructive theology. That requires not merely answering the explicit challenges that Islam has posed to Christianity through the centuries, but rather developing a constructive and creative theology that addresses these questions at a more subconscious level. I call these the "hermeneutical questions" of the rhetorical Muslim context.

One particular project, initiated by *Dār ath-Thaqāfa* in Egypt, has begun to do that in a 2007 publication titled *Towards a Contemporary Arab Theology.*[5] This collection of chapters, written by different Arab theologians and edited by Andrea Zaki, attempts to address biblical and theological issues that represent key hermeneutical questions in the Middle East context. Out of the eight chapters that constitute the volume, half of these are directly connected with the question of Israel. The remaining four chapters deal with a variety of other issues that are relevant to the Middle East context, specifically interacting with the realities of Islam.

This collected work is no doubt a first in its genre for Middle East-

---

[5]Andrea Zaki, ed., *Naḥwa Lāthūtin ʿArabiyyin Muʿaṣir* (Cairo: *Dār ath-Thaqāfa*, 2007).

ern theology. The Palestinian issue and the state of Israel clearly stand out as the object of great concern. But even though the collected pieces are important, in some ways the title does not reflect adequately the content of the book. We are promised a "contemporary Arab theology" but actually end up with a treatment of important issues primarily addressed, it would seem, to an external audience. The work attempts to clarify the position of Arab Protestants on issues with regard to which they are often misunderstood by their Muslim neighbors due to their close association with the West. That is not to say that the work will not be useful to develop a better understanding of these issues within the church, but the help that we have been offered in thinking theologically in Middle Eastern categories is still limited.

It is interesting that perhaps the Bible scholar who comes closest to offering us a Middle Eastern theological discourse is Kenneth E. Bailey, an American. By spending several decades of his life in Egypt, Palestine and Lebanon, Bailey has been able to bring a special Middle Eastern flavor to his study of the biblical text. In works such as (among others) *Poet and Peasant*, *Through Peasant Eyes*, and more recently *Jesus Through Middle Eastern Eyes*, he brings unique insight into the text by drawing from cultural observation and study of the Middle East.[6] Here we have a discourse that is uniquely Middle Eastern in inspiration without a continuous ax to grind. It is a constructive discourse for the growth and benefit of the church, rather than a reactive and defensive discourse. It is true that his works were not written in Arabic and that he is not an Arab. But we have much to learn from his approach as we seek to develop an authentic contemporary Middle Eastern theological discourse.

What would make our Arab evangelical theology more evangelical? The word *evangelical* in the Middle East carries with it some very unique connotations. To begin with, the word *Injīlī* (as it is used in Arabic) is more of a denominational rather than a theological category in the

---

[6]See Kenneth E. Bailey, *Poet and Peasant: A Literary Cultural Approach to the Parables in Luke* (Grand Rapids: Eerdmans, 1976); *Through Peasant Eyes: More Lucan Parables, Their Culture and Style* (Grand Rapids: Eerdmans, 1980); and *Jesus Through Middle Eastern Eyes: Cultural Studies in the Gospels* (Downers Grove, Ill.: InterVarsity Press, 2008).

Middle East. Furthermore, in several Middle Eastern countries, the word carries with it political connotations. A so-called Supreme Council of the *Injīlī* Churches in Syria and Lebanon gathers under its umbrella all of the various Protestant elements of the church in those two countries. Any non-Catholic or non-Orthodox Christian group without official recognition by the "Supreme Council" is not legally recognized by the Lebanese state. This is an extension of a sociopolitical categorization called the *milla*, which was imposed on all religious groups by the Ottomans and inherited from that era.

This sociopolitical reality borne out of history carries with it some very serious implications regarding the way that we define ourselves as *church* and as *Christian* in the context of the Middle East. As we have been forced into a heavily institutionalized political category, we need to be intentional about breaking out of that imposed identity when we are theologizing. I am fond of Karl Barth's reference to the "revelation of God" as "the abolition of religion" and to religion as "unbelief."[7] The question then becomes, How do we express that we belong to Christ, the supreme deconstructionist of institutional religion, when our very legal existence is dependent on our affiliation to a religious institution? When a Muslim identifies me as a Christian, there are all sorts of ethical, social and political connotations that are assumed, ones that are largely unhelpful to the gospel. In those conditions, how do we strip the gospel of such heavy dress of ethnocentrism and exclusion?

If we come back to the importance of the hermeneutical context, the sociopolitical reality of the Middle Eastern church may well require that we equip ourselves with a very strong theology of incarnation. We have a powerful model in Jesus, whose context in the Gospels was not completely unlike that of the church in the Middle East today. He too lived in a society where religious belonging was essentially assimilated into ethnic identity.

Arab evangelical theologians in the Middle East need to dissociate themselves from the idea that belonging to a Protestant sociopolitical

---

[7]Karl Barth, "The Revelation of God as the Abolition of Religion," in *Christianity and Other Religions: Selected Readings*, ed. John Hick and Brian Hebblethwaite (Philadelphia: Fortress, 1980), p. 5.

reality has anything to do with their spiritual identity of belonging to God in Christ. This has powerful implications for the Middle Eastern church's presence and mission in its Muslim context.[8] One way that this has been expressed powerfully in recent years is through some of the reader-centered Bible translations that have seen the light in Arabic. *Al-Kitāb ash-Sharīf* (The Honorable Book) is a translation that uses very carefully selected key terms to ensure that some important concepts, which have essentially become Christian jargon in our traditional Arabic translations, actually communicate their true meaning to a Muslim reader. For example, with biblical characters that have a place in the Qur'an, the *Sharīf* Bible uses the Qur'anic name rather than the biblical one—such as *Yūnus* for Jonah, instead of *Yūnān, Yaḥya* for John the Baptist, instead of *Yūhanna al-Ma'madān, 'Isa* for Jesus, instead of *Yasū'*—so that the Muslim reader would understand the references. This continues to create much controversy within the Arab church, as we have come to use even the Bible as a symbol of our exclusive tribalism. The other highly controversial issue is the suggestion that some substitute for the title "Son of God" be used, which would communicate the strong Messianic connotations of the New Testament title, rather than the shocking physical—even sexual—connotations that it communicates to the Muslim ear.

Another series of books worth mentioning is the series of Islamic-style Bible commentaries that have been coordinated by Arab poet and novelist Mazhar Mallouhi, often in collaboration with other scholars and literary people. In 1998 he published *The Gospel: An Oriental Reading*, which simply contained one of the traditional Arabic translations (the Smith-Boustany-Van Dyck in this case) written in a calligraphic style, together with a running commentary (in 2001 he did the same with the book of Genesis). In 2004, he published *The Gospel of John: A Sūfi Reading*. This time he used quite a bit of material and imagery from some of the Muslim Sufi writers and poets in his reflection on the Gospel text. Most recently, in 2008, an altogether new translation of

---

[8]I have further argued for this deinstitutionalization of the church's mission in the Muslim world in Martin Accad and John Corrie, "Trinity," in *Dictionary of Mission Theology: Evangelical Foundations*, ed. John Corrie (Downers Grove, Ill.: InterVarsity Press, 2007), pp. 396-401.

the four Gospels and Acts was published, together with a rich and extensive introductory section containing a number of articles addressing some of the main points of contention that a Muslim reader would have in mind when approaching the Bible. It is titled *The True Meaning of the Gospel of Christ.*[9] These books remain controversial and are very little used within the Arab church, but they have made their way into numerous secular bookstores of the Arab world with no restrictions, simply because they respect Arab Islamic aesthetics and contain endorsements by well-known Muslim religious leaders. In other words, these books are a genuine expression of the incarnation of the written word in the linguistic idiom of a specific region and culture.

Going Glocal

A neologism that has appeared in recent years is *glocal*. It has been used in the fields of business and academia, and it expresses beautifully what the present chapter, and more generally the present volume, is attempting to vouch for. Glocal theology implies that every local theology has the responsibility to be both context relevant and at the same time to remain in touch with the global church and the rest of the world. An Arab glocal theology will be a theological tapestry that is able to weave together global theological training and thinking with a fluid Arabic theological idiom, resulting from a vigorous translation movement and a sharp connectedness with its largely Islamic hermeneutical context and questions. It is from this standpoint that Middle Eastern theology will be able, in turn, to contribute to the global conversation about God, his Word and the world.

For Further Reading

On the Israeli–Palestinian question:
Ateek, Naim S. *A Palestinian Christian Cry for Reconciliation.* Maryknoll, N.Y.: Orbis, 2008.

---

[9]The Arabic titles of these works are, respectively: *Al-Injīl: Qirāʾa Shariqiyya; Qirāʾa Sūfiyya li-Injīl Yūhanna*; and *Al-Maʿna aṣ-Ṣaḥīh li-Injīl al-Masīh*.

Brown, Wesley H., and Peter F. Penner, eds. *Christian Perspectives on the Israeli-Palestinian Conflict.* Pasadena, Calif.: William Carey International University Press, 2008.

Maalouf, Tony. *Arabs in the Shadow of Israel: The Unfolding of God's Prophetic Plan for Ishmael's Line.* Grand Rapids: Kregel, 2003.

On Islam and Relating to Muslims:

Accad, Fouad E. *Building Bridges: Christianity and Islam.* Colorado Springs: NavPress, 1997.

Moucarry, Chawkat. *Faith to Faith: Christianity and Islam in Dialogue.* Downers Grove, Ill.: InterVarsity Press, 2001.

———. *The Prophet and the Messiah: An Arab Christian's Perspective on Islam and Christianity.* Downers Grove, Ill.: InterVarsity Press, 2002.

———. *The Search for Forgiveness: Pardon and Punishment in Islam and Christianity.* Downers Grove, Ill.: InterVarsity Press, 2004.

Part Three

NORTH AMERICAN
THEOLOGIES

NEW OLD PERSPECTIVES

THEOLOGICAL OBSERVATIONS REFLECTING
INDIGENOUS WORLDVIEWS

Terry LeBlanc

• • •

My intention in this chapter is to undertake an exercise of description. Briefly, I want to engage what we are examining—exploring various theological constructions in global context—from a Native North American perspective, focusing on a central topic of concern to many of us. I want to offer some theological reflections that I, along with others in the Native North American community, have been engaged with these past twenty or so years. Let me begin with a story.

When asked by some young ones about the meaning of the words in their language for the Creator, Magat Nisgam,[1] an elder said, "Well, it is like the word in the Bible which the Hebrew people had for their God—Yahweh. No one really knows entirely what it means." The Creator of all things is so much a mystery his name does not describe who he is but only helps us speak of him. Then he told this story.

> Way back many years ago, two men went walking. It was on the flat land. As they walked, they noticed a hill in the far West and said to each other, "Let's go up that hill over to the West; let's see what is on the other side!" So they walked and walked until they got to the hill and had climbed it to the top. On the other side they noticed yet another,

---

[1] The original story is of Lakota origin but is told in different ways among different peoples about their name for the Creator of all things.

larger hill so they decided to climb it as well. They had not even finished climbing that hill and they saw a third, even larger one behind the
one they were climbing.

One after another, hill after hill, this kept going on all day. Each hill
they climbed was followed by an even larger one. Now in those days,
people could walk great distances in a single day; so you can see, they
would have covered a lot of ground by the end of the day.

Finally, at the top of the biggest hill yet, with another looming high
above them in the distance, they said to one another, "This must be
what Magat Nisgam is like!"

Elaine Jahner notes several important dimensions to this story that
give us hints about worldview and spirituality from a *Wa'banaki* perspective: (1) The searchers (think they) are exploring the physical universe when all of a sudden they sense or realize the mysterious depth
(and interconnectedness) of the physical and spiritual one. (2) The
search is not an individual one—*two* people journey toward the West—
the search is a human search within the rest of creation, not an individual one explored in the inner sanctum of each human being. (3) The
searchers' response to their new insight is an awed response to mystery,
not an effort to fully understand it.[2] To a large extent this story describes the focal points of the challenge encountered in coming to understand some aspects of the differences between Native North American and non-Native North American peoples.

Western Christian theology finds its philosophical underpinnings
in a progressively developed series of dualisms and its biblical foundations in Genesis 3. It has, with some notable exceptions, historically
focused its inquiry on the restoration of relationship between God
and humankind: the salvation and recovery of the lost human soul.[3]

---

[2]See Elaine Jahner's discussion of this old story in J. R. Walker, *Lakota Myth*, ed. Elaine Jahner
(Lincoln: University of Nebraska Press, 1983), pp. 193-94. These have been expanded here for
the purposes of this paper.
[3]In *Sublimis Dei* (1537) Pope Paul III unequivocally declares the indigenous peoples of the
Americas to be rational beings with souls, denouncing any idea to the contrary as directly inspired by the "enemy of the human race" (Satan). He goes on to condemn their reduction to
slavery in the strongest terms, declaring it null and void for any people known or that could be
discovered in the future as well, entitles their right to liberty and property, and concludes with
a call for their evangelization. See Pope Paul III, "*Sublimus Dei*," Papal Encyclicals Online,
September 2008, www.papalencyclicals.net/Paul03/p3subli.htm.

The emphasis has almost exclusively been on the restoration of human relationship with God first, then with others in the human community. We see this in the profound theological masterworks of Augustine and Aquinas, the theologies of Calvin and Luther, which reacted to theology in their day, the attempts at recovered communities of relationship with the Anabaptists, as well as the contemporary emphases of the various emergent streams in recovering old ecclesial liturgies and understandings. As history will (for some, debatably) attest, we have more often than not failed seriously in developing relationships with others and struggled to give effective evidence to our relationship with God.

One contemporary writer, capturing the perspectives of the neo-Reformed movement in Christianity, recently offered this perspective on the nature of the gospel: "The Gospel is at once personal and social, as are we. Thus a relational approach to evangelism not only involves individual salvation, but salvation on a larger societal and social scale as well—the redemption of all creation."[4]

While on first blush this seems agreeable and inclusive in its scope, it becomes apparent in the context of the article that, for the author, "all creation" refers strictly and only to the human community—and that defined quite intentionally over the years as the growing Western cultural community.[5] Nowhere does this author, or for that matter most other Christian authors/theologians (until very recently), describe all creation as just that: all creation. Most times it reflects a tenuous conception of the redemption of all *ethnē* (peoples). I recall a conversation I had several years ago with Richard Longenecker about this issue. I was concerned that my Greek exegesis might be poorly reflecting Paul's intent about the reconciliation of all things through Christ. So I asked Richard, a fine Greek scholar, about the meaning of *all* in Colossians 1:20. His response was straightforward, almost

---

[4]Derek Flood, "An Evangelical Relational Theology: A Personal Relationship with God as Theological Leitmotif," June 2007, www.therebelgod.com/relational.html.

[5]While I would agree with Andrew Walls's description of the trajectory offered by the Jerusalem Council in this volume (pp 23-24), the reality is that the Council's decision was short-lived in its impact—as attested to by the continued struggle for the legitimacy of non-Western cultural expressions of Christian faith throughout the globe.

unremarkable except for his energized tone. He said simply that when Paul says "all," he means *"all!"*—the entirety of creation.[6]

In spite of Colossians and other passages that describe the clear intent of the Creator, and after all these years of observing the groaning of the earth, Western-rooted theologies of creation and redemption appear neither robust enough nor biblically thorough enough to effectively inform contemporary and future Christian behavior with respect to the complex issues confronting us today, let alone being prophetic in a world driven by the desire for bigger, better, more and faster! Western thought and its multifaceted dualistic framework appears unable to take us where we need to go. We as indigenous people believe we could, if we are courageous enough to do so, offer a way forward that is very much rooted in an evangelical commitment, but one that is lived within our traditions, our worldviews and our philosophical understandings.

And so my question is, Can we look back at the framework of theological understanding that has led to countless cycles of colonial mission, the haphazard devastation of the rest of creation—the whole of which is the focus of Christ's redemption on the cross—and a stunted theology of salvation, to finally understand where we are so that we might gain some perspective about where to go from here? It seems to me that if we are to do so, we must seriously and fully revisit several things that are stamped on the two sides of one coin. On the one side we find etched the philosophies on which our theologies rest, the worldview from which we do theology and our understanding of the nature of the spiritual. The other side is inscribed with our biblical starting point for Christian theology.

The Christian Scripture, as well as our own experiences if we take the time to reflect on them, is abundantly clear that redemption through Jesus' work on the cross has implications far beyond our generally limited focus on the restoration of human beings alienated from their Creator. The creation itself, Paul makes quite clear, groans in travail awaiting its own redemption (Rom 8:18-25). Yet, even as we give tacit assent

[6]Richard Longenecker, personal conversation with author, December 2, 2006.

to this in our Christian theologies, we fail miserably to account for the work of the Spirit—dare I say, the gifts of the Spirit—so abundantly evident in the rest of creation through which that groaning is becoming increasingly unmistakable and from which we might learn something about the means and trajectory of salvation were we to listen more carefully. Most times the best we seem able to offer as creation-redemption theology is a wonderful, pastoral scene or awe-inspiring panorama of the rest of creation projected on the church screen behind the lyrics of the hymns and choruses we sing.

Yet seldom in evangelical writing does the idea that Jesus came to give his life so that the rest of creation might also be redeemed find its expression. This, Native North American people would argue, characterizes the lived theology of the majority of the evangelical church today—and, I would argue, has for the Western church down through the ages. It is precisely this theological understanding that allowed Christian mission to traverse large bodies of water to places where, it seemed, God would never have been present if they had not brought him! The specific ways church authorities of the past have dealt with indigenous peoples is evidence enough of this longstanding historic trend. It is clear from the behavior of most of the folks in our pews (taught by the pastors and teachers who come from our Christian seminaries and colleges) that they do not believe other than what I am suggesting.

And, lest we be tempted to distance ourselves from this scenario, as if it is foreign to Western societies or as if our historic theologies have not been the author and arbiter of its impact, I offer the countless and constantly updated volumes of the past 150 years or more published in most Euro-Western contexts as a defense of the position. All are titled with some variation of "Christianity: A History of Our Civilization." The collective and individual behavior of Western society is predicated today, like it or not, on the thought patterns laid down by the theologies of the (not-altogether-too-distant) past, shaped in the forge of ongoing political, economic and religious alliances.

If I had the platform to do so, however, I would venture to say that it is in the rest of creation where we find the gifts of the Spirit most manifest, or perhaps better put, most consistently manifested. We find this expression in the natural way of life of creatures living in a more intuitive way with their Creator. Job's affirmation of the wisdom creation is in natural possession of, which humanity represented in the self-absorbed arrogance of his three companions seems unable to comprehend, bears testimony to this fact (Job 12).[7]

The rejection of this clearly observable interrelationship—the interdependency of the created order under its Creator—continues society's short slide toward death. Moreover, the present predilection toward understanding life in simple binaries contributes most significantly to the scenario in which we now find ourselves in the human part of our Creator's world.

Distinguishing between these dispositions, the one characterizing Western society, the other the pragmatic experience-oriented approach of Native North American people, Navajo philosopher Brian Yazzie Burkhart notes that

> Phenomenology begins with a distinction between two different attitudes: the natural attitude and the phenomenological attitude. The natural attitude is the way we are ordinarily taken up with the various things in the world. We walk down the street and pass the trees. We have conversations with our friends and talk about our jobs. What we do not do in this attitude is step back and reflect on this natural way we carry on in the world. . . . However, the phenomenological attitude is just this kind of disengagement.[8]

Edmund Husserl similarly observes that Western philosophy (we could just as accurately say Christian philosophy) effaced the notion of who we are in the "pre-given" world, replacing it with a perspective that

> saw fit to recast the idea of "knowledge" and "truth" in natural existence and to ascribe to the newly formed idea of "objective truth" a higher dignity, that of a norm for all knowledge. In relation to this, finally,

---

[7]Read with a different set of lenses, it portrays true wisdom as if set in residency within the rest of creation through its intuitive behavior, not within the deductive reasoning ability of Job's human counselors.

[8]Brian Yazzie Burkhart, "What Coyote and Thales Can Teach Us: An Outline of American Indian Epistemology," in *American Indian Thought: Philosophical Essays*, ed. Anne Waters (Malden, Mass.: Blackwell, 2004), p. 24.

arises the idea of a universal science encompassing all possible knowledge in its infinity.[9]

The Cartesian dualistic bias on which this view is predicated differenti-
ates precisely between Native North American concepts of creation and
those evidenced in Western philosophy, and between Western Christian views of spirituality largely expressed in terms of specific behaviors
and those of the Native North American community expressed in an
intuitive yet experiential embrace of the spiritual reality present in all of
creation.

I would extend this somewhat further to make it more emphatic,
asserting that the spiritual nature at the core of the entirety of creation
is the ontological design of God. For me this means that the "groaning
in travail" described by Paul in Romans 8:22-25 is neither metaphoric
nor anthropomorphic nor merely a literary device of personification.
The working of the Creator's Spirit in the rest of creation is precisely
what we find in human beings groaning in their prayer closets. It is for
Western Christian theologies to finally grasp and comprehend this
without losing the authenticity of the Christian faith or the fine balance between our understanding of the transcendence and immanence
of the Creator.

In interpreting the redemptive narrative of Scripture, Christian theologies have been famously devoid of explanation for this deeply en-
trenched concern of God—other than as window dressing for human
salvation or as an afterthought on the way to the restoration of human
beings to a new heaven and earth. This kind of theological reflection,
and the corollaries produced in such thinking, are almost exclusively
personal and human-centered.[10]

For our discussion I might make an even more emphatic point. Seldom,

[9]Edmund Husserl, *The Crisis of European Sciences and Transcendental Phenomenology: An Introduction to Phenomenological Philosophy*, trans. David Carr, Northwestern University Studies in
Phenomenology and Existential Philosophy (Evanston, Ill.: Northwestern University Press,
1970), p. 121.
[10]See, for example, Ray Aldred's discussion of the difference in perspective of the function of
story in painting a more interrelational creation context in his article "The Resurrection of
Story," *The Journal of the North American Institute for Indigenous Theological Studies* 2 (2004):
5-14.

if ever, has our pneumatology focused on the work of the Spirit of God in and through the rest of creation. We have instead focused on discussions of the gifts of the Spirit, the timing of those gifts, the possession of the gifts (individual or collective), the purposes of the gifting and so on. Rarely have we spoken of the Spirit's animation of the rest of creation in any more than a passing reference on the way to the focal point or pinnacle of God's story of the Spirit—humanity's blessing at Pentecost.

Looking Up from Below

In Genesis 1–2 the entirety of creation is described as primarily and inherently relational. This is because it is inherently spiritual, proceeding from the creative nature that we observe in the trinitarian relationship of the Father, Son and Holy Spirit. The Spirit of the Trinity broods over the waters and is instilled in the rest of creation as life is given to it. Relationship with God is the intent in the creation act. Each part of creation in its respective way through its form and function (see Gen 1:28-30; Job 12; Rom 1; 8) is nested in a set of relationships. Animals, plant life, birds and fish are linked to their Creator spiritually and intuitively—an intuition that I would suggest is retained in the rest of creation but in humans has been supplanted by ego and ethnocentrism. Unlike humanity, the rest of creation lives in constant expression of the Spirit and the intent of the Creator (acknowledging the very real breakdown Paul reflects on in Rom 8:20, the subjection to frustration), illustrating proper relationship and relatedness. We see this so clearly and compellingly in Job's reply to his counselors.

While the other beings of creation may have proven unsatisfactory to meet the full companionship needs of the human being, their spiritual relatedness to one another and to the human is nevertheless described, albeit partially, in the process of naming. These relationships were further delineated, we might imagine, in the days immediately following creation. The intrinsic, spiritual understanding of the relationship we possess with the other beings of creation—and the fact that it is of a reciprocal nature—is something that First Nations people have traditionally appreciated more than Western society.[11]

If we understand God's original intention, then we understand the Fall and restoration in the more profound terms of loss and restoration of relationship and relatedness of all things by the Spirit—not simply human soul salvation as escape from hell and entry into heaven. Our first parents descend into a state of separation from the Creator and the rest of creation as they wilfully choose to break relationship. A far-reaching pronouncement of the outcome of the breech is made, with consequences for all of creation. The curse shreds each aspect of the original relationship, and its effects implicate all of the created order. For the male, the previous idyllic relationship in creation—wanting for nothing, not having to labor unduly for sustenance—turns to toil and hardship. For the woman, egalitarian intimacy with the male and, presumably a less stressful procreation, is replaced with pain, suffering and subservience—a posture the church in history has exploited in profound ways.

And for humanity yet to come relational intimacy with the One who made them is subjected to distorted yearnings for transcendence and meaning, punctuated regularly by an idolatry that misrepresents the intended relationship between humankind, the Creator and the rest of creation. This is the curse. All of creation, Paul emphatically notes, not simply human beings, is subjected to its effect. All, he enthusiastically observes, await their future, full redemption.

A Suggested Path for Change

In good Mi'kmaq storytelling fashion, let me reiterate. First, the theological enterprise must move out of the third chapter of Genesis as the starting place for our articulation of the human situation and the situation of the rest of creation. We should, instead, examine the beginning of the story with greater care to ascertain the intention and expectation of the Creator. It is, after all, the intention of our Creator that our first

---

[11]For a discussion that describes a more holistic view of the world, see Daniel N. Paul, *We Were Not the Savages: A Mi'kmaq Perspective on the Collision Between European and Native American Civilizations* (Halifax, N.S.: Fernwood, 2000), pp. 57-67.

parents clearly departed from. So, rather than focus our efforts on scraping the barrel of original and subsequent collective sin to see what lies at the bottom, we might be better served by engaging first in a vigorous investigation of the original intent and plan of the Creator.

It would seem that the penchant for beginning our theological reflection in Genesis 3 and overemphasizing creation's depravity obscures the primal state of harmony and goodness in Eden too thoroughly. This has led to more circumscribed evangelical theologies that articulate the need for a Savior as being strictly about blood price[12] and anthropocentric redemption, not at all about the restoration of the multilayered relationships resident in the rudimentary creation, set as the goal for its restoration. This is curious given that the core elements of the announced curse in Genesis 3, which lie at the heart of sin's consequence, address themselves to change in relationship—God with humanity, humanity with the others in the spiritual world (represented in the serpent), man with woman, and, of course, least understood in the West, humanity with the rest of creation—not the total eradication of any goodness initially instilled in the creation, be it human or other.

Second, Western theology has consistently focused its theological efforts through the lens of a stacked set of philosophical dualisms—a theoretical foundation that has had weight and substance added to it because of my first premise in a chicken and egg fashion. Whether observed in the deep embrace of classical dualism, the Gnostic variations in the era of the early church and beyond, or that which has been offered in the Enlightenment, dualism is comfortably embedded in the foundations of Western Christian theology. As a consequence it has become increasingly difficult for Western Christians to make sense of what we are discovering, by means of contemporary science, to be a far more interrelated cosmos than we had ever imagined.

I am reminded of a commercial by the Manitoba Public Insurance

---

[12]The issue here for the author is not at all the need for a Savior—clearly central to our faith as per 1 Cor 15—but rather the emphasis placed on the depraved nature of the post-Gen 3 creation, the way the saving work of Jesus is understood in, within and through creation and the spectrum of relationship which is restored by the Savior through his death on the cross.

Corporation against drinking and driving. Using empty beer glasses stacked in front of the camera to make their point, the advertisement portrays the problems of depth perception that the driver of a motor vehicle experiences following the consumption of successive beers. After one, a perceptible but manageable difference in vision; after two, a blurring of vision and diminishment of depth perception; following the third, a serious difficulty discerning the reality behind the glasses; after four, a foggy haze and the noise of a crash. Christian theology, in my experience, has been somewhat like that. Stacked dualities have caused a great crash theologically and societally—and we still do not offer as a corrective anything other than a tweaked set of old theologies premised on the same foundations.

Third, if we were to successfully navigate the issues that one and two raise, we could see that the presence and gifts of the Spirit have been in evidence in all of creation since the beginning and are there for our instruction. Longtime friend and Cree leader Kenny Blacksmith, when confronted with the devastation that the Great Whale hydro-development project was about to unleash on the traditional homelands of his people, inquired of his mother what he should do. She replied, as if echoing Job in Job 12:12, "Ask the trees, Kenny, and they will tell you!" His mother was reflecting the historic understanding the Cree people have regarding the spiritual. Kenny took note of this admonition and, when next he went out on the land, the trees, spoke to him. Kenny's mother knew intuitively what Paul wrote emphatically: all of creation groans by the same Spirit that created and gifted it. Due to our limited capacity to comprehend that this is indeed real, the epithet is hurled at those who might assert this to be true—that they are at best subscribing to panentheism or at worst pantheism. Perhaps we need new language to begin to address these ideas so that we can move beyond the name-calling.

Fourth, there is the potential to do it all over again with greater enthusiasm. Emerging theologies that proceed in their articulation from an admirable desire to address these and other issues, seem to me to be entirely incapable of arriving at a different place, because they begin again by asking the same or similar questions, predicated on the same or similar assumptions, using the same or similar philosophical constructs. I point to two of Einstein's oft-quoted dictums (no, one is not E=MC²). Attributed to him on what he believed might be the brink of atomic disaster is the comment that "Insanity is doing the same thing over and over again and expecting different results." Powerfully germane to our discussion here, he is also known for the quip "The significant problems we face cannot be solved at the same level of thinking we were at when we created them."[13]

An example from a presentation that I was to give in 1997 further outlines some of the differences between Native North American and non-Native North American peoples' worldviews. Searching for an illustration to help communicate the difference in time orientation, specifically the different value placed on past, present and future, I happened on a story in *Field and Stream* magazine that seemed fitting. It concerned the collapse of the cod fishery in the East and the salmon fishery in the West. The article, as we might expect in 1997, painted a dire picture complete with statistics of the impending collapse and assignment of various levels of fault. Its conclusion was: if something was not done, the fisheries would be all but totally decimated in short order. This was not an unexpected conclusion. To my shock, however, in fine print at the bottom were the words, "This article is a reprint from *Field and Stream*, May, 1913." The question at the forefront of my mind was: "Did the system get changed?" The answer, as you might imagine, was no!

It is precisely because we do not understand these things by the intuition of the Spirit that we have resorted to a reductionist, categorical thought process and a series of propositional truths about the Spirit's work and manifestations in our theologies. The response in such frameworks is clear when such things as happened to my friend Kenny take place—this must be animism or spiritism! When the rest of creation acts outside our prescription that it is strictly instinctual or inanimate, we do not know how to respond.[14] In what I have always found to be a

---

[13]Albert Einstein, as paraphrased by Michael Amrine, "The Real Problem in the Heart of Man," *New York Times*, May 25, 1946, p. 13.
[14]Trees speaking to a Westerner and to an indigenous person would be very likely to elicit an

statement of simple wisdom in this regard, my grandfather and others of his generation used to say, in one form or another, that animals are indeed persons—they are just not people. Perhaps, if I may suggest it, Balaam's ass and Kenny's trees were really just speaking in tongues in hopes that someone might hear and obey.[15]

Conclusion

In Jesus, the curse is practically and prophetically broken. We may now live out from under its effects—at least in theory. While this is clearly a "now but not yet" reality—one in which we both receive now and wait for a later fulfillment of the promise—the capacity for right relationship has at least been restored. This ought to have implications for the way we live our lives within all of God's creation—not just the way we treat human beings. We are expected to demonstrate right relatedness with all of creation because the Holy Spirit has animated all and placed within all a spiritual nature that, while qualitatively different from that which is instilled in humanity, is nonetheless clearly present in all if we will but look and listen. Its groans are as those of human beings animated by the Spirit in their prayer closets—perhaps in some of our cases, more so. In these times it seems to me that human recipients of God's Spirit must not simply be focused on orality—the communication to others of what we say we believe about God and

---

entirely different response. The Westerner would more likely deny this as a sign from the Creator, assigning it instead to an experience manifest by the evil one. The indigenous person would be more likely to ask if the tree was speaking to him or her and what it wished from him or her.

[15]Note the elements of the story of Balaam and his ass. The donkey sees what is obscure to Balaam, and Balaam's response is to blame the ass—creation suffers because humans cannot see! "When the donkey saw the angel of the LORD standing in the road with a drawn sword in his hand, she turned off the road into a field. Balaam beat her to get her back on the road. . . . Then the LORD opened the donkey's mouth, and she said to Balaam, 'What have I done to you to make you beat me these three times?' Balaam answered the donkey, 'You have made a fool of me! If I had a sword in my hand, I would kill you right now.' The donkey said to Balaam, 'Am I not your own donkey, which you have always ridden, to this day? Have I been in the habit of doing this to you?' 'No,' he said. Then the LORD opened Balaam's eyes, and . . . the angel of the LORD asked him, 'Why have you beaten your donkey these three times? . . . The donkey saw me and turned away from me these three times. If she had not turned away, I would certainly have killed you by now, but I would have spared her'" (Num 22:23-33).

God's creation—but also, perhaps more profoundly and extensively, on aurality—listening to what God is actually saying to us through the groaning of the Spirit in the rest of creation.

For Further Reading

Irwin, Lee. *Native American Spirituality: A Critical Reader*. Lincoln: University of Nebraska Press, 2000.

Jenkins, Philip. *Dream Catchers: How Mainstream America Discovered Native Spirituality*. New York: Oxford University Press, 2004.

Kidwell, Clara Sue, Homer Noley and George E. Tinker. *A Native American Theology*. Maryknoll, N.Y.: Orbis, 2001.

Paul, Daniel N. *We Were Not the Savages: A Mi'kmaq Perspective on the Collision Between European and Native American Civilizations*. 3rd ed. Halifax, N.S.: Fernwood, 2007.

Twiss, Richard. *One Church Many Tribes*. Ventura, Calif.: Regal, 2000.

Woodley, Randy. *Living in Color: Embracing God's Passion for Ethnic Diversity*. Downers Grove, Ill.: InterVarsity Press, 2004.

11

"OUTSIDE THE GATE"

EVANGELICALISM AND
LATINO PROTESTANT THEOLOGY

Juan Martínez

• • •

After finishing high school, I attended a Spanish language Bible Institute in south Texas. In chapel we usually sang translated hymns. Once the chapel director invited a group from Miami to participate. They sang with a light Cuban beat and some of their songs were written originally in Spanish. In the next chapel service the president of the school, a Euro-American, got up and apologized for having the group in chapel. He wanted to assure the students that this was not the type of service that the institute encouraged. The only acceptable worship style was one that looked Euro-American.

Nonetheless, as a U.S. Latino Protestant I also learned a parallel story; I was an *evangélico*, so my community of believers was broader than the conservative evangelical definition of the Bible institute. The Pentecostals were also *evangélicos*, even though that Bible institute did not accept them as evangelicals. That broader community was teaching me that there were expressions of the faith that were more culturally relevant, more incarnated, than the faith I had been raised with.

Latino theology asks the question that was raised by my mixed experience: What is unique about being Christian and Latino? Latina/o theology developed as both Protestant and Catholic theologians drew from the experiences that are common to most Latinos, whether Catholic or

Protestant. Most Latino/a theology expresses understandings of Christian faith that both Protestants and Catholics can affirm. But several Protestant theologians have also drawn on teachings and experiences that are more specifically Protestant to describe Latino Protestantism.

Latino theology, like all contextual theologies, creates tensions for evangelicals in the United States. The Latino Christian experience in the United States not only raises questions of contextualization but also forces us to address how Latinos became Protestant Christians in the United States. Issues of conquest and mission, racism, internal colonialism, the benefits that the U.S. economy gains from having undocumented "disposable labor" and related topics all come to the fore if one includes Latina/o theology in the conversation. This not only raises many questions but also calls for a significant reinterpretation of the narrative of evangelical Protestantism in the United States.

Context of Latino Theology

Latino theology was born in the imperial expansion of the nineteenth-century United States. The takeover of the Southwest in 1848 made 100,000 Mexicans U.S. citizens, and the next major imperial expansion, the Spanish-American War (1898), made Puerto Rico a U.S. colony and its inhabitants U.S. citizens. The Mexicans of the Southwest became "strangers in their own land"; the new immigrants from the Eastern Seaboard were now the citizens, and those who had been born in the Southwest were now considered foreigners. Puerto Ricans became U.S. citizens who were considered immigrants and outsiders when they came to the mainland.

Before the war with Mexico, many Christians spoke up against the war and its potential consequences. But once the Southwest was conquered, even those who had been against the war saw the takeover as a God-given opportunity. Protestant mission agencies hoped that the conquest would make it easier to reach Mexico. They were less sure about what to do with the Mexicans who were now U.S. citizens. Protestants were afraid that these new citizens would cheapen the birthright of U.S. citizens. These people needed to be evangelized because of the gospel mandate, but they also needed to be Americanized so that they might become good citizens.

During World War I, the United States welcomed Mexicans fleeing the Mexican Revolution to take the place of those sent to war. Puerto Ricans were made U.S. citizens in 1913 so that they could be drafted into the U.S. military. When the Depression began, thousands were deported to Mexico, including many born in the United States. World War II saw the creation of the *Bracero* Program to provide Mexican labor to take the place of U.S. workers who had been sent to war. The previous pattern was repeated in the 1950s with Operation Wetback.

U.S. interventions in Latin America created new migratory patterns, be it Cubans fleeing the revolution, Dominicans after the United States sent marines to Santo Domingo (1963), or Central Americans as the United States supported the military dictatorships in various countries of the region during the 1970s and 1980s. Each intervention brought new migrants to the states, which is why Juan González calls his book about the history of Latinos *Harvest of Empire*.[1]

In the midst of all of this, Protestants have continued to evangelize Latinos. While evangelicals and mainline churches continued to link the gospel and Americanization, the Pentecostal movement turned that project on its head. They never "got the memo" that stated that Latinos could only be the objects of mission, not missionaries themselves. So they began doing mission and reflecting on who God was in their own lives. That reflection began with testimonies, and then continued with hymns written by the people in the idiom of the people.

Latinos in mainline denominations began to formally reflect on their experience as they sought a space in light of the civil rights movement and the development of liberation theology in Latin America. This often was a more formal conversation, done in the academy, though seeking to reflect on the popular aspects of the Latina experience.

Meanwhile, a number of things have been making the Latino Protestant experience much more complex. The growth of Latin American Protestantism means that a growing number of the new

---

[1]Juan González, *Harvest of Empire: A History of Latinos in America* (New York: Viking, 2000).

immigrants to the United States are Protestants. Also the impact of assimilation has created a generation of Latinos that do not easily identify with the framework common to a previous generation of Latina scholars. Globalization and transnationalism have created new types of migrants and people with a more fluid sense of identity. So Latinos are both people with a long history in the United States and recently arrived undocumented aliens. They are also the face of 2040, the year that it is estimated that the minorities will become the majority in the United States.

Common Latino Experiences

Miguel de la Torre and Edwin Aponte argue that there are common cultural themes within the Latino community that create the environment for a community-based theology. Most Latinas share similar cultural roots, similar cultural influences on their theology and common understandings of God.

Most Latinos have experienced exile or have been treated like outsiders, even if they have their historical roots in this country. Though this experience is more personal and direct for some than for others, just about all Latinas have either experienced this or are the descendants of people who have.

Most have also lived in the same types of neighborhoods or communities. Barrios or poor farming communities have been their common lot or background. Only very few have no links, personal or historical, to these places where the schools are deficient, social services limited and crime higher. Though an increasing number of Latinas are well off economically, this is still the common lot of a large percentage.

Latinos are *mestizos*. The vast majority are the children of multiple cultural, ethnic and racial encounters. Our Spanish forbearers forcibly procreated among the indigenous. People of African descent were brought into the mix as slaves. People from other latitudes have joined through migration. Today just about all Latinos are multiracial, even if they can claim one "race" as the one that principally defines them.

This *mestizaje* is also reflected in Latino religions that reflect medieval Islam, Catholicism, native religions and African religious practices. But it is a faith strongly tied to the people. The poor listen to God and do not allow the powerful and the official religious elites to define them as mere spectators or receptors. For example, many Latinos have found that Pentecostal faith best addresses their search for ultimate meaning, provides them a way to worship God that connects with their lived experience and allows them to be subjects of their service to God.

Spirituality is another common influence. There is a clear openness to the spiritual and a sense of God's presence in the world. Worship services often feel like a fiesta where God's presence and mighty acts are celebrated in the gathering of the extended family.

Religion is also lived out in community. Community is closely linked to the extended family, not only in the sense of blood relatives but of all of those who are connected to the family. Among Catholics one sees that popular religious practices are tied to family life. Among Protestants the church community often becomes the extended family. Religion is not something experienced individually; it is something practiced in relationship with others.

These common experiences, influences and social location create the space for reflection on who God is and what God is doing in the world. Latino/a theology cannot be separated from the lived experiences of real people. Latina/o theologians recognize that there is no such thing as "objective" theology, an understanding of God separated from how people concretely experience God. It is in this setting that one needs to address the issue of Latino Protestant theology.

Latino Protestants as Contextual Theologians

Latino Protestants began reflecting on their experiences soon after the first conversions in the nineteenth century. But the first signs of Latino theological reflection that was ethnically unique happened in tension with Euro-American Protestants in the early twentieth century. Several of the early Latino Protestant leaders found that they had to tell their stories not only in contrast to Roman Catholicism but also in tension with their Protestant brothers and sisters. Some of the early Latino Pentecostal leaders spoke about their differences with Euro-Americans, but leaders like Francisco Olazábal, Antonio Nava and Juan Lugo mostly lived out their unique theology by separating from the Euro-American leadership of their denominations or traditions.

It was in this environment that Pentecostal Latinas began to write their own hymnology. These songs used popular instruments and common musical styles. While many Protestant missionaries were sure that a guitar was too sensual and erotic for Christian worship, Latino Pentecostals were using it because it was from their culture and it fit their economic reality. Antonio Nava, one of the founders of the Apostolic Assembly, once stated: "La guitarra . . . pa'al pobre . . . la guitarra" (the guitar . . . for the poor . . . the guitar).

These songs were an important step toward a Latino Protestant theology because they were written in the idiom of the people and reflected the people's experience with God. While mainline and evangelical Latinos were mostly singing translated hymns, Latino Pentecostals were singing their own songs. Several of the Latino Pentecostal groups developed their own hymnals filled with songs written by their people. Because of the transnational nature of the people, these songs also migrated north and south, mostly between Mexico and the Southwest, and between Puerto Rico and the Eastern Seaboard.

The 1960s created a new context for Latino theological reflection. The civil rights movement pushed many mainline denominations to acknowledge the minority voices among them. The growth of Latino Pentecostals and evangelicals was creating a critical mass that would not be easily ignored in those denominations. The birth of Latin American liberation theology also created a space for Latinos to think about their own situation and to develop their own theology.

Reading Through González

Justo González and Orlando Costas were the first Latino Protestants to write theology from a distinctively Latino perspective. Both were influential in Latin America and among U.S. Latinos. Justo González has contributed to Christian theological reflection far beyond what he has written about Latino theology. His books are used in many seminaries in the United States, and his work has been translated into many languages. He is a key leader in the Latino Christian community. Orlando Costas served as a pastor in Puerto Rico and the United States, and as a seminary professor and academic dean in both Costa Rica and the United States. His influence was somewhat more limited because he met an untimely death in 1987.

Justo González has written several books and articles on Latino Protestant theology. Two books in particular frame his understanding of the unique contributions of Latino Protestant theology: *Mañana: Christian Theology from a Hispanic Perspective* and *Santa Biblia: The Bible Through Hispanic Eyes*.[2]

The Latino Protestant experience provides a unique lens through which to read the Bible. In the first place, Latinos have a noninnocent reading of the Bible and of history. Latin Americans and Latinos have experienced the reality that all human structures, including the U.S. government and Protestant churches and missionaries, are fallen. This is an extremely important contribution to U.S. Protestantism, which has often fallen into the trap of believing in "American exceptionalism." Reading the Bible through noninnocent eyes also means facing the difficult parts of Scripture with the clarity that God works in broken human history.

The Bible is also a book that can be read by all, including those with limited education. Latina Protestants have demonstrated that the Bible is not the exclusive purview of those with a college or seminary education. Simple people can read the Word and also preach it.

Latinos also bring a series of unique experiences that make it possible for them to see things in Scripture that others might not see, due to a different set of experiences. To read the Bible *en español* is not only about language, though that is important. But reading *en español* also has to do with how some of the common experiences of Latina Protestants have shaped their reading of Scripture. González identifies five common ex-

---

[2]Justo González, *Mañana: Christian Theology from a Hispanic Perspective* (Nashville: Abingdon, 1990); *Santa Biblia: The Bible Through Hispanic Eyes* (Nashville: Abingdon, 1996).

periences: marginality, poverty, *mestizaje*, exile and solidarity.[3] Each of these allows Latinas to grasp teachings from the Bible that might not be obvious to those who have not had similar experiences. By reading from this perspective, Latinos receive insight and strength from the Bible for dealing with injustice that is often justified "biblically," but also a clear sense that God walks with the marginalized.

Standing with Costas

Orlando Costas was born in Puerto Rico but raised on the mainland. He became a believer while in the United States, but returned to the island where he married and served as a pastor. Later he pastored Latino congregations in the United States. From there he went to Costa Rica in 1970 to teach at the Latin American Biblical Seminary. He arrived there as that seminary was beginning to go through tensions related to the growing influence of liberation theology. During his time in Costa Rica, liberation theology, the Latin American Theological Fraternity and the church growth movement influenced him. His area of expertise was evangelism, and he began to develop a perspective on evangelism and mission that took into account all of these influences. After service in Latin America he decided to return to the United States to serve the Latino community once again.

After he returned to the United States, Costas published *Christ Outside the Gate: Mission Beyond Christendom*.[4] In this book Costas brought his Latin American experience to bear on his developing missiology, but also on his understanding of ministry in the Latino community. His last major publication was *Liberating News: A Theology of Contextual Evangelization*, which was published after he died in 1987.[5] These books lay out his theology of mission and evangelism that had already been expressed in previous publications in Spanish. But he also presented key components of a Latino Protestant understanding of mission and theology.

---

[3]González, *Santa Biblia*.
[4]Orlando Costas, *Christ Outside the Gate: Mission Beyond Christendom* (Eugene, Ore.: Wipf & Stock, 2005).
[5]Orlando Costas, *Liberating News: A Theology of Contextual Evangelization* (Grand Rapids: Eerdmans, 1989).

Costas's principal concept is that mission has to be contextual. The gospel is good news to those who are in need. But only those who recognize their own need can effectively share it. Only the beggar can tell another beggar where to find bread, because only a person that recognizes their own need for bread will understand the value of sharing that message. This speaks to both the missionary strategy and to the missionary. Christ is outside the gate of power and privilege; therefore those who want to share the gospel in ways that will truly be good news have to be willing to leave the comforts and privilege of Christendom so that the gospel can transform both the missionary and the one accepting the message. This is much more than connecting the gospel to the context of the hearer; it means communicating the good news from the "margin" where we find the absentees of history, the most vulnerable and needy. This perspective implies returning the evangelistic ministry to the grass roots of the church and establishing a preferential option for the marginalized of society.

Costas recognized that as a "Hispanic missiologist" he needed to help Protestantism in the United States understand the perspective of the "absentees" of U.S. missionary history: Latinos, African Americans, Asians and Native Americans. His role was to do missiology from the periphery. One of the key contributions of Latino Protestantism, particularly Pentecostalism, is that it works on the margins. Latino Pentecostalism is good news to the poor because it is working from among the poor, outside the gates of power. The call of Latino missiology is that one can only be faithful to the gospel if one is willing to let go of the "comfort and security of our ecclesiastical compounds, . . . in order that we might serve the world and witness to the new creation."[6]

Other Important Voices

Eldin Villafañe builds on González and Costas, but works specifically from the perspective of Latino Pentecostalism. He develops his thought in books like *The Liberating Spirit: Toward a Hispanic American Pente-*

---

[6]Costas, *Christ Outside the Gate*, p. 194.

*costal Social Ethic, Seek the Peace of the City: Reflections on Urban Minis-
try,* and *Fe, Espiritualidad y Justicia: Teología Posmoderna de un Boricua
en la Diáspora.*[7] Villafañe was born in Puerto Rico and formed in the
Puerto Rican Pentecostalism of New York. He brings together the
marginality of Latino Pentecostalism and the exile theme, common to
most Latino immigrants, and calls Latino Pentecostals to be a community of the Spirit for the world so that they will avoid the negative
elements of upward social mobility, that is, becoming a "church" in the
sociological sense, a part of Christendom.

Villafañe also develops that thought for the church's mission in his
appeal to the exile motif and to the Old Testament prophet Jeremiah's
letter to the Israelites in exile. All Christians need to take seriously an
understanding of exile as a motif for the Christian life. They need to
seek the peace of the city they live in, even as they recognize that their
goal and vision is the city of God, not the incomplete visions of any
earthly city.

Recently, younger Latino and Latina theologians have taken Latino
theology in new directions. Many of these Latino/a theologians have
worked *en conjunto,* "working together," reflecting on *lo cotidiano,* "daily
lived life," of the Latina experience. From their perspective, these are
another two key contributions that Latinos give the larger Christian
community. Theology is the reflection of how a concrete community of
believers experiences God and how that community articulates its experience. In addition, the theological task is the task of the people who
experience God in their day-to-day situations. In other words, all theology is contextual and communal.

Many of the newer works of Latino theological reflection have been
collections, often put together as part of conferences. Three representative collections from a Protestant perspective are *Teología en Conjunto: A Collaborative Hispanic Protestant Theology, Protestantes/Protes-
tants: Hispanic Christianity with Mainline Traditions,* and *Vivir y Servir*

---

[7]Eldin Villafañe, *The Liberating Spirit: Toward a Hispanic American Pentecostal Social Ethic*
(Grand Rapids: Eerdmans, 1993); *Seek the Peace of the City: Reflections on Urban Ministry* (Grand
Rapids: Eerdmans, 1995);Villafañe, *Fe, Espiritualidad y Justicia: Teología Posmoderna de un Bo-
ricua en la Diáspora* (Río Piedras, Puerto Rico: Palabra y más, 2006).

en el Exilio: Lecturas Teológicas de la Experiencia Latina en los Estados Unidos.[8] Each of these collections seeks to take seriously the concept of working *en conjunto* while reflecting on *lo cotidiano.* The first was born out of a conference of Latino/a theologians who came together in 1995 to address historical Christian doctrines from a distinctively Latino perspective. The second looked at the Latino Protestant experience as the basis for understanding Latino theology. The third collection developed in the theological reflections of the Los Angeles chapter of the Latin American Theological Fraternity. The specific focus of each collection is how Latinas experience God within the complexities of our *cotianidad.*

Issues for Latino Protestant Theological Reflection

Latino theology has to deal with important internal issues, such as who should be a part of the conversations. Even as Latino theologians need to reflect with those outside the community, there are also important voices within the community that are not always recognized. For example, Latino theology has been influenced by Latin American theology. Yet most of the books and articles published by Latina theologians have been written with the U.S. scholarly community in mind and published in English. They have served as an "explanation" of who we are to the Euro-American Christian community.

But Latino theology needs to strengthen the relationship with two conversation partners. On the one hand, it needs to talk consciously to the south. Latino Protestantism is influenced by its southern background, but also by the movement of religious ideas in the globalized and transnational reality of those Latinos who move between the United States and Latin America. Latina Protestants are doing popular theology with Latin Americans as they move north and south.

---

[8]José David Rodriguez and Loida I. Martell-Otero, eds., *Teología en Conjunto: A Collaborative Hispanic Protestant Theology* (Louisville: Westminster John Knox, 1997); David Maldonado Jr., ed., *Protestantes/Protestants: Hispanic Christianity with Mainline Traditions* (Nashville: Abingdon, 1999); Jorge E. Maldonado and Juan F. Martínez, eds., *Vivir y Servir en el Exilio: Lecturas Teológicas de la Experiencia Latina en los Estados Unidos* (Buenos Aires: Ediciones Kairós, 2008).

The other conversation partners that need to be more consciously in-cluded are the Spanish-language dominant in the Latina community and those who do not read scholarly material. Latino theologians are commit-ted to doing theology *en conjunto* and *en lo cotidiano*. But they also need to be more intentional in interacting with those in the church and commu-nity, allowing them to be agents of their own theological reflection.

Because Latina identity is fluid, there is also the need to reflect on the changing identity of those who have been in the United States for generations. Is *exile* still a term that helps them understand how they experience God in the world, or do we need new terms to describe their experience? Since culture is not static, Latina theology will need to expand its lexicon to help all the community reflect on its encounter with God.

Some Latin American scholars see popular Pentecostalism as a sub-versive Protestantism that seeks radical change in life and society. The temptation from this perspective is to assume that Pentecostalism is "merely" a reflection of the struggle of the excluded that are trying to find a "way in" to the structures of power. But are they something more profound: a different way of thinking about social order, one in which the biblical eschatological vision of God's reign, where social, political and economic justice for all, is central? Might this type of popular Pentecostalism offer an answer for a postmodern reality that is looking for spiritual answers but that recognizes that they will not be found in the structures of Christendom? Orlando Costas invited Christians to find their mission outside of the structures of comfort, and Eldin Villafañe has warned Latinos about the dangers of wanting to "fit." That seems to be the place where Latino Protestants are today, wanting to know how to fit in U.S. society or whether that is the right way to frame the issue.

Issues for Evangelicals

Latino theology raises important issues for evangelical theological re-flection in the U.S. context. But standing "outside the gate" will mean continuing to move toward "the margins" even as Latino theology is being accepted in the theological and academic center. Because of the unique nature of the Latino experience, this process will continually have much to contribute to the theological task. I want to briefly mention some of the types of issues Latino Protestant theology raises for Euro-American evangelicals.

The undocumented. One of the key motifs of Latino theology has been exile. But currently the most clearly defined struggle among Latinos is that of the undocumented. Most Latino Protestants have identified themselves with the struggles of the undocumented and are working for immigration reform. But are Latino evangelicals ready to incorporate "undocumented" into the theological lexicon, with all the marginalization that this implies? The experience of the undocumented offers a powerful way to read the migration narratives of the Old Testament patriarchs and matriarchs, but also the "sojourners" and "diaspora" language of the New Testament.

For many Latino Protestants and most evangelicals the undocumented also raise difficult questions about the role of the state, how Christians understand law and order, ethics and national identities. Yet the transnational movement of peoples, documented or undocumented, raises these questions for Latino theology. Is the concept of being undocumented a theological metaphor that Latino Protestant theologians are ready to embrace? Incorporating it into the core of Latino theological reflection will place Latino theology firmly at the margins but will raise many serious questions, particularly for Latino evangelicals and Pentecostals.

Conquest and gospel. Latino theology calls for a noninnocent reading of U.S. history and of U.S. mission history, a recognition that mission is always a divine and human exercise. Latino Pentecostals have models of mission from below. But many Latino evangelicals are products of evangelical missions. Will Latino evangelicals be able to bring a noninnocent reading to evangelical theology? Or will the cost of "fitting" be "accepting" an American exceptionalism narrative of evangelical mission work among Latinos?

Culture and gospel. U.S. evangelicalism has had an outsized influence on the global evangelical movement. The problem is that U.S. evangelicals have taken U.S. dominant culture with them in the process. The globalization process has increased the influence, such that one sees a homogenization of worship and theology among evangelicals around the world. Will Latino evangelicals bring their cultural distinctives to the larger evangelical table? Will U.S. evangelicals be ready to accept the cultural influences of others and take active steps to limit U.S. evangelical cultural hegemony?

Visions of the eschaton and visions of the future of the United States. The biblical vision of the future is one in which the rich diversity of humanity is joined in the worship of the Lamb (Rev 7:9-10). Yet this goes against the assumed models for the unity of U.S. society. Both the Anglo-conformity and Melting Pot models subsume the diversity into the commonality. Most U.S. Protestants, be they evangelical or mainline, assume uniformity over diversity.

As the United States becomes more diverse, which model will guide U.S. evangelicals as they envision the place of Latinos and other minority groups in U.S. society? How will U.S. evangelicalism interpret Revelation 7 and its role in helping diverse peoples in the United States form a society together? What vision will U.S. evangelicals have for churches in the United States in the future?

Multicultural, multiethnic, multiracial realities. Latinos are a *mestizo* people. We are the result of many ethnic and racial encounters. Here in the United States a significant percentage of Latinos are marrying non-Latinos. This means that we are contributing to the increasing *mestizaje* of the United States, both as a people and in our own intermarriages.

Some in the United States sought to claim that with the election of Barack Obama as president we were now postracial. But the reality is that race is still a very strong social construct in this country. Latinos have demonstrated that one can have a common identity without a common, or even clearly defined, race. Will we be able to show a way forward in which diversity is celebrated, instead of questioned?

Latin American missionaries to the North. How will U.S. evangelicals respond to the growing number of migrants from the South that are evangelizing as they migrate and who see themselves as missionaries to the increasingly pagan North? Will they be seen as partners in God's mission?

Euro-American evangelical contextual theology. One of the most important contributions contextual theologies can make to U.S. evangelical theology is to help it name itself as a contextual theology. Because of the outsized influence of U.S. evangelicalism, it will be particularly difficult for it to name its theologies as contextual. But until that happens all "minority" theologies will be marginalized.

That task is also crucial because dominant-culture evangelicalism also needs to recognize how it has been shaped by its context. Militarism, individualism, materialism and the U.S. story of racism and imperial expansion have all had an influence on evangelical theology. Until evangelicalism can name itself as a contextual theology it will be very difficult to recognize the influence the U.S. experience has had on how theology is done by evangelicals.

The stories of U.S. Protestantism not yet told. Will Latino Protestants become part of the narrative of U.S. evangelicalism, or will the story always be told in ways that either exclude or marginalize Latino Protestants? Pentecostalism is likely to have an increasingly important role in global Christianity. Will U.S. evangelicalism learn to retell its story in such a way that Latino Pentecostalism plays a role in its self-definition or will it be excluded because of a European slant or a Calvinist restriction?

Conclusion

As Latinos join the theological conversation in the larger U.S. evangelical world, it will be tempting to either adopt the dominant perspective or to talk at or past each other. Will evangelicalism be able to go outside the gate or will it attempt to draw Latino theology into the center?

For Further Reading

Costas, Orlando. *Christ Outside the Gate: Mission Beyond Christendom.* Eugene, Ore.: Wipf & Stock, 2005.

de la Torre, Miguel, and Edwin Aponte. *Introducing Latino/a Theologies.* Maryknoll, N.Y.: Orbis, 2001.

González, Justo. *Mañana: Christian Theology from a Hispanic Perspective.* Nashville: Abingdon, 1990.

Villafañe, Eldin. *The Liberating Spirit: Toward an Hispanic American Pentecostal Social Ethic.* Grand Rapids: Eerdmans, 1993.

12

Asian American
Evangelical Theology

Amos Yong

• • •

My charge is threefold: to describe the main themes and major developments in Asian American theology, to critically evaluate these proposals from an evangelical perspective, and to suggest next steps for evangelical theology in response. The three sections of this essay will attempt to fulfill, in order, this threefold charge. My thesis is that this exercise of thinking about Asian American aspects of the evangelical tradition is important not just for Asian American evangelicalism in particular but also for the evangelical theological enterprise as a whole.

ASIAN AMERICAN THEOLOGY
Major Developments

Any survey of Asian American theology within the space constraints of this essay will necessarily have to be selective. Fortunately, Jonathan Tan's recent book has already overviewed the field, which frees me to focus on the discussions I feel may be most pertinent to our own constructive theological task later.[1] I thus highlight the following three trajectories, reserving comment on Asian American evangelical theologies for the next section.

---

[1]Jonathan Y. Tan, *Introducing Asian American Theologies* (Maryknoll, N.Y.: Orbis, 2008).

First, we begin with Asian American theologians in mainline Protestant circles. There have been a few in the last generation who began their theological work focused on "accepted" theological tasks and topics rather than on articulating a specific Asian American theological vision. Most prominent here has been Korean American Sang Hyun Lee, who achieved his reputation as a Jonathan Edwards scholar.[2] Although Lee has published a number of articles and essays on Asian American theological issues over the years, by and large his contributions have been in Edwardsean scholarship. In general, Lee is better known as a Reformed theologian who happens to be Asian American than as an Asian American theologian who does Reformed theology.[3] More recently his book on Asian American theology highlights the themes of marginality and liminality central to the Asian American experience.[4] It is here that Lee's Asian American identity comes to the forefront, even if one might ask what is unique to the Asian American experience of either marginality or liminality from that of other ethnic groups in our age of globalization. On the other hand, it may also be precisely insights into marginality and liminality that enable Lee to contribute as an Asian American to a discourse with wider theological purchase beyond his ethnic community.

Parallel to Lee in the Reformed tradition but moving in a very different direction has been the Taiwanese American Choan Seng Song. Song began with a doctoral dissertation on Barth and Tillich (Union Theological Seminary, 1965) but gradually was convinced about the need to theologize more explicitly and intentionally from Asian sources. By the time he arrived to teach at the Pacific School of Religion in 1985, he was firmly committed to a research and writing program that

---

[2]Sang Hyun Lee, *The Philosophical Theology of Jonathan Edwards* (Princeton, N.J.: Princeton University Press, 1988).

[3]This is exemplified in Sang Hyun Lee, "Jonathan Edwards's Dispositional Conception of the Trinity: A Resource for Contemporary Reformed Theology," in *Toward the Future of Reformed Theology: Tasks, Topics, Traditions*, ed. David Willis and Michael Welker (Grand Rapids: Eerdmans, 1999), pp. 444-55. Otherwise, Lee has published a handful of essays on Asian American theology. See his "Pilgrimage and Home in the Wilderness of Marginality: Symbols and Context in Asian American Theology," *Princeton Seminary Bulletin* 16, no. 1 (1995): 49-64.

[4]Sang Hyun Lee, *From a Liminal Place: An Asian American Theology* (Minneapolis: Fortress, 2010).

involved the retrieval and appropriation of Asian traditions for the theological task.[5]

For Song, however, that did not mean that his theological work was relevant only in Asian contexts. Rather, Song emphasized the importance of local or contextual theologies that were pertinent across the Asian diaspora in a globally shrinking world, while he also insisted that Asian sources invited a narrative hermeneutical and methodological approach to theology that was applicable not only to the formulation of Asian theology but also to the theological enterprise as a whole.[6] In other words, Song has never understood his working with Asian materials and ideas as thereby circumscribing his audience. Instead, the what and the how of Asian theological reflection is relevant both to Asian Americans and to the wider theological conversation. The response to Song's *oeuvre*, however, has been mixed: some are appreciative of his efforts to think consistently and deeply from out of Asian sources, while others are leery about what they feel are uncritical deployments of such for Christian theological reflection.

In the meanwhile other Asian American Protestants have also begun registering specifically Asian perspectives in their theological work. Jung Young Lee, Rita Nakashima Brock and Andrew Sung Park among many others have brought Asian voices into the theological arena, in the process proposing that the Christian theological tradition as a whole has much to gain from engaging Asian viewpoints.[7] In ef-

---

[5]See Choan Seng Song, *Christian Mission in Reconstruction: An Asian Analysis* (1975; reprint, Maryknoll, N.Y.: Orbis, 1977); *Tell Us Our Names: Story Theology from an Asian Perspective* (Maryknoll, N.Y.: Orbis, 1984); *Theology from the Womb of Asia* (Maryknoll, N.Y.: Orbis, 1986); and *Third-Eye Theology: Theology in Formation in Asian Settings*, rev. ed. (Maryknoll, N.Y.: Orbis, 1991). Song's theological trilogy will no doubt constitute his legacy: Choan Seng Song, *Jesus, the Crucified People* (1990; reprint, Minneapolis: Fortress, 1996); *Jesus and the Reign of God* (Minneapolis: Fortress, 1993); and *Jesus in the Power of the Spirit* (Minneapolis: Fortress, 1994).
[6]For example, Choan Seng Song, *The Believing Heart: An Invitation to Story Theology* (Minneapolis: Fortress, 1999).
[7]For example, Jung Young Lee, *The Theology of Change: A Christian Concept of God in an Eastern Perspective* (Maryknoll, N.Y.: Orbis, 1979); *Marginality: The Key to Multicultural Theology* (Minneapolis: Fortress, 1995);*The Trinity in Asian Perspective* (Nashville: Abingdon, 1996); Rita Nakashima Brock, *Journeys by Heart: A Christology of Erotic Power* (New York: Crossroad, 1988); Rita Nakashima Brock, Jung Ha Kim, Kwok Pui-Lan and Seung Ai Yang, *Off the Menu: Asian and Asian North American Women's Religion and Theology* (Louisville: Westminster John Knox, 2007); and Andrew Sung Park, *The Wounded Heart of God: The Asian Concept of Han and the Christian Doctrine of Sin* (Nashville: Abingdon, 1993).

fect, these can be understood as responding to the rhetorical question, What if Paul had gone to China (instead of to Rome)?[8]

Second, a few comments should be made about Asian American theologians in the Roman Catholic tradition. Here we find Korean Americans like Anselm Min, who teaches at Claremont Graduate School, sitting across the ecumenical table from those like Sang Lee. But while Lee's focus has been on Edwards, Min, nurtured in a classical Roman Catholic theological education, is as comfortable with philosophers like Hegel as he is with magisterial philosophical theologians like Aquinas. Nevertheless, Min brings these major voices of the tradition to bear on questions and issues most relevant to the Catholic Church's global experience, like development and liberation, globalization and religious pluralism.[9]

Perhaps the most prominent, and certainly the most prolific, Asian American Catholic theologian today is Peter C. Phan. Like other senior Asian American theologians, Phan also cut his theological teeth on the major thoroughfares of the tradition, writing his first books on the church fathers and important contemporary theologians.[10] Upon establishing himself, however, he has gradually turned his gaze to Asia, beginning with a study of Christian/Catholic theological inculturation in his homeland Vietnam.[11] In the last decade Phan has increasingly written on Asian and Asian American theological issues, traversing fluently between Asia and America, between the theological tradition

---

[8]I adapt here the title of the essay by Gerald R. McDermott, "What If Paul Had Been from China? Reflections on the Possibility of Revelation in Non-Christian Religions," in *No Other Gods Before Me? Evangelicals and the Challenge of World Religions*, ed. John G. Stackhouse Jr. (Grand Rapids: Baker Academic, 2001), pp. 17-35.

[9]Anselm Kyongsuk Min, *Dialectic of Salvation: Issues in Theology of Liberation* (Albany: State University of New York Press, 1989); *The Solidarity of Others in a Divided World: A Postmodern Theology After Postmodernism* (New York: T & T Clark, 2004); and *Paths to the Triune God: An Encounter Between Aquinas and Recent Theologies* (Notre Dame, Ind.: University of Notre Dame Press, 2005).

[10]Phan's books in the 1980s were *Social Thought*, Message of the Fathers of the Church 20 (Wilmington, Del.: Michael Glazier, 1984); *Grace and the Human Condition*, Message of the Fathers of the Church 15 (Wilmington, Del.: Michael Glazier, 1988); *Culture and Eschatology: The Iconographical Vision of Paul Evdokimov*, American University Studies Series 7: Theology and Religion 1 (New York: Peter Lang, 1985); and *Eternity in Time: A Study in Karl Rahner's Eschatology* (Selinsgrove, Penn.: Susquehanna University Press, 1988).

[11]Peter C. Phan, *Mission and Catechesis: Alexandre de Rhodes and Inculturation in Seventeenth-Century Vietnam* (Maryknoll, N.Y.: Orbis, 1998).

and its contemporary horizon, between Catholic and ecumenical environments, between global and local contexts, and, in terms of theological disciplines, between missiology and systematic theology.[12]

From an Asian American theological perspective, Phan's work is path breaking precisely because of his ability to cross what to most others would be insurmountable chasms. This can be appreciated from his essay "The Dragon and the Eagle: Toward a Vietnamese American Theology," wherein he provides phenomenological depth and existential richness to the interstitiality and liminality that characterizes the immigrant experience, and wherein he is able to give voice to the exilic sense of journeying between two cultures and two churches.[13] Thus the theological themes that surface tap into Asian cosmological intuitions on the one hand (for example, with the themes of heaven-earth-humanity playing a central role), while sketching a Christology that bridges traditional concepts with those drawn from the Asian and immigrant experiences on the other hand (for example, Jesus Christ the Son of God now viewed also as the marginal immigrant, elder brother and the divinely incarnate ancestor). The result, at least in part, calls for a contemplative spirituality suitable for the Asian American mind and heart, a liturgical inculturation relevant to transnational and globalization trends as these are being played especially in the North American context, and a kingdom-centered ecclesiology that nurtures hope and anticipation without minimizing the importance of the church in the present time. In each of these ways, Phan models how Asian American themes are relevant not only for Asians, nor only for Asian Americans, but also for the enrichment of the church Catholic/catholic—all the while without denying the distinctiveness and par-

---

[12]For example, James H. Kroeger and Peter C. Phan, *The Future of the Asian Churches: The Asian Synod and Ecclesia in Asia* (Quezon City, Philippines: Claretian Publications, 2002); Peter C. Phan, ed., *The Asian Synod: Texts and Commentaries* (Maryknoll, N.Y.: Orbis, 2002); Peter C. Phan, *Vietnamese-American Catholics* (Mahwah, N.J.: Paulist Press, 2005); and Peter C. Phan, ed., *Christianity in Asia* (Oxford: Wiley-Blackwell, 2010). Phan has also written a trilogy: *Christianity with an Asian Face: Asian American Theology in the Making* (Maryknoll, N.Y.: Orbis, 2003); *In Our Own Tongues: Perspectives from Asia on Mission and Inculturation* (Maryknoll, N.Y.: Orbis, 2003); and *Being Religious Interreligiously: Asian Perspectives on Interfaith Dialogue* (Maryknoll, N.Y.: Orbis, 2004).
[13]See Phan, *Christianity with an Asian Face*, chap. 11.

ticularity of the Vietnamese American experience.

A third trajectory of Asian American theology consists of advances made in biblical scholarship. Here I will only very briefly mention the major contributions, since this is perhaps more tangentially related to the theological task strictly defined.

- The work of established and senior biblical scholars like K. K. Yeo, while not intended to be limited specifically to Asian American issues, has implications not only for crosscultural biblical scholarship but also for the Asian American evangelical theological endeavor more specifically.[14]

- Collections of essays produced by those working within the orbit of the Society of Biblical Literature are currently at the vanguard of what is happening among Asian American biblical scholars.[15]

- A number of younger scholars working at the interface of biblical studies and postcolonial studies or at the intersection of biblical studies and Asian American studies particularly have begun to produce monographs in conscious dialogue and substantial engagement with the Asian American experience.[16]

- There have also been a good number of Asian American evangelicals who have earned their Ph.D.s in biblical studies, but who have not yet begun to publish explicitly from an Asian American perspective.[17]

---

[14]Khiok-Khng Yeo, *Rhetorical Interaction in 1 Corinthians 8 and 10: A Formal Analysis with Preliminary Suggestions for a Chinese, Cross-cultural Hermeneutic* (New York: Brill, 1995); *What Has Jerusalem to Do with Beijing: Biblical Interpretation from a Chinese Perspective* (Harrisburg: Trinity Press International, 1998); *Chairman Mao Meets the Apostle Paul: Christianity, Communism, and the Hope of China* (Grand Rapids: Brazos, 2002); *Navigating Romans Through Cultures: Challenging Readings by Charting a New Course* (New York: T & T Clark, 2004); and *Musing with Confucius and Paul: Toward a Chinese Christian Theology* (Eugene, Ore.: Cascade, 2008).

[15]For example, Tat-Siong Benny Liew and Gale A Yee, eds., *The Bible in Asian America*, Semeia 90-91 (Atlanta: Society of Biblical Literature, 2002); and Mary Foskett and Jeffrey Kah-Jin Kuan, eds., *Ways of Being, Ways of Reading: Asian American Biblical Interpretation* (St. Louis: Chalice, 2006).

[16]For example, Uriah Y. Kim, *Decolonizing Josiah: Toward a Postcolonial Reading of the Deuteronomistic History* (Sheffield, U.K.: Sheffield Phoenix, 2005); *Identity and Loyalty in the David Story: A Postcolonial Reading*, Hebrew Bible Monographs 22 (Sheffield, U.K.: Sheffield Phoenix, 2008); and Tat-Siong Benny Liew, *What Is Asian American Biblical Hermeneutics? Reading the New Testament* (Honolulu: University of Hawai'i Press, 2008).

[17]Leading the way here are the biblical studies faculty at Logos Evangelical Seminary (Silas Chan, Hing Wong, John Wu, Jeffrey Lu and Chloe Sun) and International Theological Sem-

I turn momentarily to consider this lack of interaction with Asian American perspectives among these and other evangelical scholars.

Insofar as biblical studies inevitably informs theological reflection, those interested in the evolution of Asian American theology should pay close attention to the work that is being done by Asian American biblical scholars. This is especially important since the lines between biblical scholarship and theological thinking are increasingly blurred and since few Asian American biblical scholars see their work as limited to the exegetical issues of "what the text meant" as opposed to the more theological tasks of deciphering "what the text means."

The preceding does no more than highlight some of the major developments in the field of Asian American theology. Depending on how one defines *evangelical,* the achievements noted here have involved scholars with evangelical sympathies if not commitments. Yet institutionally speaking, the major steps forward have taken place in mainline Protestant and Roman Catholic environments. Evangelical participants therein, then, have not been recognized as contributing explicitly to the Asian American theological cause, so to speak.

ASIAN AMERICAN EVANGELICAL THEOLOGIES
Struggling for Emergence

I now turn to overview the state of the discussion in Asian American evangelical theology. The short version is that there is not much to tell. One edited volume has appeared, and even here, the title admits we are at the beginning stages of the conversation.[18] While the six essayists reflect the diversity of the Asian American evangelical community, none are theologians, strictly considered. David Yoo and Tim Tseng are historians. They urge that religion needs to be factored into immigration and racial analyses of Asian American communities, and that the "color blindness" of American church history should be acknowledged so as to enable moving beyond orientalist or assimilationist mod-

---

inary (Kyu Sam Han), both in El Monte, California, among others.

[18]D. J. Chuang and Timothy Tseng, eds., *Conversations: Asian American Evangelical Theologies in Formation* (Washington, D.C.: L2 Foundation, 2006). See www.L2Foundation.org.

els of the Asian American Christian experience. There are also essays by Peter Cha, who discusses the challenges involved in identity formation among second-generation Asian Americans, and by James Zo, who analyzes how structural and power issues complicate the assessment of racism, prejudice and discrimination on both sides of the American and Asian American equation. Finally, there are essays by two historical theologians: Paul Lim, who specializes in early modern England, reveals the importance of biography in the construction of any Asian American evangelical theology, and Jeffrey Jue, a post-Reformation historian, seeks a way beyond both modernist experientialism and postmodernist subjectivism by returning to the gospel. As should be evident from this overview, Asian American evangelicals are presently more engaged in sociological and historical analyses than with constructive, dogmatic or systematic theological reflection.

New developments may be on the horizon, however. The first issue of *SANACS Journal*, published by the Society of Asian North American Christian Studies, features a number of exploratory theological articles. One remains at a high level of abstraction in rethinking race in a postmodern and postcolonial context in ways that are suggestive for how Asian American identity formation can provide missiological impetus, while another operates concretely on the Laotian American ground in thinking about a theology of migration and exile.[19] For the moment, however, we note that the task of thinking theologically as Asian American evangelicals is only barely beginning. Thus the preceding overview raises the question, why have Asian American evangelicals lagged behind in substantive theological reflection when compared to their mainline Protestant and Roman Catholic counterparts? I believe there are some fairly evident reasons. Note, though, that the following are presented as hypotheses to be tested rather than as dogmatic certifications about the Asian American evangelical theological academy.

First, Asian Americans with roots in East Asian or Confucian cul-

---

[19]See, respectively, Jonathan Tran, "Identity as Missiology," *SANACS Journal* 1 (2009): 29-40, and Sharon Stanley, "Theology from Bamboos, Borders, and Bricks," *SANACS Journal* 1 (2009): 41-58.

tures (especially Chinese, Korean, Japanese, Vietnamese, among others) are, in general, traditionalists and conservatives. Sociologically, many of these Asian Americans are drawn to evangelical Protestantism because it provides a similarly conservative worldview, albeit one that enables their acculturation into American society.[20] Thus, among Asian American Protestants, Confucian conservatism morphs into a form of evangelical conservatism, and Asian American evangelicals tend to attend solidly evangelical seminaries because of their conservative commitments. So whereas mainline Protestant seminaries are much more focused on corporate identities sorted out in ethnic, political and sociocultural terms, evangelical seminaries and their curricula focus more on personal identities, particularly the formation of spiritual lives in relationship to Jesus Christ.[21]

But what else does evangelical conservatism entail? Drawing from the classical *Christ and Culture* study of H. Richard Niebuhr, North American evangelicalism has historically been ensconced in the "Christ against culture" stance, albeit more recently shifting more toward the "Christ transforming culture" posture.[22] This involves either at worst the rejection of culture, which has traditionally characterized evangelical sectarianism, or at best an ambiguous relationship with culture, one featuring what might be called a cultural hermeneutics of suspicion that is always concerned about syncretism with the world. Asian American evangelicals have thus usually understood their Christian conversion to involve either a turning away from their Asian cultural roots or a minimizing of such aspects of their identity, emphasizing instead their new life in Christ and as Christians.[23]

---

[20]For example, Janelle S. Wong with Jane Naomi Iwamura, "The Moral Minority: Race, Religion, and Conservative Politics in Asian America," in *Religion and Social Justice for Immigrants*, ed. Pierrette Hondagneu-Sotelo (New Brunswick, N.J.: Rutgers University Press, 2007), pp. 35-49.

[21]Russell Jeung, "Evangelical and Mainline Teachings on Asian American Identity," in *The Bible in Asian America*, ed. Tat-Siong Benny Liew and Gale A Yee, Semeia 90-91 (Atlanta: Society of Biblical Literature, 2002), pp. 211-36, reprinted in Viji Nakka-Cammauf and Timothy Tseng, eds., *Asian American Christianity: A Reader* (Castro Valley, Calif.: The Institute for the Study of Asian American Christianity, 2009), pp. 197-216.

[22]See H. Richard Niebuhr, *Christ and Culture* (1951; reprint, San Francisco: Harper Torchlight, 1956).

[23]Thus Taiwanese immigrants see Christian conversion and Americanization conjointly as in-

This fundamental worldview orientation is reinforced in evangelical seminary education in various ways. Epistemologically, for example, evangelicals up until recently have embraced a modified foundationalism characteristic of the Enlightenment quest for universal knowledge, one tempered by a biblical presuppositionalism and propositionalist theory of language.[24] This brings with it, so it has been assumed, a universal standpoint, with the resulting resistance to the pluralism endemic in the postmodern context. Thus the diversity of cultures might be celebrated, but not if such is thought to threaten the foundations of evangelical certitude. Similarly, at the hermeneutical level, modernist emphases on historical-grammatical interpretation have been assumed to be central (foundational!) to identifying the scriptural authors' message, which is then seen as the norm for Christian belief. This means that biblical interpretation focuses primarily, if not solely, on exegesis—the identification and retrieval of what the biblical authors meant—upon which the secondary steps of contemporary meaning and application are extrapolated. Perennially, then, evangelical hermeneutics has always been concerned about *eisegesis*, precisely what is understood as infecting or contaminating reader-response approaches which skew and distort the pristine message of the Bible.[25] These epistemic and hermeneutical assumptions have undergirded evangelical theological method, long guided by the *sola scriptura* commitments of Reformation traditions.[26] This is not to diminish the role of tradition, reason or even experience, particularly among Wesleyan evangelicals, but it is to point out that in general, evangelicals have emphasized the primacy of Scripture in ways that have minimized (at best) or ignored (at worst) the various roles and interplay of sources from out of which theological reflection inevitably emerges.

---

volving a jettisoning of much of Taiwanese culture—see Carolyn Chen, *Getting Saved in America: Taiwanese Immigration and Religious Experience* (Princeton, N.J.: Princeton University Press, 2008)—and this attitude is quite prevalent across the Asian American scene.

[24]As summarized in Gary J. Dorrien, *The Remaking of Evangelical Theology* (Louisville: Westminster John Knox, 1998), pp. 107-14.

[25]In mainline Protestant circles, of course, there has long been recognition that the traditional line between exegesis and eisegesis is much more blurry than previously thought; see Jay G. Williams, "Exegesis-Eisegesis: Is There a Difference?" *Theology Today* 30, no. 3 (1973): 218-27.

[26]For example, R. C. Sproul, *Scripture Alone: The Evangelical Doctrine* (Phillipsburg, N.J.: P&R Publishing, 2005).

Hence theologically, evangelicalism insists on a biblical orientation that maps the totality of the human experience, regardless of cultural particularities. Thus, for example, humankind suffers from one overall problem, that of sin against God, and that one problem demands basically one solution, the substitutionary atonement of the Son's death on the cross. It does not matter that Asians have a shame rather than guilt culture since, in this evangelical framework, there is no need to rethink the inherited theology of atonement from Asian perspectives.[27] My point is that evangelical theological tendencies generally urge a universalistic horizon, and in this paradigm, there is no need to articulate Asian, Asian American or other cultural and ethnic perspectives since these are all subsumed within the biblical framework when read in an evangelical way.

I suggest that Asian American evangelicals, formed theologically with such sensibilities, have internalized the American evangelical worldview and in that sense mostly do not see the need to think explicitly from an Asian American vantage point. Rather, the Bible addresses all human beings, and so any plain reading of it will or should be able to access the Word of God at any and all times and places. Hence, while there remains an important role for sociological or other disciplinary analyses of the Asian American experience in particular or of Christian life in general, theologically—at least in this Asian American perspective that has been deeply shaped by the (white) North American evangelical theological establishment—there is little work needed to be done. The basic theological and doctrinal truths of the Christian faith have already been formulated and can be found in any evangelical systematic theological text.[28] If Asian Americans were to write their own theologies, these would be parochial undertakings, with marginal relevance from the evangelical perspective only for "those" people (maybe

---

[27]Asian Americans are beginning to do just this, however—for example, Rachel Y. Lei, "Saving Significance of the Cross in the Asian American Context," *SANACS Journal* 1 (2009): 95-116.

[28]As communicated, for example, in Timothy Larsen and Daniel J. Treier, *The Cambridge Companion to Evangelical Theology* (Cambridge: Cambridge University Press, 2007), and compare my critical review: "Restoring, Reforming, Renewing: Accompaniments to *The Cambridge Companion to Evangelical Theology*," *Evangelical Review of Theology* 33, no. 2 (2009): 179-83.

immigrants, refugees or exiles) who have not yet assimilated into the broader American evangelical culture. Little wonder, then, that few Asian Americans have ventured into this theological territory.[29]

THE FUTURE OF EVANGELICAL THEOLOGY
Asian American Questions, Hopes and Aspirations

In this final section I can do no more than sketch briefly some possible avenues of exploration for the Asian American project in evangelical theology. Here I would urge both my Asian American evangelical associates in particular and my evangelical colleagues in general to take Asian cultural, philosophical and religious resources seriously in our global context. The retrieval and reappropriation of the Confucian tradition among biblical scholars like Yeo is one positive example of how the East-West encounter is being negotiated in the wider academy. My point is not to impose Confucianism on the evangelical theological agenda but to say that there is no good reason for evangelicals in general to neglect Asian traditions in the theological task.[30] And with biblical scholars such as K. K. Yeo leading the way, there are even fewer excuses for ignoring the promise and challenges of Christian-Confucian dialogue for evangelical theology in global context.

But why take Asian traditions seriously in the North American context? The short answer is that the forces of globalization, immigration and transnationalism have produced an Asian diaspora not only in the West but also around the world.[31] Without dismissing the import of biblical scholarship for the work of theology, I want to emphasize the "on the ground" nature of the Asian American experience and how this

---

[29]The preceding analysis is a short version of what I have elsewhere argued in greater detail—for example, Amos Yong, "The Future of Evangelical Theology: Asian and Asian American Interrogations," *Asia Journal of Theology* 21, no. 2 (2007): 371-97, esp. 376-81, reprinted by *SANACS Journal* 1 (2009): 5-27, esp. 11-17; see also my "Asian American Historicity: Problems and Promises for Evangelical Theology," *SANACS Journal* (forthcoming).

[30]I applaud the efforts of Young Lee Hertig, "Why Asian American Evangelical Theologies?" *Journal of Asian and Asian American Theology* 7 (2005-2006): 1-23, to retrieve Daoist resources for evangelical theology.

[31]See Amos Yong, "Asian American Religion: A Review Essay," *Nova Religio: The Journal of Alternative and Emergent Religions* 9, no. 3 (2006): 92-107.

invites a religious and theological solidarity with those on the underside of history.[32] I am also reminded that theology ultimately not only attempts to scale the heights of understanding the divine but also that the central dictum of evangelical theology is that the divine has accommodated to the human experience and been revealed below, in the flesh, amid the messiness of human history. If that is the case, then theology needs not only to emerge from out of our worshiping the exalted and transcendent One, but it also needs to discern the traces of the God who is also immanent in our lives. Theology, in short, cannot remain merely an exercise in philosophical speculation and abstraction, but must be touched by and get its hands dirty with the concreteness of the flesh and the historical process that God has entered into.

It is also at this point that I very briefly supplement the Christocentric emphases of much of evangelical theology with a Pentecostal and pneumatological accent. By "Pentecostal" I am referring not only to the modern charismatic renewal movement related in many minds to the revival birthed out of Azusa Street in the early twentieth century, a movement that is certainly a formative aspect of my religious life and my theological DNA, but I am also following out the narrative of the gospel story in which the Christ who was incarnate in the flesh died, was resurrected and ascended into heaven, then poured out from on high the Spirit of God upon all flesh (Acts 2:17, 33).[33] My claim is that evangelical theology should be fully trinitarian, which means Christ-centered *and* pentecostally oriented. It is from this trinitarian vantage point that I see the languages of all flesh, Asian and Asian American dialects included, to have been caught up in the Pentecostal outpouring of the Spirit.[34]

---

[32]See Amos Yong, "The Im/migrant Spirit: De/constructing a Pentecostal Theology of Migration," *The Journal of World Christianity* (forthcoming), and "Informality, Illegality, and Improvisation: Theological Reflections on Money, Migration, and Ministry in Chinatown, NYC, and Beyond," *Journal of Race, Ethnicity, and Religion* (forthcoming), www.raceandreligion.com.

[33]See Amos Yong, *The Spirit Poured Out on All Flesh: Pentecostalism and the Possibility of Global Theology* (Grand Rapids: Baker Academic, 2005), and *In the Days of Caesar: Pentecostalism and Political Theology* (Grand Rapids: Eerdmans, 2010).

[34]I build here on previous work—for example, Amos Yong, "Whither Asian American Evangelical Theology? What Asian? Which American? Whose *Evangelion*?" *Evangelical Review of Theology* 32, no. 1 (2008): 22-37, and "The Future of Asian Pentecostal Theology: An Asian

This means that the American evangelical theological conversation ought to be characterized by at least three interwoven strands: (1) a trinitarian framework, one that takes normatively the scriptural witness and is deeply embedded in the great theological tradition; (2) a global horizon, one that is dialogically albeit no less critically open to engaging the great cultural, philosophical and religious traditions of the East; (3) a local sensitivity, one that is attuned to the practical realities of Asian American life in particular, including the travails of migration, the burden of being a moral minority, the challenges of ethnicity in a world of "whiteness,"[35] and the task of living betwixt and between, which oftentimes means neither "here" nor "there."[36] Asian Americans and other evangelicals who take up this theological charge will in turn challenge, perhaps overhaul, but certainly enrich the evangelical theological conversation, at least for those who are ready and willing to receive gifts both from the Eastern shore and from the suburbs and downtowns across the multicultural world we call North America.[37]

For Further Reading

Alumkal, Antony William. *Asian American Evangelical Churches: Race, Ethnicity, and Assimilation in the Second Generation*. New York: LFB Scholarly Publishers, 2003.

Jeung, Russell. *Faithful Generations: Race and New Asian American Churches*. New Brunswick, N.J.: Rutgers University Press, 2005.

Toyama, Nikki A., et al. *More Than Serving Tea: Asian American Women on Expectations, Relationships, Leadership and Faith*. Downers Grove, Ill.: InterVarsity Press, 2006.

American Assessment," *Asian Journal of Pentecostal Studies* 10, no. 1 (2007): 22-41.

[35]See J. Kameron Carter, *Race: A Theological Account* (Oxford: Oxford University Press, 2008); see also Carter's chapter, "Race and the Experience of Death: Theologically Reappraising American Evangelicalism," in *Cambridge Companion to Evangelical Theology*, pp. 177-98.

[36]See Jung Young Lee and Peter C. Phan, eds., *Journeys at the Margin: Towards an Autobiographical Theology in American-Asian Perspective* (Collegeville, Minn.: Liturgical Press, 1999).

[37]Thanks to the following for their comments on a previous draft of this paper: Timothy Lim, Teck Ngern, Peter C. Phan, Jonathan Tan and Young Lee Hertig. I also appreciate the editorial assistance of Jeffrey Greenman and Gene Green of Wheaton College for helping shorten a much longer version of the paper for publication.

Tseng, Timothy, and Nakka-Cammauf, Viji, eds. *Asian American Christianity Reader.* Castro Valley, Calif.: Pacific Asian American & Canadian Christian Education Project and the Institute for the Study of Asian American Christianity, 2009.

Young Lee Hertig, and Chloe Sun, eds. *Mirrored Reflections: Reframing Biblical Characters*, Eugene, Ore.: Wipf & Stock, 2010.

13

African American Theology

Retrospect and Prospect

Vincent Bacote

• • •

The 2008 presidential election campaign was the context for introducing black theology to a nationwide audience. The selectively edited clips of the Reverend Dr. Jeremiah Wright provoked significant controversy, especially because Wright was the pastor of then candidate Barack Obama. As members of the news media inquired about the beliefs of Wright, black liberation theology moved to center stage and became part of the national consciousness; this was the theological framework of the man who was pastor to Obama. What was this black theology and was it a unique strain of theology, perhaps radical and out of the mainstream, with the implication that someone running for president could hold a version of Christian beliefs that was militant and even un-American? My task here is to consider African American theology and ultimately to reflect on how this brand of contextual theology might stimulate our theological reflection as we strive to live with greater Christian faithfulness.

Black liberation theology is not the only expression of African American theology. Indeed, one can argue that African American theology began the moment when African slaves first encountered Christianity on American soil and subsequently began to develop modes of Christian expression that mingled their indigenous practices with the gospel they learned from slave owners. In recent centuries there is certainly a great tradition of preaching and music that emerged from the various African American denominations and these traditions express theological commitments, but not significantly in the manner of theological monographs and articles. For this essay, black liberation theology will be the primary focus because it is perhaps the most developed expression of African American theology, certainly in terms of the academy. After a brief survey of black theology, I will present briefly the thought of two prominent representatives, note the response of womanist theology, and then summarize two recent critiques before suggesting a way forward for evangelical theology as it faces the concerns raised by this tradition.

Black Liberation Theology

According to one version of the narrative,

> Black liberation theology originated on July 31, 1966, when 51 black pastors bought a full page ad in the *New York Times* and demanded a more aggressive approach to eradicating racism. They echoed the demands of the black power movement, but the new crusade found its source of inspiration in the Bible.[1]

These members of the clergy resisted the idea that Black Power was nihilistic and impossible to reconcile with Christianity. One significant motivation was that African Americans in the North had disagreements with the strategy of the civil rights movement; Black Power was a response of those frustrated by the pace of the civil rights struggle as well as the theology linked to the Southern African American churches that gave leadership to the movement. A younger group of civil rights activists wanted transformation more quickly and Black Power was the name given to this newer movement. Black Power was also the name given to the statement issued by the National Committee of Negro Churchmen that appeared in the *New York Times* on July 31, 1966.

The pioneers of Black Theology were determined to extrapolate from

---

[1]Barbara Bradley Haggerty, "A Closer Look at Black Theology," *All Things Considered*, NPR, March 18, 2008, www.npr.org/templates/story/story.php?storyId=89236116.

the concept of Black Power a theological referent that would not only vindicate the young civil rights workers laboring in the rural South, who wanted to apply more severe sanctions against white die-hards, but would also galvanize the left wing of the Southern-based civil rights movement and reassemble it within the province of Black Christians who lived in the urban North.[2]

It would not be an overstatement to regard black liberation theology as a response to a particular set of despisers of religion who would only find Christianity viable if it took their concerns for equality and social transformation seriously. Black liberation theology emerged as an attempt to answer the question, How can a person be Christian and also committed to addressing the oppressive legacy of racism in the United States? How can you have a gospel that is not only about going to heaven but also about being concerned with justice and peace in the present? Can you have a Christian faith that changes the way that black people see themselves? Can you have a faith that proclaims justice and proper self-regard? The Black Power statement was a public document aimed toward validating the concerns of those associated with the Black Power movement. The work of James Cone emerged as a way to speak the concerns of those for whom Christianity was discredited because of its failure to be relevant to the black consciousness and Black Power movement.

Before we focus on Cone, two comments are in order. First, it is interesting to observe black liberation theology emerged around the same time as feminist theology and Latin American liberation theology, though all three emerged without knowledge of the others. Second, it is important to note some of the other prominent writers in black theology who are sometimes obscured by the length and width of Cone's shadow. For example, J. Deotis Roberts is a very important figure who was already writing a version of black theology before Cone's work emerged, and who places a significant emphasis on reconciliation as part of the agenda.[3] Another figure who emphasized black

---

[2]Gayraud S. Wilmore, introduction to *Black Theology: A Documentary History*, vol. 1: *1966-1979*, ed. James H. Cone and Gayraud S. Wilmore, 2nd ed. (Maryknoll, N.Y.: Orbis, 1993), pp. 15-16.
[3]See J. Deotis Roberts, *Liberation and Reconciliation: A Black Theology*, rev. ed. (Maryknoll, N.Y.: Orbis, 1994). The first edition was 1971. In conversation, Roberts once remarked that he was writing about black theology long before Cone had begun to think about it.

religions as a critique of black theology was Charles Long, who claimed the blacks practiced religion but did not do theology because it is a Western construct. Other figures include Major Jones, Gayraud Wilmore, Albert Cleage Jr., William R. Jones and Vincent Harding.[4] These figures have a range of opinion and emphasis in black theology, even as there is a common concern for the liberation of African Americans. Turning back to Cone, it is helpful to note the following statements that reveal his mindset as he moved toward writing *Black Theology and Black Power* (1969):

> While reading Martin Luther King, Jr., and Malcolm X, the blackness in my theological consciousness exploded like a volcano after many dormant years. I found my theological voice. . . . The turn to blackness was an even deeper metanoia-experience than the turn to Jesus. It was spiritual, radically transforming my way of seeing the world and theology. Before I was born again into thinking black, I thought of theology as something remote from my history and culture, something that was primarily defined by Europeans whom I, at best, could only imitate. Blackness gave me new theological spectacles, which enabled me to move beyond the limits of white theology and empowered my mind to think wild, heretical thoughts when evaluated by white academic values. Blackness opened my eyes to see African American history and culture as one of the most insightful sources for knowing about God since the Bible was declared a canon.[5]

The black experience became a valid primary source for Cone's theological reflection, and the production of *Black Theology and Black Power* was an experience that liberated him from his liberal and neo-orthodox professors and from writing theology that was irrelevant to the concrete life and death concerns of African Americans. In this text Cone's central claim is that the Black Power movement is a legitimate expression

---

[4]It is also important to highlight the work of Dr. William H. Bentley, who was a pivotal figure in the National Black Evangelical Association. Bentley was very familiar with the terrain of black theology. See William H. Bentley, "Factors in the Origin and Focus of the National Black Evangelical Association," in *Black Theology*, 1:233-44.

[5]James H. Cone, "Looking Back, Going Forward: Black Theology as Public Theology," in *Black Faith and Public Talk: Critical Essays on James H. Cone's Black Theology and Black Power*, ed. Dwight N. Hopkins (Maryknoll, N.Y.: Orbis, 1999), p. 251.

of Christianity because it is a religion that is focused on the liberation of the poor and oppressed as revealed in Luke 4:18-19. Reflecting on the book's aim Cone states,

> Any theology . . . that takes this religion as its starting point must also be accountable to the oppressed community in its struggle for freedom. It was in this theological and political context that the task of Black Theology was defined as that of analyzing black [people's] condition in the light of God's revelation in Jesus Christ with the purpose of creating a new understanding of black dignity among black people, and providing the necessary soul in that people to destroy white racism.[6]

For Cone, Black Power was a manifestation of Christ that could emancipate blacks from self-hatred and whites from racism.

More recently, Cone's "Strange Fruit: The Cross and the Lynching Tree" expresses his ongoing desire for a Christianity that addresses the ongoing challenges of racism in America. By linking the death of Christ on the cross and the deaths of African Americans by lynching, Cone hopes to make clear that God cares for their plight by identifying with those who are crucified today. He states,

> The cross and the lynching tree need each other: the lynching tree can liberate the cross from the false pieties of well-meaning Christians. The crucifixion was a first century lynching. The cross can redeem the lynching tree, and thereby bestow on upon lynched black bodies an eschatological meaning for their ultimate existence. The cross can also redeem white lynchers, and their descendants too, but not without profound cost, not without the revelation of the wrath and justice of God, which executes divine judgment, with the demand for repentance and reparation, as a presupposition of divine mercy and forgiveness. Most whites want mercy and forgiveness, but not justice and reparations; they want reconciliation without liberation, the resurrection without the cross.[7]

While lynching is rare today, for Cone the lynching tree symbolizes race in America, because it reflects the fact that black people had no

---

[6]Cone, epilogue in ibid., p. 428.
[7]James H. Cone, "Strange Fruit: The Cross and the Lynching Tree," *Harvard Divinity Bulletin* 35, no. 1 (2007): 53.

choice about being lynched even as Christ had no choice in the face of the Roman state. For Cone, the good news is that just as God transformed the cross into a victory, the same hope can be present today for Americans if they confront the legacy of white supremacy with repentance and reparation.

I have barely touched on Cone's work and not drawn attention to emphases such as his assertion that a person must become "black" in order to be saved ("black" as a symbol for taking on the plight of the poor and oppressed), but now briefly I would like to draw attention to Dwight Hopkins, a former student of Cone who now teaches at the University of Chicago Divinity School. Writing in 1993 about an agenda for black theology, he states that the task of the theologian is to

> make the church and the community accountable to what God had called the church and community to do as coagents in the current divine kingdom inbreaking for the poor on earth. . . . The doing of a systematic Black theology of liberation is in response to God's call to covenant with poor people in a divine-human movement for freedom and full humanity. . . . [A] constructive Black theology of liberation is a mediation between what poor African Americans of faith believe and do by force of habit, on the one hand, and a systematic tradition where oppressed Black folk self-consciously struggle for full humanity in God's divine realm, on the other hand.[8]

He further identifies priorities such as a commitment to the poor in resistance to a bourgeois status quo among those who have "made it," the importance of preserving positive ties to the black church (which does not have a strong relationship to black liberation theology), a greater focus on black women and a challenge to a monopoly capitalist system. What is clear from these statements and other essays is that Hopkins wants to focus more intently on the poor and disenfranchised with the aim of promoting a theology that leads to a society that is equal in every sense, what Hopkins regards as a balanced, full humanity.

---

[8]Dwight N. Hopkins, "Black Theology and a Second Generation," in *Black Theology: A Documentary History*, vol 2: *1980-1992*, ed. James H. Cone and Gayraud S. Wilmore, 2nd ed. (Maryknoll, N.Y.: Orbis, 1993), pp. 65-66.

While black liberation theology had an area of consistent emphasis, it came under criticism because of its inattention to African
American women. Scholars such as Delores Williams, Katie Cannon,
Renee Leslie Hill and Kelly Brown-Douglas are among those who
began writing womanist theology as a response to their frustrations
with white feminist theology and black liberation theology. The term
womanist theology is inspired by Alice Walker's *In Search of Our Mothers' Gardens: Womanist Prose.* What exactly is a womanist? According
to Delores Williams:

> Her origins are in the black folk expression "You acting womanish,"
> meaning, according to Walker, "wanting to know more and in greater
> depth than is good for one . . . outrageous, audacious, courageous and
> willful behavior." A womanist is also "responsible, in charge, serious."
> . . . She loves, she is committed, she is a universalist by temperament.[9]

Brown-Douglas says, "Womanist symbolizes Black women's resistance
to their multidimensional oppression as well as their self-affirmation
and will to survive with dignity under dehumanizing social-historical
conditions."[10] This approach aims to bring theology into contact with
the unique experiences of African American women, with a resultant
theological articulation that modifies Christian discourse as necessary,
such as critiquing a cross-centered theology because of its possible use
in sanctioning the victimization of women and children.[11]

Black liberation theology and womanist theology are contextually
derived theologies that clothe the Christian message in language that
attends to varieties of oppression. I now move to two critiques of black
theology, from Alister Kee on the more liberal side and Anthony Bradley on the more conservative side.

---

[9]Delores Williams, "Womanist Theology: Black Women's Voices," in *Black Theology*, 2:265.
[10]Kelly Delaine Brown-Douglas, "Womanist Theology: What Is Its Relationship to Black Theology?" in *Black Theology*, 2:290.
[11]Cone notes, "When I read Rita Brock, Rebecca Parker, Elisabeth Schüssler Fiorenza, and
especially my colleague Delores Williams, I had to go back and rethink the theological meaning of the cross. When one considers how corrupt and misguided Christian preachers and
theologians have used the cross of Jesus to oppress marginal people, especially women and
children, urging them to accept passively their suffering in home, church, and the society, who
can blame womanists and feminists for saying, 'no more crosses for me'" ("The Cross and the
Lynching Tree," pp. 51-52).

Kee's *The Rise and Demise of Black Theology* leaves nothing to the imagination with these opening words:

> Many theologies describe themselves as contextual: they arise within a certain socio-cultural context and respond to it. But frequently they are not contextual enough. Contexts change, but the theologies continue, repeating their original forms. So it is with Black theology. Its dominant form emerged in the 1960s and 1970s, an important movement which displayed courage and creativity. By the 1990s the context had entirely changed, but this contextual theology did not reposition itself. Far from exhibiting a new flourishing of creativity, commitment and imagination, it has been content to repeat the mantras of a previous period.[12]

One way that Kee establishes his claim is by critiquing the 1998 conference that produced the volume *Black Faith and Public Talk: Critical Essays on James H. Cone's Black Theology and Black Power*.[13] While affirming the significance of Cone's important text, he regards the great majority of the book's essays as uncreative and insufficiently critical; they fail to help establish a new direction for black theology. What is this new direction that Kee would like to see? He pleads for a more direct emphasis on the plight of the poor everywhere, along with a critique of capitalism and its effects on the continent of Africa. In spite of the agenda expressed in Hopkins's previous comments, Kee concludes that essentially nothing new has been said. Kee is a white European, thus some may wonder why he has such concern about black theology. His answer:

> Why? . . . Because the forces of oppression and exploitation are increasingly taking control of the world through the processes of global capitalism. They cannot be successfully opposed simply by progressive Europeans. It requires an alliance of men and women of goodwill throughout the world. In this black Americans could play a vital part, if they read the new context and move their agenda forward.[14]

---

[12]Alistair Kee, *The Rise and Demise of Black Theology* (London: SCM Press, 2008), p. xiii.
[13]Dwight N. Hopkins, ed., *Black Faith and Public Talk: Critical Essays on James H. Cone's Black Theology and Black Power* (Maryknoll, N.Y.: Orbis, 1999).
[14]Kee, *Rise and Demise of Black Theology*, p. 216.

Kee's claim is that black theology as it currently exists is dead, hence he uses the word *obituary* in the title of his concluding chapter.

Anthony Bradley's *Liberating Black Theology: The Bible and the Black Experience in America* also echoes the critique that black theology is limited by its identification with a particular contextual moment.[15] From Bradley's perspective, the work of Cone, Hopkins and others relies on the view that African Americans are perpetually victims. One of the obvious limitations of victimologist anthropology is that it runs aground when confronted by African Americans who are middle class and above, and more significantly it veers theological reflection away from historic orthodoxy when it is the primary theological starting point. One can ask, What are the prospects for black theology when the contextual moment has significantly changed and the immediate challenges are different? Is it necessary to articulate salvation as a particular form of liberation, as the emancipation for specific forms of injustice in the experience of African Americans? Bradley also critiques the view of Marxism espoused by some black theologians, arguing that in fact the Marxism of black theologians is different from the thought of Marx himself. For example, Bradley states:

> Cone equates his understanding of "the oppressed" with the Marxist idea of alienation, resulting in a misapplication of what Marx intended. Marx believes that workers are alienated because they have no control over their employment decisions, thus leaving them humiliated. Cone, on the other hand, is not as concerned about the relationship between management and employees as he is about the relationship between races. A more accurate application of Marxist thought regarding social structures would lead to an evaluation of the relationship between church leaders and parishioners in hierarchical church bodies. . . . The critical question never fully examined by black theologians who promote the use of Marx is whether the black condition in America is analogous to the socioeconomic condition of the proletariat of whom Marx wrote. Otherwise, serious problems abound.[16]

---

[15]Anthony Bradley, *Liberating Black Theology: The Bible and Black Experience in America* (Wheaton, Ill.: Crossway, 2010).
[16]Ibid., p. 117.

While Bradley concurs with the concerns about racism and white supremacy expressed in black theology, he finds the project to be flawed.

Conclusion: Looking Forward

Where do we go from here? What is the current task ahead for the evangelical world in light of the concerns raised by black liberation theology and important critiques? First, it is important to recognize that we live in a cultural context that presents new challenges for addressing seriously the ongoing legacy of racism. The United States has elected a biracial president, a man who is half African, and this reality leads some to believe that we are past the need to give significant attention to the ongoing ripple effect of slavery, Jim Crow laws, institutional racism and the more invisible forms of racism that remain at work. Perhaps one way to frame the question is to ask, If racism is such a thing of the past and if there is nothing left for us to do, then why is it that in the United States, evangelicalism as a movement remains predominantly white? Why is it that in evangelical institutions and organizations, minorities are not consistently part of the population? Why is it that I can count fewer than twenty African American Ph.D.s in theology who will identify as evangelical, and why is it that some who do would rather hang their hat elsewhere?

In this regard, my point is not that evangelicals have decisively failed in their efforts to address the legacy of racism but to inquire about the level of priority given to addressing the multifaceted contemporary challenges linked to racial and ethnic concerns. This is not a case of asking for special attention but an inquiry into how evangelicals understand the priorities of the mission of the church. Evangelicals are "people of the book," a population that gives greater attention to reading the Bible than many other Christian demographics. If evangelicals have a desire to be truly biblical people, it is important to revisit how we read the Bible, construct our doctrine and articulate our mission. Perhaps one way to think of this is by considering how we understand part of the gospel mission to be a Christian witness that constantly seeks to live out the full dimensions of the first and second greatest commandments. If the first commandment is to love God with all of our heart, soul, mind and strength, does it prompt us to ask whether there are ways that facets of our identity (cultural, political, racial, socioeconomic, national and so on) impede our ability to truly worship God alone? Likewise, if the second commandment compels us to love our neighbors as ourselves, are we constantly looking for ways to seek the good of our neighbors (all other human beings) in the same way that we seek our own flourishing? More specifically, have we considered how obedience to the second greatest commandment might lead us to give greater priority to engaging and addressing the challenges of race, poverty and class that remain?

Another consideration that arises for us is proper regard for context. How do we consider the place of context in articulating a truly faithful theology? This is an area of great challenge, I believe, because it is very easy to validate a strategy that overcompensates for the preeminence of European and white North American perspectives in theology. It is certainly true that many minorities within evangelicalism arrive at a place of frustration because certain theological questions are assumed to be simply "biblical" while the questions of minorities are labeled as questions of "black theology" or "Latino theology" and so on. In response, sometimes those in the minority desire to articulate their biblical interpretation and theology in a manner that accords with their cultural lenses; this is not necessarily problematic but can run the risk of switching one form of privilege for another. In my view, a better path is one where we are constantly asking how to better deepen and broaden our understanding of the faith by a constant process of refinement. This refinement arrives by the continual interrogation of our theological method and articulation; we ask questions such as, What might be missing in the tradition as passed on to us? How do I faithfully articulate the truth of the faith in each locality? What do I keep from what was handed down to me? And what contributions for other contexts can bring greater illumination to our faith and compel us toward greater fidelity to the gospel? The role of context is important so we can speak the faith clearly everywhere we take it, but it is also important that we resist the temptation toward idolatry.

Other challenging questions for us are: How are we to move forward without being confined by the legacy of race? How do we affirm common humanity and cultural distinctiveness and particularity without finding ourselves limited by the discourse of race? It is important to tell the story about the modern construction of "race" as one means to expose the idolatry of white supremacy, yet this is ultimately not sufficient because very often the theological response will still operate according to the racial logic that frames the way many of us think of identity in the modern West. Willie James Jennings's *The Christian Imagination* proposes that we reckon with the fact that our capacity to truly understand ourselves as creatures created by God has been compromised by modern racial thinking, particularly because we have separated identity from geography.[17] He recognizes that this is a hard concept to grasp, precisely because we struggle to imagine a concept of identity that regards place and space as important; our modern tendency is to construe identity according to the fiction of race that is severed from our actual relationship to the creation. Think of it this way: God's promise to Abraham was that he would be the father of a nation identified with a land, and as Christians today we anticipate the coming of kingdom and taking up residence in space that has realized the full potential of the creation, the New Jerusalem. Jennings' project prompts me to ask whether I have given much consideration at all to the fact that our ultimate identity is not separate from place. What is the goal if we desire to be free of the gravitational pull of race-based thinking? The goal is neither colorblindness nor a tribalism that creates unique domains for theological expression, but a robust creaturely identity that embraces particularity without being confined by it.

As a theologian, for me, a final question is how does our doctrine relate to our ethics? In this regard I wonder how the entirety of our doctrinal beliefs, from creation to eschatology, facilitates and prioritizes certain ethical concerns. We have to ask ourselves if our beliefs and our practices are actually connected, given the bifurcation of theol-

---

[17]Willie James Jennings, *The Christian Imagination: Theology and the Origins of Race* (New Haven, Conn.: Yale University Press, 2010).

ogy and ethics that is the legacy of the modern world. For example, does sanctification only compel me to be a person of inward holiness and have nothing to do with my public commitments? Does my ecclesiology lead me into or away from engaging the machinery in our society that still produces glass ceilings and disparities in public education? Does my eschatology prompt me to only look heavenward and not regard the much-needed reform of our prison system as worth the investment of time? And on it goes.

African American theology had to be formed in the crucible of the legacy of racism in the United States, and now we find ourselves in a time where we must address that legacy in a different way. Evangelicals have an opportunity to live up to their identity as people of the book who strive to live with greater fidelity to the triune God and the gospel. This is an opportunity to be a living witness in the face of great challenge. Will we rise to it?

For Further Reading

Fields, Bruce. *Introducing Black Theology: Three Crucial Questions for the Evangelical Church*. Grand Rapids: Baker Academic, 2001.

Metzger, Paul Louis. *Consuming Jesus: Beyond Race and Class Divisions in a Consumer Church*. Grand Rapids: Eerdmans, 2007.

Williams, Delores. *Sisters in the Wilderness: The Challenge of Womanist God-Talk*. Maryknoll, N.Y.: Orbis, 1995.

Yancey, George. *Beyond Racial Gridlock*. Downers Grove, Ill.: InterVarsity Press, 2006.

Part Four

NEXT STEPS

14

SOME IMPLICATIONS OF GLOBAL THEOLOGY FOR CHURCH, MINISTRY AND MISSION

Mark Labberton

• • •

A PRIMARY QUALITY
Humility

Humility should be the first "implication for church, ministry and mission" arising from the explorations in this volume. The richness of the chapters has underscored that no one sees without distortion. And what is more, no one acts with full wisdom. The staggering diversity of the world as portrayed by the authors here would be more than enough to end any illusion of comprehensively or exhaustively grasping a part of the global theological story, let alone the whole. The diversity, range and subtlety of contexts, history, issues and challenges is breathtaking. Global theology demands particularity. And that very particularity is itself "global," not least given the wonder and mystery of human beings who bear the *imago Dei*.

In addition to our finitude before the global theological task, we should also be humbled by our fallenness. The story of global theology includes many tales of human self-interest, tribalisms, power abuse and much more. And this is not just the past but also the present. We are not just inadequate to the task; we are unfit. God's providential grace exceeds the failure and sin of the church, but our sinfulness establishes a ground for caution, repentance, restraint, self-critique and patience.

Annie Dillard captures some of these colliding themes in an essay she calls "An Expedition to the Pole."[1] In it she weaves two story lines, one about explorers seeking the Arctic Pole, and one that focuses on her stuttering return to a Roman Catholic Church, if only "to avoid Protestant guitars." She describes, to her shock, the presence and impact at this church of a contemporary musical group that calls itself "Wildflowers." At one point, she recounts how this unlikely, eclectic, eccentric and ordinary group leads in the singing of the *Sanctus*. Annie Dillard says this is painful enough. She would rather experience the dark night of the soul than endure "the dread hootenanny."[2] Yet, in this very ordinariness and inadequacy is, ironically, the very presence of God at work in the "ice floes" of our human expedition to get to the heavenly Pole. We can, in the end, only share in the *Sanctus* as the "Wildflowers" we are or are near. It is the floe on which our journey can and must be lived.

We are made for the *Sanctus*. As human beings—in this generation and every generation, in every tribe, tongue and nation—we are people made for the glory of God and created to reflect it in every dimension of who we are. Every relationship, every expression of our being is meant to be an enactment of worship that acknowledges and reflects the reality and the goodness of the God who has made us. That same God has now sought us and redeemed us in Christ, and has a purpose for us which is nothing less than to be partners, in some sort of mysterious and remarkable way, in the work of God's salvation of the whole world. It is an amazing and humbling and staggering thing, but we only ever get to do it together with the "Wildflowers."

So when we engage in this kind of global conversation, we need to ask, What does it mean to give our best selves to the deepest and most profound work of God in the world? In what way do we come to that exercise?

It has somehow been God's unlikely plan from the start to choose the "Wildflowers," people of shuddering skills, often self-conscious and awkward. We are to do in our own culture and location and place

---

[1]Annie Dillard, "An Expedition to the Pole," *Teaching a Stone to Talk: Expeditions and Encounters* (New York: HarperCollins, 1982), pp. 29-64.
[2]Ibid., p. 45.

the things that will never be perfectly done this side of glory, that will never be the consummation of all that could possibly be imagined, that will not always sound like anything that we could ever in our best theological and spiritual dreams really imagine. And it is still worth doing as we sing the *Sanctus*. And it is still worth doing as the "Wildflowers," who bear witness to the glory of God in this strange gaggle of people, known as the community of God's people, the body of Christ, the church in the world, "Wildflowers" who have varying gifts and abilities and skills and capacities and places and circumstances.

This does not mean we collapse in despair or cease our reflection and action. It does mean we need to remember that in doing theology we are in over our heads—however brilliant some of those heads may be, as are those of the people who have authored chapters in this book. Our insight is always partial and transitional, the only way human beings can dare witness to the eternal, triune God. Though we may bring our very best self in community with other best selves to this complex task of doing theology, it is freeing and honest to admit we are embodying the folly of God's wisdom to use such earthen vessels to do kingdom work. Thankfully, astonishingly, God uses "Wildflowers."

I want to underline the relevance of all of this for me, as the white, male, American, Presbyterian, all-too-human and fallen person who has been asked to suggest some "implications for church, ministry and mission." Whatever positive things I may or may not bring to this task, I am neither neutral in myself nor neutral as a symbol. I stand inescapably in the long line of white, male Americans who are given privileged speech, telling and naming for others (most of whom are not white, male or American) the implications of global realities like those we have been considering. This is precarious and problematic at best. It is inadequate by definition. It is also the task I have been given and have accepted—with humility.

A PRIMARY TASK
Paying Attention

Psalm 8 provides us with a powerful guide as we ask about our human vocation, including doing theology globally: What is our primary task?

This very familiar psalm falls into two important pieces. The first part of the text has to do with the way God pays attention to us (Ps 8:1-4). The second has to do with the way we are called to pay attention to the world in God's name (Ps 8:5-9). The two sections together hold the pieces of what we have been exploring in this volume. Wherever we may be, we are engaged in these two great acts: the discovery of God's attentiveness to us and our call to pay attention to God's world around us. Human existence, including global theology, involves acts of paying attention to God and paying attention to the world in God's name.

In what way does God pay attention? The Lord pays attention by his creation. The Lord pays attention in ways that are evident by the significance, subtlety and variation of that creation. God attends to it. Yahweh pursues the world in its brokenness. The Lord doesn't pay dispassionate attention like a neutral observer of the Enlightenment model, but instead exercises intensive, prejudicially passionate engagement, and then not just engagement, but identification and participation in the reality of that work.

The discovery and affirmation of this God's attentiveness to us and to all of creation is what grounds this whole pursuit of global theology. We take time to consider a global theology because the God we believe we have been thinking about is a God who pays attention. And God does not, it turns out, pay attention to just part of the world, or a certain tribe of people, or a certain gender, or a certain class, or a certain background, or a certain personality or a certain layer of gifts, but instead pays radical attentiveness to a whole world, at all times and in all places. That is the context out of which the incarnation becomes the most concrete expression of God's attentiveness—its proximity, its imminence, its presence—and God's participation in what and how we actually see.

This brings us to the second part of the psalm. The psalmist's astonishment that the Lord, Adonai, pays attention to us then brings the psalmist to affirm that we who have been made a little lower than the angels have been given significant responsibility: dominion. What is that dominion? It is participation in the attentiveness of God, turning to the world around us and seeing that world in the attentiveness that mirrors the God who has made us.

We exercise this attentiveness, as the psalmist says, in relationship to the natural order of animals and species. But I want to suggest that as the Bible's wider narrative unfolds, we also exercise our dominion by our attentiveness to our family and our neighbors and our enemies. We do it among the part of the world that we know and the part of the world that we have yet to discover. We do it with people who are like us and people who are not in any way like us. It is all part of the attentiveness that is a mirror of the attentiveness of God.

To live attentively to the world in God's name is our human vocation. This is what constitutes our worship: being attentive to and engaged with God and God's world. This is why we have been made in the *imago Dei*. This is how we demonstrate and enact the distinctive qualities of our true humanity. Though theological debate continues about the definition of *imago Dei*, it is not too much to suggest that our capacities to know and be known, to love and be loved, to think and to think about thinking, to imagine and to create are among the prime contenders for defining the *imago Dei*. In its own distinctive way, each of these involves paying attention.

Ministry beckons God's people to pay attention to the particular world of people, relationships, culture, economics, religion, sociology, power, art, land and more. If you do this as an insider to that setting, it means seeing things more clearly than an outsider might, while also not seeing some things as clearly as an outsider might. A pastor, a theologian, a church member in their own settings see in similar and varied ways, and no one sees all that can and should be seen. This is why paying attention is a continuous, communal act that is meant to be part of how our diversity of gifts enables the body of Christ to attend to God and the world more faithfully.

If paying attention is an act of worship—that is, committed, compassionate consideration and service—then it means we are to attend to what *is* in light of what is *meant to be*. This double consideration means we do not just observe how life is going and take it seriously, albeit that would be a huge improvement over many current patterns many times. It means we see and engage in light of God's intention for flourishing life. This is a weighted attentiveness shaped by hope. When we see

diminished, beleaguered lives—impoverished, tormented, abused, oppressed, alienated—we pay attention to the immediate and evident factors and respond by offering mercy and seeking justice. And we also
care about attending to the whole context (local and global) that creates
such circumstances, and to the past, present and future hope that God
would have for enabling human flourishing to grow for all people in
physical, social, economic and spiritual terms.

This volume has highlighted in specific ways the difference in contexts and circumstances for people around the world. The various authors have reminded us of global diversity at a high demographic level
and at a personal level. We have dwelt at times on the longer and larger
historical story into which every person arrives and participates. It has
felt a bit like a slice of "the state of the church in the world." Few people
can have this conversation and fewer can sustain it. Doing this work is
the specialization of those who are authors and some others. However,
each of us is not called to this type of specialization. More commonly,
the church in the world is meant to bear witness to the truth that "the
Word became flesh and blood, and moved into the neighborhood"
(John 1:14 *The Message*). This means that paying attention is usually
done at very close range, in the midst of the daily realities of time, place
and people. That is where the cup of cold water, the visit to the pris-
oner, the care for the widow, the making of disciples can and must
occur. This is the gift and this is the challenge.

A PRIMARY PROBLEM
Distraction

The dual themes in Psalm 8 of paying attention to God and to the
world in God's name provide an encompassing framework. This is why
these chapters have been assembled: to enable us to reflect on our attentiveness to God and to the world in God's name. The difficulty, of
course, is that there are so many things that affect our vision and distort
our willingness and capacity to pay attention. Issues such as culture,
personality, education, economics and class are part of the focus of our
attention, and they also distract our attentiveness. In a fallen world it is

predictable that left to our own devices we can become so distracted that our vision is not just particular, which it must be, but also smaller and smaller, which it need not be.

This is part of the way sin operates. It always takes something great and makes it less than it was ever intended to be. And here, certainly this is one of the great challenges for global theology, whatever the specific context or time. How do we maintain a global theology? How do we live as a church in a world where the gravitas of self-interest, of culture, of absorption and of consumption just causes us to so easily fall prey to small and myopic distractions?

When I think about the challenges of taking home and living what this book presents, it is the force of domestication as much as any other single thing that will make a global perspective very hard to sustain. To live in the expansiveness of the kingdom of God, to live with a heart and mind that is being opened up without the same mechanisms of self-defense, without the same commitment to personal safety, without the same myopic preoccupations that are part of our lives, to actually live in a greater, larger, freer space, which is what the kingdom of God invites us into—that is a lot harder to do than to settle into my own smallness. It is just more comfortable to allow the gospel, and my flavor of the gospel, and my friend's flavor of the gospel, to become a smaller and smaller, more and more domesticated reality, until finally it just feels like me again. How do we get free of this small prison of a land that, in my case, is called "Mark: North, South, East and West"?

Some years ago I was in a major bicycle accident that gave me a lot of opportunity to think about the way I see. My left eye was pushed back through the back of the eye socket about an inch and down about an inch as well. I had four operations over the course of a year to repair the orbital socket and to realign the muscles of both eyes to return to binocular vision. Many weeks went by following each of these operations when I was in bed, eyes closed, slowly and painfully recovering. After the second operation it began to be imaginable that my sight would be restored due to the marvelous skill of the surgeons. But what slowly emerged for me was that I had to face a deeper need than restored sight. What I needed even more was renewed vision. That is, what I needed in the world was altered perception that would enable me to perceive God, my neighbor, the world and myself in ways that were closer to God's perception. This would mean paying attention in some radically different ways.

The most compelling and complex issues in global theology demand this sort of personal transformation. The viewpoints that have been shared in this book underline just how true that is. They also raise questions about how this kind of broader and deeper faith can be encouraged and sustained in the lives of ordinary disciples and churches, not least in a consumer-shaped culture like that in the United States. This is a work of the Holy Spirit through the power of God's Word, and we all need it. Seeing our world clearly and faithfully is at the core of our greatest needs, especially if we take the kingdom of God seriously. We are meant to see everyone and everything through a lens of truth and grace, and that is meant to be demonstrated not just inside our head, but also in the action in our lives in the context of real life. That is the challenge of living a global theology.

A PRIMARY GOAL:
Kingdom Sociology

This book offers a vision of a God who sees a world of incredible creativity, of amazing imagination and diversity, a world filled with people made and fashioned, each one knit together in his or her mother's womb, treasured, valued, affirmed, celebrated and loved. It is into that world that this vision of the kingdom is meant to somehow arrive as the good news that calls us into this place of paying attention. Of paying attention to God who sees us to the very core, who frees us from our smallness in order to be able to see and perceive and engage and love a world that is larger and more diverse and unlike us.

To do that will mean that we have to take the road that Jesus says is exactly the road that we have to take. Following him on this road is going to mean going to the people who are like and unlike us, and doing so again and again. It means learning along the way all of the things that God wants to teach us about what it means to be people who pay attention in God's name.

I really love paying attention to the things I love to pay attention to and then saying those are the things that God has given me to attend to daily. But then I come back to the Gospels and realize that God wants more than that. God wants us to pay attention to the things and people that matter to the heart of God, and often that means people and circumstances that are not my sociology. I discover that the kingdom of God is about a new sociology, a sociology that acknowledges my own location, my own context, my inescapable whiteness and maleness and tallness—all of those things that are just inescapably pieces of who I am in the world. And then God says, "Now I want you to pay attention to things that are so different from that, and from which you have so much to learn, and into which I call you to go in order to be a person who shares at least more of my heart than you do now."

It is that vision that makes these conversations so compelling and so urgent. Important on an academic level, a theological level, important on the most interpersonal level, important in a way that simply enlarges our heart and helps to grow our sense of perception about the world and the God we see and that we claim to worship. A God who, it turns out, doesn't look very much like me. A God who is actually quite other than me, but who sees me and says, "Now will you pay attention to the world in my name?"

If I am the pastor of a church, which I have been for almost thirty years, then what is my vocation? I think my vocation as a pastor is to help people discover that God pays attention to them in every dimension. But if God does that, then the implications of that are meant to cause us to pay attention to the world in God's name. And that's going to cause us to have to do and consider and weigh all kinds of things that would not be part of our sociology. It is going to be part of a new sociology—a new sociology of the kingdom that enlarges and grows and increases our sense of who we are and what we are about in the world.

A PRIMARY VISION
Hope

It is easy in the face of the diversity, complexity and enormity of global realities to withdraw or to become paralyzed. These responses are understandable, even defensible, however ineffective they may be. Whether we consider personal, institutional or governmental responses to global realities over decades and centuries we have no grounds for easy optimism. This means that we must consider the prospects of our reflections and actions with greater theological care. We are not engaged in this endeavor out of spiritual naiveté or from theological utopianism. If the world is anything like what has been depicted in these chapters, and if the layers of response, distortion and suffering inside and outside the church are as convoluted, intertwined and pervasive as they appear, is there hope?

While hope is "not yet seen," neither is it a matter of abstract conviction. We are called to a living hope (1 Pet 1:3), and God's people are meant to be evidence of that living hope embodied in the world. God's people are to pay attention by leaning into lives that are fully present in time and place and beyond time and place. This is part of what Jesus had in mind when he said we should be in the world but not of it. It is what it means to live as salt (that does not lose its saltiness) and as light (that does not get hidden under a bushel). We engage in the world in incarnational and eternal terms, we are fully present "in the neighborhood," even as we are also "in the kingdom of God."

Part of the underlying questioning, thoughtfulness, creativity, comparative reflections, self-searching and historical inquiry is to take time and place seriously enough to be able to bring all this to today, and then beyond today to questions of tomorrow.

Clearly, hope is not that God's people are the only locus of God's grace in the world, nor is it that only the work of God's people can bring hope into reality. God uses the church, but God is also at work beyond it. Therefore, our attentiveness to the workings of the Spirit, that the people of God might discern, affirm, encourage and celebrate, reminds us that God is not captive to the church. This means that the discernible presence of God in the world, and in the affairs of humanity generally, reassures us of God's deep and broad lordship.

What is true about hope, however, is that as people of God, we have received the down payment of the Holy Spirit in our lives. The one who holds the future and who is leading us into the future is present in us now. This implies that, like earnest money that underlines the assurance of hope, the church is meant to be the living assurance of the future, that the Lord reigns in hope and shows that hope primarily through the life and witness of the church. This is meant to be evident by how we love our world.

Acts of sacrificial love, service and courage that come in the name of Christ are our standard (Mt 25:31-46). Seeking to call and invite "all the nations" into life as Christ's disciples, whose identity is formed and established by the triune God, and whose obedience further extends God's witness into the world—all this is the stuff of hope to which God's people are to give themselves. When this is carried out with special commitment to pay attention to those at the margins—the lost, the forgotten, the unseen, the poor, the widow, the imprisoned—we bear witness to our God whose peculiar hope is specially mindful and attentive to those who may seem or feel least hope-full.

This is what reminds the church, not least in a culture of consumption, privilege and technique, that God's thoughts are not our thoughts, and his ways are not our ways (Is 55:8). Hope is not constituted by circumstances, but by God's truth and character. The church trusts folly when it forgets to let this be the guide and rule for the grounds of hope that we are to make tangible.

In these terms, and before the world's great needs, we end now where we started. Hope is an expression of humility. It is a laying down of presumption and a grounding in a theological reality far beyond our imagination and design. The work of global theology that is centered in and reflective of the God revealed in Jesus Christ will be profoundly vested in hope because we are profoundly mindful of the "surpassing worth of knowing Christ Jesus my Lord" (Phil 3:8 ESV) before whom one day "every knee should bow, in heaven and on earth and under the earth, and every tongue confess that Jesus Christ is Lord" (Phil 2:10-11 ESV).

For the local and global theology of the church, working out this salvation is our daily task as we pay attention, stay focused and live it out with tangible hope. Our call is not to finish this project. Our call is not to complete this work in our generation. Our call is to inhabit the kingdom, even as the "Wildflowers" we are.

For Further Reading

Haugen, Gary. *Just Courage: God's Great Expedition for the Restless Christian.* Downers Grove, Ill.: InterVarsity Press, 2008.

Labberton, Mark. *The Dangerous Act of Worship: Living God's Call to Justice.* Downers Grove, Ill.: InterVarsity Press, 2007.

McNeil, Brenda Salter. *Credible Witness: Reflections on Power, Evangelism and Race.* Downers Grove, Ill.: InterVarsity Press, 2008.

Rah, Soong-Chan. *The New Evangelicalism: Freeing the Church from Western Cultural Captivity.* Downers Grove, Ill.: InterVarsity Press, 2009.

Scandrette, Mark. *Practicing the Way of Jesus: Life Together in the Kingdom of Love.* Downers Grove, Ill.: InterVarsity Press, 2011.

15

LEARNING AND TEACHING GLOBAL THEOLOGIES

Jeffrey P. Greenman

• • •

Conspicuously absent from our survey of global theologies in this volume is any representative of Western academic theology. No one has mapped the landscape of contemporary European and North American theological approaches, reviewed their critical debates and offered some evangelical assessment. In principle, such a chapter could have been included. Doing so would have made the point that Western theology should be interpreted as a contingent, contextual theology comparable to those originating in Africa, Latin America and everywhere else. Western theology is just that—Western. But it has been exported effectively for a long time, such that the influence of Western theology, for better or for worse, is an undeniable feature in any evaluation of the past, present and future of global theology or theologies. The center of gravity in Christian vitality has shifted decisively to the Majority World, and Global South theologies emerging from regions such as Africa, Asia and Latin/South America are blossoming, but the power and prestige of academic institutions, scholars and publications from Europe and North America continue (at least for now) to exercise a powerful influence on the global theological landscape.

This convergence of factors suggests that we need to ask, When it comes to biblical and theological scholarship, what do the heartlands of Nairobi or Beijing or Buenos Aires have to do with the margins in Wheaton or Tübingen or Aberdeen? Why and how should students and scholars in North America and Europe engage seriously with theologies from the Global South? What might global theological dialogue look like in the coming generation?

In order to address these questions, this chapter will briefly describe Western academic theology as a contextual theology, offer four reasons why Western students and scholars should give priority to engaging seriously with non-Western theologies, recommend ways to approach learning and teaching global theologies, and suggest some concrete steps forward for students, teachers and educational institutions.

Western Theology as Western

I come not to bury Western academic theology, nor to praise it, but rather to locate it within a particular historical narrative, namely, the modern or Enlightenment period that began in seventeenth-century Europe. Like any other form of theology—past, present or future— Western academic theology arises from a particular cultural context, operates with a particular set of assumptions and seeks to answer a particular set of questions. Like any other form of theology, it has its share of blind spots.

The main contours of the modern worldview are well documented. I will follow David Bosch's analysis.[1] The Enlightenment emphasized the centrality of human reason over against the claims of faith or tradition; interpreted the empirical world as "nature" (rather than "creation"), understood as an object to be investigated through examination of its discrete parts; advocated the elimination of purpose from scientific explanation and operated with a mechanistic view of causation in a closed universe; endorsed an optimistic view of social progress, especially through technology, assuming that all problems were in principle solvable; championed a view of knowledge as factual, value-free and neutral; distinguished sharply between facts and values, assigning religion to the realm of opinion or belief rather than truth; and regarded human beings as "emancipated, autonomous individuals"

---

[1]See David J. Bosch, *Transforming Mission: Paradigm Shifts in Theology of Mission* (Maryknoll, N.Y.: Orbis, 1991), chap. 9.

who are to be given priority over community, and who are to be afforded maximal freedom to live as they please. Bosch asserts that "what distinguishes our culture from all cultures that have preceded it" is that its public philosophy is atheist.

Bosch expounds marvelously (and disturbingly) the influence of the modern worldview on theology. He shows how Christianity morphs under the pressures of the Enlightenment, and how theology responds in various ways to its profound challenges. From this perspective it is easy to see why apologetics emerges as a major preoccupation. Defending the very possibility of faith becomes paramount when it is being "severely questioned, contemptuously repudiated, or studiously ignored."[2] In addition, Bosch elaborates a variety of ways that "even where [Christianity] resisted the Enlightenment mentality it was profoundly influenced by it."[3] Similarly, Andrew Walls claims that "a Christianity shaped to fit the Enlightenment world-view" arose, hence, "modern western theology is Enlightenment theology."[4]

As Walls points out, "Christian scholarship follows Christian mission and derives from Christian mission."[5] Therefore the types of scholarship that emerged have been ones conditioned by the church's intellectual responses to its mission context. Some of the best features of Western academic theology are attributable to habits of mind that have been sharpened on account of operating within a basically hostile cultural environment. For example, its attention to detail, penchant for comprehensive examination, concern for rigorous argumentation, strenuous work to understand biblical languages, and probing into the ancient cultural world that shaped the biblical text were necessary, given its situation, for modern Western theological scholarship to attain credibility and to commend the Christian faith. The good fruit of this work over centuries should not be taken for granted. Almost all scholarship from outside the West draws deeply on the resources provided by this Western tradition.

---

[2]Ibid., p. 268.
[3]Ibid., p. 269.
[4]Andrew F. Walls, "Christian Scholarship in Africa in the Twenty-First Century," *Transformation* 19, no. 4 (2002): 223.
[5]Ibid., p. 217.

At the same time, some of the worst features of Western academic theology typically are traceable to the manner in which biblical and theological scholars have adopted key features of a basically alien worldview. Some of the foremost examples are the dependence on reductionist and rationalistic methodologies, and the endorsement or at least implicit support for a privatized, individualistic faith. While it would be simplistic to suggest that Western academic theology is simply a long tale of capitulation to the pressures of an antagonistic framework, it would be unwise for Westerners to deny these characteristic weaknesses that are so widely observed by scholars from the Global South.

Even so, in fairness to the tradition of Western academic theology, it should be said that they are answering their own contextual questions, thinking through the meaning of faithfulness to Christ in their political, economic and religious circumstances. The problem is that too many Westerners appear to assume that *their* contextual questions automatically have *universal* importance. A Jesuit theologian from Chile once asked, "Why is it that when you speak of *our* theology you call it 'Latin American Theology' but when you speak of *your* theology you call it 'theology'?"[6] Western issues are not necessarily the same ones that actually concern Christians elsewhere. For instance, Gustavo Gutiérrez has famously remarked:

> The question we face . . . is not so much how to talk of God in a world come of age, but how to proclaim God as Father in an inhuman world? How do we tell "non-persons" that they are the sons and daughters of God? These are the key questions for a theology that emerges from Latin America, and doubtless for other parts of the world in similar situations.[7]

Gutiérrez is not denying the validity of Western questions about how to speak of God's existence in a secular society. Rather, he is observing that Western and Latin American theologians are asking different

---

[6]This remark is attributed to Gonzolo Arroyo, cited in Robert McAfee Brown, *Gustavo Gutiérrez: An Introduction to Liberation Theology* (Maryknoll, N.Y.: Orbis, 1990), p. xix.
[7]Gustavo Gutiérrez, "The Task and Content of Liberation Theology," trans. Judith Condor, in *Cambridge Companion to Liberation Theology*, ed. Christopher Rowland (Cambridge: Cambridge University Press, 1999), p. 28.

questions, ones that arise naturally from their contexts, and he is defending the validity of his questions arising from his context.

So I propose that the first step toward profitable learning and teaching of global theologies is for Westerners to realize more self-consciously who they are and where they are, and to understand their own tradition as just that: a particular tradition. Western scholars will be better positioned to enter fruitfully into and benefit from global theological dialogue if they are increasingly self-aware that their theology is not necessarily a universally adequate theology, a superior variety of theology or the only way of doing things, but it is a Western perspective with its own strengths and weaknesses that arise from its contextual shaping. Despite our Western cultural mythology of superiority and self-sufficiency, it should be obvious that Western ways of doing theology cannot satisfy the global church's search for truth and for faithful service.

Reasons Why Westerners Should Take Global Theologies Seriously

Agreeing with the argument so far, someone might well conclude, "Okay, then I will stick to my own context and dig into Western theology. That is a huge job in itself, since there are whole libraries filled with that alone. And besides, it sounds like Western theology is what will be most relevant to the church's mission here in the West anyhow. I think that I simply will leave all this global theology to specialists or to people who happen to be interested in it. If I were thinking of being a missionary, I would want to learn about theology from whatever place I was going. But I am going to live in the West. So all this is really not necessary—it is just an optional extra that I can leave aside." In other words, "Why bother?" In response, I want to offer four reasons why contemporary Western students and scholars should make it a priority to engage deeply and broadly with global theologies.

First, the deepest rationale is simply that we belong together in a global church. We each are joint members in a universal body of Christ with brothers and sisters from a remarkable array of cultures. My assumption is that Christian theology first and foremost is a servant of the church's life and witness rather than a discipline of the university. As such, for Christian students and Christian scholars, taking an active interest in global theologies is an implication of their membership in a global body of Christ and their commitment to the broadest possible witness of the gospel. As one of my students said in class, "God calls together believers from every nation to make us all members of one family. You don't ignore family." Moreover, the global body of Christ is very much present in the West. The church down your street in Wheaton or Pasadena or Toronto might well be a church plant from a Pentecostal megachurch based in Ghana, a congregation of Romanian Baptists or Korean Presbyterians, or a Roman Catholic congregation composed of Mexican immigrants. The global church is literally next door—not "over there" but "right here." Anglo churches in North America typically have operated in almost total isolation from ethnic minority Christian communities, and truly multiethnic congregations are disturbingly rare.

The strongest spiritual motivation for Westerners to make a priority of learning global theologies is to honor and enter into deeper fellow-ship with people with whom we share a common allegiance to Christ and common calling to represent Christ faithfully in our respective contexts. Evangelical Protestants in North America have been slower to engage global theologies than have other Christian traditions, typically due to the misperception that Majority World theologies are, by definition, inevitably liberal or dangerously unorthodox. Evangelicals should work to catch up on the lively dialogue among their evangelical cousins around the world. In fact, Majority World evangelicals have played a key role in shaping theological discussions in recent decades; Samuel Escobar's chapter in this volume documents one important dimension of a broader contribution.

This exhortation is based on the conviction that theologians of every race, tribe and tongue have a common stake in advancing the cause of Christ worldwide through attending carefully to the church's speech, especially its preaching, teaching and apologetic discourse. Westerners have a vested interest in the theological vibrancy and cogency of non-Western theology, and vice versa, particularly since there are so few boundaries around theological ideas. (Witness the all-too-easy international transmission of the prosperity gospel.) Through sophisticated telecommunications, in some respects the world grows smaller and smaller, making possible new ways of ongoing global theological discourse and closer connections between scattered Christian communities. Andrew Walls appears entirely correct when he suggests that the "great ecumenical issues" of the twenty-first century "will be about how African and Indian and Chinese and Korean and Hispanic and North American and European Christians can together make real the life of the body of Christ."[8] It is incumbent upon theologians to offer their own distinctive gifts in service of the global body of Christ as it faces decisions concerning how best to "make real" the oneness of God's people in the Spirit. A pressing question is whether Western scholars can come alongside their brothers and sisters as servants, as co-laborers and fellow pilgrims without insisting on dominating the theological agenda.

Second, engaging non-Western thinkers and theological trends is necessary given the increasing internationalization of theological education. Many theological colleges and seminaries in North America and Europe have a very significant contingent of non-Western students. It's not that unusual these days for a Nigerian to be studying in Wheaton in preparation for service as a missionary to Poland. My assumption is that theological teaching at its best is undertaken for the sake of formation for ministry.[9] It is more learner-centered than information-centered, although deep interaction with substantive content is essential. As such, teachers should actively engage with the learners in their midst by taking the students' cultural backgrounds, previous experience and existential questions seriously. To treat non-Western students as tacit Westerners who should be satisfied with entirely Western approaches and assumptions is to "ignore family" by disrespecting and

---

[8]Andrew F. Walls, *The Cross-Cultural Process in Christian History: Studies in the Transmission and Appropriation of Faith* (Maryknoll, N.Y.: Orbis, 2002), p. 69.

[9]For more on theology as formation for mission, see Jeffrey P. Greenman, "Spiritual Formation in Theological Perspective: Classic Issues, Contemporary Challenges," in *Life in the Spirit: Spiritual Formation in Theological Perspective*, ed. Jeffrey P. Greenman and George Kalantzis (Downers Grove, Ill.: InterVarsity Press, 2010), pp. 23-35.

silencing them, claiming the center for Western categories and questions rather than creating space for non-Western ones.

Third, Western students and scholars should—better, *must*—study non-Western scholarship in order to obtain a comprehensive picture of contemporary theological discussion. This is a matter of intellectual integrity in an age of internationally distributed and connected Christian scholarship. Quality scholarship is being redefined in global terms. The day has long since passed when anyone in the West could dismiss non-Western scholarship as inferior and capable of being ignored without much loss. Sticking to Western sources and Western debates might make our lives easier, but it is a shortcut that betrays a lack of curiosity and smacks of willful ignorance.

For example, suppose your interest is Christology. If you are a student who is writing an essay or a professor teaching a course on Christology, naturally it is legitimate to narrow the focus to certain figures. There is no offense in working with standard thinkers of the Western canon. It is widely agreed that there is value for people of all cultures in wrestling with Aquinas or Luther or Barth on Christology. But it is now clear that working exclusively with Western figures means choosing to ignore some of the most fascinating and important theological discussions currently happening. If our investigation of Christology has overlooked the African questions about Jesus as Ancestor, the Latin American interpretation of Jesus as Liberator, or the Indian identification of Jesus as a Dalit, then our Christological horizons have been narrowed too quickly. These are just some of the topics under discussion in global Christologies, and similar contextual factors of Christology surely will feature prominently in global discussions in the future. It is time to agree that there is value for people in all cultures in wrestling with Gutiérrez or Nyamiti or Nirmal on Christology. Again hear the wisdom of Walls: "The discoveries about Christ that are made in the African, Asian and Latin American heartlands will belong to us all."[10] To be content simply to study Western approaches exclusively is either a sign of sloppiness or of a parochial or even chauvinistic mindset. Knowing the Western de-

---

[10]Walls, "Christian Scholarship," p. 227.

bates is not enough anymore. Global South scholars know the Western debates and engage in their own work with reference to the Western perspectives. But if they need to know Western debates, then the shifting patterns of scholarship mean that Westerners equally need to know the Global South debates, simply to be considered current with contemporary scholarly discussions on a given topic.

Fourth, we should take seriously non-Western theologies in order to address our Western blind spots in biblical interpretation and theological formulation. More than matters of style are at issue. If every theology is contextual and contingent to some degree, then every theology is partial rather than complete. Any monocultural theology will need supplementation. This means that Western theology needs the challenges and correctives of non-Western theology just as much as non-Western theology needs the challenges and correctives of Western theology. Any given cultural orientation enables its readers to see certain important aspects of Scripture but simultaneously prevents them from seeing other important features.

For example, more individualist cultural readings of Scripture draw attention to its emphasis on personal responsibility in sin, salvation and ministry; more collectivist readings draw attention to the Bible's emphasis on corporate solidarity, structural sin and communal witness. Each monocultural reading will miss critical elements in the overall message of Scripture that hold both emphases together in dynamic tension. Each group should welcome the opportunity to test their own insights against those emerging from readers with different worldview assumptions and social values. Walls observes that

> the great advantage, the crowning excitement which our own era of Church history has over all others, is the possibility that we may be able to read [the Scriptures] together. Never before has the Church looked so much like the great multitude whom no man can number out of every nation and tribe and people and tongue. Never before, therefore, has there been so much potentiality for mutual enrichment and self-criticism, as God causes yet more light and truth to break forth from his word.[11]

---

[11]Andrew F. Walls, *The Missionary Movement in Christian History: Studies in the Transmission of Faith* (Maryknoll, N.Y.: Orbis, 1996), p. 15.

There is reason for being optimistic about the productive possibilities of such collaboration, if interpreters are genuinely open to what Walls calls "self-criticism." This requires not only self-awareness but also sincere openness to correction and willingness to admit a need for change. These are easier said than done, especially among academics who so easily become so personally wedded to their preferred interpretive schemes and their favorite ideas. Once again, Walls offers an astute insight: "Shared reading of the Scriptures and shared theological reflection will be to the benefit of all, but the oxygen-starved Christianity of the West will have the most to gain."[12]

Taking Up the Challenge

At the outset of the previous section I said that students and scholars should make it a priority to engage broadly and deeply with global theologies. The key words there are *broadly* and *deeply*—as opposed to *narrowly* and *superficially*. It is worth remembering that a little bit of knowledge is a dangerous thing. Theological tourism can be unhealthy. Westerners need to slow down, spend time and stay a while in order to benefit from theologies of the Global South. Some occasional dabbling in non-Western theologies in order to accumulate more decorative footnotes is not the goal.

Nor am I advocating a relativist view of theology where, by definition, the entire project involves constant seeking but never finding, according to which all that can be done are increasingly sophisticated comparative studies. Rather, my assumption is that learning from non-Western theologies is crucial in seeking better biblical understanding and better theological expression in the pursuit of truth. I am fond of G. K. Chesterton's quip "Merely having an open mind is nothing; the object of opening the mind, as of opening the mouth, is to shut it again on something solid."[13] John Howard Yoder's warnings about "the ordinary ethos of liberal Western ecumenism" are worth bearing in mind.

---

[12] Walls, *Cross-Cultural Process*, p. 47.
[13] G. K. Chesterton, *The Autobiography*, vol. 16, The Collected Works of G. K. Chesterton (San Francisco: Ignatius, 1988), p. 212.

Yoder rejected the version of "good-mannered" ecumenism wherein "one listens to them on one's own terms and at one's own convenience," an assumption which is rooted in a view of pluralism that can "replace the truth question with a kind of uncritical celebration of diversity."[14]

Yoder's point is that authentic ecumenical dialogue must assume that the views of other people, from other times and other cultures, are capable of having a "hold on us because they can claim to be true or biblical or prophetic."[15] From that standpoint, students and scholars operating from the assumption of a high view of Scripture's authority and from the perspective of historic, orthodox creedal commitments have a distinct advantage. Someone is more likely to have an open mind and to engage in a genuine search when they believe that God's truth cannot reside fully in any particular human formulation of truth, but in a transcendent source. Frail and partial theologies can be remarkably useful to those who seek to grasp the truth of God's revealed Word, but these theologies are never promising substitutes for it. Those who believe that there is "yet more light to break forth" from God's Word are far more likely to find it than those who believe that their system has captured all the light already, or that Scripture offers only interesting varieties of fog rather than light.

These concerns raise questions about what attitudes or dispositions are most conducive to fruitful engagement with global theologies. Many Western students react negatively at first to an encounter with the unfamiliar Other of global theologies. But within weeks, these same students sometimes have shifted from a defensive resistance to the discomforting challenges of the Other to an uncritical and sometimes quite zealous advocacy of everything proposed by the Other, including some devastating critiques of Western Christianity. How quickly the pendulum can swing! There are some basic spiritual and intellectual hazards in rushing too quickly toward an evaluative conclusion. On quite a few occasions I have said to a class: "Okay, before we decide whether we agree with this point, are we sure that we really have un-

---

[14]John Howard Yoder, "The Kingdom as Social Ethic," in *The Priestly Kingdom* (Notre Dame, Ind.: University of Notre Dame Press, 1984), p. 81.
[15]Ibid.

derstood the author's argument?" Fear, defensiveness, arrogance and rigidity stand in the way of genuine thinking and therefore in the way of fruitful engagement with the Other.

What is needed most critically is the exercise of deeply Christian interpretive virtues: humility, sympathy, patience and charity. Humility creates an attitude of receptivity and respect. It makes possible a teachable spirit that is capable of self-criticism. Sympathy in this context refers to the capacity to understand and value the pressing concerns of the Other and to feel the urgency of their questions. Patience is particularly important because much Majority World scholarship does not address our concerns or answer our questions. Often it speaks in an unfamiliar idiom. Sometimes it prefers a personal or narrative mode of expression over a more sequential, analytical approach. It takes unhurried time to enter meaningfully into a distant cultural world and to discern the significance of new questions. Charity means operating with fairness while ascribing the best motives and goals to the Other. The challenge is to cultivate the interpretive disposition and skills necessary for scholarly engagement that is astute and appreciative yet critical and discerning.[16]

Next Steps for Students, Faculty, Schools, Donors and Publishers

Let me offer some advice for college or seminary students, especially those from evangelical Protestant backgrounds, who are digging into church history, biblical studies, theology or Christian ethics and wanting to get started in this direction. The best place to start is reading everything you can get your hands on by Andrew Walls, Lamin Sanneh and Philip Jenkins.[17] Acquire some basic reference tools, such as

---

[16]For much more along similar lines concerning interpretive virtues, see Kevin J. Vanhoozer, *Is There a Meaning in this Text: The Bible, the Reader and the Morality of Literary Knowledge* (Grand Rapids: Zondervan, 1998), esp. chap. 7.

[17]For Walls, see footnotes 8 and 10. Lamin Sanneh, *Translating the Message: The Missionary Impact on Culture*, 2nd ed. (Maryknoll, N.Y.: Orbis, 2009); *Disciples of All Nations: Pillars of World Christianity* (New York: Oxford University Press, 2007); Philip Jenkins, *The Next Christendom: The Coming of Global Christianity*, rev. ed. (New York: Oxford University Press, 2007); *The New Faces of Christianity: Believing the Bible in the Global South* (New York: Oxford Uni-

the *Global Dictionary of Theology*, *Global Bible Commentary* and *Africa Bible Commentary*.[18] Watch for the one-volume *Latin America Bible Commentary* currently being written under the direction of general editor C. René Padilla. John Parratt's edited volume *An Introduction to Third World Theologies* is quite helpful in providing both historical background and theological orientation to the global landscape.[19] Read some of the theologically astute, classic "bridge" books written by Westerners through long experience overseas, such as Vincent Donovan's *Christianity Rediscovered*, E. Stanley Jones's *The Christ of the Indian Road* or John A. Mackay's *The Other Spanish Christ*.[20] Similarly, an orientation to important Global South theological conversations comes in works by Western scholars such as Timothy Tennent's *Theology in the Context of World Christianity* and Veli-Matti Kärkkäinen's books tracking global perspectives on key doctrines such as Christology, ecclesiology and Trinity.[21] Be aware of the high quality current scholarship to be found in key journals such as the interdisciplinary *Studies in World Christianity*, *Asia Journal of Theology*, *The Journal of Theology for Southern Africa*, the evangelically oriented *Journal of Latin American Theology*, the Roman Catholic *Journal of Hispanic/Latino Theology* and many others. Focus on reading primary sources. Steer clear of secondary source summaries or evaluations (especially by Westerners) until you have carefully read the originals.

For scholars who write and teach in fields such as church history, biblical studies, theology or Christian ethics, perhaps some of that ad-

versity Press, 2008); *The Lost History of Christianity: The Thousand-Year Golden Age of the Church in the Middle East, Africa, and Asia—and How It Died* (San Francisco: HarperOne, 2009).

[18]Daniel Patte, ed., *Global Bible Commentary* (Nashville: Abingdon, 2004); Tokunboh Adeyemo, ed., *Africa Bible Commentary: A One-Volume Commentary Written by 70 African Scholars*, 2nd ed. (Grand Rapids: Zondervan, 2010).

[19]John Parratt, ed., *An Introduction to Third World Theologies* (Cambridge: Cambridge University Press, 2004).

[20]Vincent J. Donovan, *Christianity Rediscovered*, 25th anniv. ed. (Maryknoll, N.Y.: Orbis, 2003); E. Stanley Jones, *The Christ of the Indian Road* (New York: Grosset & Dunlap, 1925); John A. Mackay, *The Other Spanish Christ* (Eugene, Ore.: Wipf & Stock, 2001).

[21]See three works by Veli-Matti Kärkkäinen: *Christology: A Global Introduction* (Grand Rapids: Baker, 2003); *Introduction to Ecclesiology: Ecumenical, Historical & Global Perspectives* (Downers Grove, Ill.: InterVarsity Press, 2002); and *The Trinity: Global Perspectives* (Louisville: Westminster John Knox Press, 2007).

vice applies to your situation if you consider yourself a genuine new-comer to global theologies. For faculty it is always an act of courage to step out into unfamiliar terrain. No one wants to be dilettante, but needless timidity can prevent professional growth. I would challenge such people to take some small but significant steps in a globalizing direction. Devote time and energy to expanding your scholarly hori-zons by intentionally seeking books or articles related to your current interest areas that come from non-Western sources you could interact with in your writing or teaching. Make it a goal to include some Global South perspectives in each course you offer unless such a practice would mean forcing something artificial.

For example, I am sure that many college and seminary courses dis-cuss the church's response to issues like human trafficking or the global HIV/AIDS crisis, but I wonder how many of them assign readings from Majority World theologians and church leaders on the topic. Here at Wheaton College we have found that our students are helpfully chal-lenged and sometimes rather strongly provoked by assigning books like Justo González's *Mañana: Christian Theology from a Hispanic Perspective* or portions of the materials like the *Postcolonial Commentary on the New Testament Writings*. It is very helpful to bring in guest speakers from non-Western backgrounds in our classes for dialogue; "real people" make a vivid impression and bring to life the ideas that students en-counter on paper. Admittedly, we have a geographical advantage in the Chicago area with its population of scholars and pastors from around the world. Not every school has ready access to such people, but a real-istic alternative is to use Skype or video clips or other technologies to open your classroom to voices from the Majority World. Make it your goal to cultivate global instincts in your students—that they would find it utterly natural to seek out and take seriously non-Western perspec-tives on the wide spectrum of topics they encounter in their studies.

For department chairs, deans, provosts or presidents of colleges and seminaries in the Western world, my recommendation is to review your curricula to ascertain the extent to which it is predominantly Western and to discover where Global South perspectives and issues are being considered seriously. Some schools are experimenting with requiring an overseas or at least crosscultural immersion experience for theology students or seminarians. Also ask whether your library holdings and journal subscriptions are keeping pace with the leading representatives of global scholarship in the areas of curriculum that you cover. In terms of faculty development, focus a future conversation on how faculty members perceive the globalization of scholarship in their fields. Consider using faculty development funds, albeit always scarce, to foster a process of deepening your faculty's discourse about ways to appropriate Global South perspectives in their research and teaching. At an institutional level explore mutually beneficial developmental relationships with Global South colleges or seminaries to facilitate student and faculty exchanges, travel study, collaborative academic programs and sharing of resources. Those in administrative leadership roles in Western institutions should resist the temptation to recruit Majority World scholars away from their home contexts. Although diversifying Western faculties with non-Westerners might seem appealing at first glance, this practice actually undermines the continued growth of nuanced, contextualized theologies around the world and steals key leaders who are critical for the success of developing (yet often fragile) institutions around the globe. Ultimately, importing Majority World scholars jeopardizes the development of theological colleges and seminaries that are critically needed to equip the pastors and lay leaders for rapidly growing churches.

Finally, I have two suggestions for scholarly societies, charitable foundations and publishing houses. First, there need to be strategic initiatives to broaden global access to electronic resources in biblical and theological studies. It is impossible for non-Western colleges and seminaries to reduplicate the traditional libraries of Western institutions. The digital age has already arrived, yet theological publishing lags behind. Second, if Western and Majority World biblical and theological scholars need each other's challenges and corrections, and if the future of theological scholarship is inevitably going to be increasingly internationalized, then the question becomes, What opportunities could be created to enable a fruitful, in-depth global dialogue? Face-to-face interaction in an extended seminar format (preferably in person but potentially via videoconferencing) between a wide cross-section of global scholars dealing with major theological issues, central doctrines, hermeneutical challenges or specific biblical texts would not only provide immense enrichment for those directly involved in such dialogue, but could yield published materials that offer an unusually rich expression of Christian scholarship to a global audience.[22]

For Further Reading

Dyrness, William A., and Veli-Matti Kärkkäinen, eds. *Global Dictionary of Theology: A Resource for the Worldwide Church.* Downers Grove, Ill.: InterVarsity Press, 2008.

Kirk, J. Andrew. *The Mission of Theology and Theology as Mission.* Valley Forge, Penn.: Trinity Press International, 1997.

Newbigin, Lesslie. *Foolishness to the Greeks: The Gospel and Western Culture.* Grand Rapids: Eerdmans, 1986.

Ott, Craig, and Harold A. Netland, eds. *Globalizing Theology: Belief and Practice in an Era of World Christianity.* Grand Rapids: Baker, 2006.

Tennent, Timothy C. *Theology in the Context of World Christianity: How the Global Church Is Influencing the Way We Think About and Discuss Theology.* Grand Rapids: Zondervan, 2007.

---

[22]I want to express my gratitude to my colleagues who share with me the joys and challenges of teaching global Christianity at Wheaton College for what I have learned from our ongoing discussions around many of the topics broached in this chapter: Jeff Barbeau, Gary Burge, Lynn Cohick, Beth Felker Jones, Gene Green and David Lauber.

CONTRIBUTORS

. . .

Martin Accad is the director of the Institute of Middle East Studies at the Arab Baptist Theological Seminary in Beirut, Lebanon, and associate professor of Islamic studies at Fuller Theological Seminary. He is the author of multiple articles on topics including Christian-Muslim relations and dialogue, Islamic studies and Middle-Eastern Christianity.

Vincent Bacote is associate professor of theology and director of the Center for Applied Christian Ethics at Wheaton College. He is author of *The Spirit in Public Theology: Appropriating the Legacy of Abraham Kuyper*. His research interests include issues of Christianity and culture, and political theology.

Samuel Escobar teaches at Theological Seminary of the Spanish Baptist Union in Madrid, Spain. He has served as president of several organizations, including the Latin American Theological Fraternity, the United Bible Societies, and the International Fellowship of Evangelical Students. He was recently chairman of the Advisory Council for Lausanne III. He has published seventeen books in Spanish and English, among them *Changing Tides: Mission in Latin America*, *The New Global Mission* and *La Palabra: Vida de la Iglesia*.

Ken Gnanakan is president of the International Council for Higher Education and chancellor of William Carey University in northeast India, where he heads up the ACTS Group of ministries, which engages in development projects in education, environment and healthcare. His books include *Kingdom Concerns*, *The Pluralist Predicament*,

Proclaiming Christ in a Pluralistic Context, God's Word: A Theology of the Environment and *Responsible Stewardship of God's Creation.*

Gene L. Green is professor of New Testament at Wheaton College in Wheaton, Illinois. Previously he served as professor of New Testament as well as academic dean and rector of the Seminario ESEPA in San José, Costa Rica. He is the author of four biblical commentaries written in Spanish and English. His research interest is the intersection of the Christian faith and cultures, both ancient and contemporary.

Jeffrey P. Greenman is associate dean of biblical and theological studies and professor of Christian ethics at Wheaton College in Wheaton, Illinois. He is the author of numerous articles and book chapters, the editor of six books, and coauthor of *Unwearied Praises: Exploring Christian Faith Through Classic Hymns.* His research interests focus on theological ethics and global Christianity.

James Kombo is associate professor of systematic theology and deputy vice-chancellor of academic affairs at Daystar University, Nairobi, Kenya. An ordained minister in the Anglican Church of Kenya, he is the author of *The Doctrine of God in African Thought: The Doctrine of the Trinity, Theological Hermeneutics and the African Intellectual Culture.*

Mark Labberton is the Lloyd John Ogilvie Associate Professor of Preaching and director of the Lloyd John Ogilvie Institute of Preaching at Fuller Seminary. Previously he served as senior pastor of First Presbyterian Church of Berkeley, California. He has published *The Dangerous Act of Worship: Living God's Call to Justice* and *The Dangerous Act of Loving Your Neighbor: Seeing Others Through the Heart of Jesus.*

Terry LeBlanc is Mi'kmaq/Acadian, who serves as director of My People International as well as the North American Institute for Indigenous Theological Studies (NAIITS). In addition to grassroots ministry in the Native North American context, he has taught courses at numerous colleges and seminaries. Author of numerous articles, theological papers and book chapters, Terry writes and works to build bridges between aboriginal people and the majority cultures.

Juan Martínez is associate dean for the Center for the Study of Hispanic Church and Community and associate professor of Hispanic studies and pastoral leadership at Fuller Theological Seminary. His current research focuses on the history of Latino Protestantism, ministry in Latino Protestant churches, and Latino and Latin American Anabaptists. Most recently Martínez has published *Los Evangélicos: Portraits of Latino Protestantism in the United States* and coedited the *Global Dictionary of Theology*.

Ruth Padilla DeBorst is involved in leadership development and theological education for integral mission in her native Latin America as a missionary with Christian Reformed World Missions. She currently serves as general secretary of the Latin American Theological Fellowship, directs the Ediciones Certeza Unida publishing house, and leads the Institute for the Promotion of Christian Higher Education in Latin America.

Lamin Sanneh is D. Willis James Professor of Missions and World Christianity and professor of history at Yale Divinity School. He is the author of numerous articles and books, including *Translating the Message: The Missionary Impact on Culture, Disciples of All Nations: Pillars of World Christianity* and *Whose Religion is Christianity? The Gospel Beyond the West.*

Andrew Walls currently serves as honorary professor in the University of Edinburgh, professor of the history of mission at Liverpool Hope University and professor at the Akrofi-Christaller Institute in Ghana. Previously he was professor of religious studies at the University of Aberdeen and the founding director of the Centre for the Study of Christianity in the Non-Western World at the Universities of Aberdeen and Edinburgh. Among his many influential writings are *The Missionary Movement in Christian History* and *The Cross-Cultural Process in Christian History.*

Khiok-Khng (K. K.) Yeo was raised in a Confucianist family in Malaysia. He is Harry R. Kendall Professor of New Testament at Garrett-Evangelical Theological Seminary and visiting professor at the philosophy and religious studies department of Peking University in Beijing, China. He is also the academic director of the graduate Christian studies programs at Peking University. He has published numerous books in English and in Chinese on crosscultural hermeneutics, spirituality and New Testament studies, including *Chairman Mao Meets the Apostle Paul: Christianity, Communism, and the Hope of China* and *Musing with Confucius and Paul: Toward a Chinese Christian Theology.*

Amos Yong is J. Rodman Williams Professor of Theology at Regent University School of Divinity in Virginia, where he also is director of the Ph.D. in renewal studies program. He has authored or edited a dozen books, including *The Spirit Poured Out on All Flesh: Pentecostalism and the Possibility of Global Theology* and *Theological Hermeneutics in Trinitarian Perspective.*

Name Index

Abraham, 221
Accad, Martin, 13, 148
Adeyemo, Tukunboh, 141, 146
Akinola, Peter, 145
Aklé, Yvette, 144
Aprāhāt, 151
Aponte, Edwin, 182
Appasamy, A. J., 116-17, 119
Aquinas, Thomas, 167, 198, 244
Arana, Pedro, 68, 70, 72
Aristotle, 104
Athenagoras, 44
Augustine, 103, 167
Bacote, Vincent, 10, 210
Bailey, Kenneth E., 158
Banerjee, K. M., 119, 120
Bar Hebraeus, 151
Barbosa, Ricardo, 97
Barth, Karl, 90, 159, 196, 244
Bastian, Jean Pierre, 93
Bedford, Nancy, 96
Bediako, Kwame, 25, 58, 136, 138-39, 141
Belloc, Hilaire, 46
Berdyaev, Nikolai, 70
Berg, Mike, 89
Blacksmith, Kenny, 175
Blomberg, Craig, 50
Boesak, Alan, 141-142
Bonino, José Míguez, 71-72, 79, 90, 93, 96
Bosch, David, 238-39
Bradley, Anthony, 216, 218-19
Brandel-Syrier, Mia, 144
Brock, Rita Nakashima, 197
Brown-Douglas, Kelly, 216
Bruce, F. F., 69
Bujo, Bénézet, 143
Burkhart, Brian Yazzi, 170
Buthelezi, Manas, 141
Byaruhanga-Akiiki, Anatole, 141
Calvin, John, 167
Cannon, Katie, 216
Carvalho, Esly, 97

Casas, Bartolomé de las, 89
Cha, Peter, 202
Chakkarai, V., 117
Chenchiah, P., 117, 119
Chesterton, G. K., 246
Chikane, Frank, 141-42
Cleage, Albert, Jr., 213
Clement of Alexandria, 44
Coe, Shoki, 53
Cone, James, 212-15, 217-18
Confucius, 61, 102, 104, 106-14, 202-3, 206
Constantine, 29-30
Cook, Guillermo, 89, 95-96
Costas, Orlando, 72-73, 79, 96, 184-87, 190
Crowther, Ajayi, 135-36
Cyprian of Carthage, 44
DeBorst, Ruth Padilla, 12, 86
Deissmann, Adolf, 35
Denton, Charles, 72
Devanandan, Paul, 120-21
Dillard, Annie, 226
Diocletian, 29
Donovan, Vincent, 249
Dube, Musa, 60
Eboussi-Boulaga, Fabien, 143
Edwards, Jonathan, 196, 198
Éla, Jean-Marc, 143
Ellul, Jacques, 67
Ephrem, 29, 151
Escobar, Samuel, 11, 67, 90, 94, 96, 242
Farquhar, J. N., 119
Feghālī, Būlus al-, 151-52
Fonseca, Juan, 84
Freston, Paul, 84, 100
Freud, Sigmund, 67
Fuller, Thomas, 36
Gitari, David, 143
Gnanakan, Ken, 13, 116
Gondim, Ricardo, 83
González, Juan, 181
González, Justo, 9, 52, 62, 72, 80, 96,

181, 184-87, 250
Graham, Billy, 69
Grau, José, 68
Green, Gene, 9, 50
Greenman, Jeffrey, 14, 237
Guenther, Titus, 90
Gutiérrez, Gustavo, 11, 51, 54-56, 72, 76, 78, 93, 240, 244
Guzmán, Angelit, 84
Hallum, Anne Motley, 91
Harding, Vincent, 213
Harnack, Adolf, 41
Heaney, Sharon E., 82
Hegel, G. W. F., 198
Hill, Renee Leslie, 216
Hopkins, Dwight, 215, 217-18
Huddleston, Trevor, 141
Husserl, Edmund, 170
Idowu, Bolaji, 135
Jacob of Serug, 151
Jahner, Elaine, 166
James, 23
Jenkins, Philip, 139, 145, 248
Jennings, Willie James, 221
John XXIII, 76
John Paul II, 81
Jones, Major, 213
Jones, William R., 213
Jue, Jeffrey, 202
Justin Martyr, 25, 44
Kagame, Alexis, 138
Kalilombe, Patrick, 141
Kärkkäinen, Veli-Matti, 249
Katanacho, Yohanna, 51
Kato, Byang, 141, 145-46
Kee, Alister, 216-18
Kepler, Johannes, 38
Kibicho, Samuel, 141
Kierkegaard, Søren, 70
King, Martin Luther, Jr., 213
Kirk, Andrew, 76
Kitamori, Kazoh, 125
Kombo, James, 12, 134
Labberton, Mark, 14, 225
Leblanc, Terry, 10, 165
Lee, Jung Young, 197
Lee, Sang Hyun, 196, 198

Lim, Paul, 202
Long, Charles, 213
Longenecker, Richard, 167
López, Darío, 83, 97
Lugo, Juan, 184
Luther, Martin, 12, 167, 244
Mackay, John A., 70-71, 249
Magesa, Laurenti, 141, 143
Mallouhi, Mazhar, 160
Martinez, Juan, 10, 179
Marx, Karl, 67-68, 218
Masimiyu-Wasike, Anne, 144
Maskīn, Matta al-, 151-52
Matthew (apostle), 12
Mbiti, John S., 63, 135, 138, 141
Min, Anselm, 198
Mondragón, Carlos, 84
Montemayor, Rebeca, 84
Moreno, Pablo, 84
Mouw, Richard, 82
Mugambi, J. N. K., 143
Mullins, E. Y. S., 68
Mulrain, George, 61
Najīb, Makram, 152
Narsai, 151
Naude, Beyers, 141-142
Nava, Antonio, 184
Newbigin, Lesslie, 127
Njoroge, Nyambura J., 144
Niebuhr, Richard H., 203
Nietzsche, Friedrich, 67
Nirmal, Arvind P., 123, 244
Nolan, Albert, 141-42
Núñez, Emilio Antonio, 77
Nyamiti, Charles, 135, 141, 244
Obama, Barack, 192, 210
Oduyoye, Mercy Amba, 143-45
Olazábal, Francisco, 184
Origen, 25-26, 44
Ortiz, Juan Carlos, 72
Padilla, C. René, 15, 51, 68-69, 72-74, 78-79, 84, 95-96, 249
Pagura I, Federico, 87, 99
Panikkar, Raymundo, 118-19
Park, Andrew Sung, 197
Parratt, John, 54, 56, 249
Paul (apostle), 10, 12, 24-25, 33, 58, 69,

108-14, 125, 128-30, 149, 167-68,
171-73, 175, 198
p'Bitek, Okot, 141
Perobelli, Rachel, 84
Peter (apostle), 10, 20-21, 40
Phan, Peter C., 198-99
Phiri, Isabel, 144
Powell, Elsie, 96
Pretiz, Paul, 89
Roberts, J. Deotis, 212
Romero, Oscar, 81, 93
Roy, Raja Ram Mohan, 122
Salinas, Daniel, 82, 93
Samartha, Stanley, 122
Sanneh, Lamin, 9, 35, 104, 138-39,
248, 255
Saracco, Norberto, 83
Schaeffer, Francis, 68
Segovia, Fernando, 59
Segundo, Juan Luis, 78
Segura, Harold, 96-97
Seng Song, Choan, 196
Setiloane, Gabriel M., 135
Shankara, 118
Smith, Wilfred Cantwell, 129
Solano, Lilia, 84
Steuernagel, Valdir, 76, 97
Stinton, Diane, 62
Sumithra, Sundand, 52
Stoll, David, 93
Stott, John, 69
Sugirtharajah, R. S., 60

Tamez, Elsa, 51, 54
Tan, Jonathan, 195
Tempels, Placide, 138
Tennent, Timothy, 249
Theodore of Mopsuestia, 151
Thiselton, Anthony, 57
Thomas, M. M., 121-23
Tillich, Paul, 196
Torre, Miguel de la, 182
Tseng, Tim, 201
Tutu, Desmond, 141-42
Ukpong, Justin, 56-59
Unamuno, Miguel de, 70
Vanhoozer, Kevin, 52
Villafañe, Eldin, 83, 187-88, 190
Walker, Alice, 216
Walls, Andrew, 9, 12, 19, 137-38, 239,
243-46, 248, 255
Watts, Isaac, 19
White, Lynn, Jr., 127
Whitman, Walt, 37
Williams, Delores, 216
Williams, Rowan, 46
Wilmore, Gayraud, 213
Wright, Jeremiah, 210
Wyclif, John, 36
Yeo, K. K., 11, 53, 102, 200, 206
Yoder, John Howard, 246-47
Yong, Amos, 10, 195
Yoo, David, 201
Zaki, Andrea, 157
Zo, James, 202

Subject Index

African American Theology/black theology, 10, 210-22

African Independent Church, 140

African theology, 12-13, 25, 50, 57-58, 62, 134-40, 141-46, 244

African traditional religions, 51, 61, 134-40, 141, 183

alien, 60, 101, 182

All Africa Conference of Churches, 144

ancestors, theology of, 12, 29, 57-58, 137

Anglican Church of Nigeria, 145

anthropology, 112, 218

anthropomorphism, 22, 171

Antioch, 10, 20-23, 31

apartheid, 141-143

apologetics, 155, 157, 239, 242

apostles, 20, 23, 30, 39, 89, 92, 114, 129-30, 149

Argentina, 68, 77, 83, 87

Armenians, 30, 155

Asia, 9, 27-33, 50, 73, 95, 148, 187, 196-99, 202-3, 205-7, 237, 244, 249

Asian American
    biblical scholarship, 200-201
    community, 10, 201
    evangelicalism, 195, 200-203, 205-6, 208
    experience, 196, 199-200, 202, 205-6, 208
    Protestantism, 197, 203
    Roman Catholicism, 198-99
    studies, 200
    See also Korean American, Vietnamese American, Laotian American

Asian American theology, 10-11, 195-208

assimilation, 41, 159, 182, 201, 206

Association of Evangelicals in Africa, 144

atonement, 205

baptism, 39, 67-68, 152

Belhar Confession, 142

Bhakti, 116

Bible. *See* Scripture

biblical exegesis, 50, 56, 74, 104, 151-152, 155, 167, 204

Biblicism, 48

Billy Graham Evangelistic Association, 94

Black Power movement, 211-14, 217

Bogotá Congress on Evangelism, 69, 73

Buddhism, 29, 61, 118, 130

Calvinism, 193

charismatics/charismatic movement, 31, 37, 90, 207

China, 27, 32, 115, 198

Chinese theology, 29, 102-15, 126, 203, 243

Christianity, 10, 25-27, 32, 35-36, 40-46, 49, 51, 104, 116-19, 136-39, 142-43, 145, 157, 167, 169, 210-12, 214, 239
    African, 51, 134-40, 142-143, 145
    Arab, 150-56
    Asian, 29
    Coptic, 32
    and culture, 39-40, 95
    European, 27, 30, 32-33, 40, 42, 46, 60, 73, 76-77, 95, 104, 136, 138-39, 151, 153-54, 193, 213, 217, 220, 237-38, 243
    global/world, 27, 30-31, 33, 46, 94, 135, 138, 140, 193
    Greek, 32
    Indian, 117-19, 121-22
    Latin, 32
    Hispanic/Latin American, 88, 90, 93-95, 100, 180, 185, 188
    Middle Eastern, 157
    North American, 100
    Syriac, 32, 151
    Western, 27, 32, 46, 114, 169, 246-47

Christology, 21, 31, 62, 80, 83, 108, 111, 143, 199, 244, 249

church, 12, 14, 19-23, 29-30, 32-33, 35,
    39-42, 46, 48-49, 55, 62-63, 69,
    72-73, 79, 82-83, 91, 94-96, 98-100,
    104, 114-15, 117, 125-26, 128,
    142-45, 152, 156-58, 169, 181,
    187-88, 190, 199, 215, 218-19,
    225-27, 229-36, 239, 242, 250-51
    African, 140-45
    African American/black, 211, 215,
        218
    Afrikaner Reformed, 142
    Arabic/Middle Eastern, 152, 153,
        156-61
    Asian, 199
    center of, 9, 30
    Chinese, 104, 114
    Coptic , 152
    early church, 10, 20-23, 27, 29-33,
        136-37, 174
    Ethiopic, 31
    evangelical, 76, 100, 169
    four-self, 9, 52
    global, 9-10, 12, 14, 88, 98, 161,
        241-42
    Hispanic/Latin American, 83, 92,
        94, 255
    history of, 124, 140, 173, 201, 245,
        248, 249
    Indian, 125
    Jerusalem, 20-23
    in the Majority World, 9, 52, 63
    missiology of, 74
    mission of, 48, 83, 95, 160, 188, 219,
        241
    missionary, 9, 74
    multicultural, 10, 20-22
    Pentecostal, 82, 90, 181, 242
    Protestant, 83, 89, 183, 185, 255
    Roman Catholic, 72, 76-77, 81-82,
        89, 140, 198, 199, 226
    Syriac, 29-31, 155
    "Third Church," 82
    United States, 192, 201, 242
    Western/Westernization of, 9-10,
        36, 156, 169, 241-42
Church and Society (movement), 72, 67
church fathers, 45, 58, 103, 150, 198

Church Growth movement, 186
Church of North India, 123
Church of South India, 116
civil rights movement, 181, 184, 211,
    212
Colombia, 68, 72, 82, 84, 87, 89, 93-94
colonialism, 60-61, 77, 168, 180
communism, 67
Conference of the Latin American
    Bishops, 72, 78, 81
Confucianism, 61, 102, 104, 106-14,
    202-3, 206
Congress on Evangelism (CLADE),
    76, 84, 94, 96
contextual theology, 11-12, 43,
    52-53-57, 59, 61, 63, 69-73, 80, 82,
    88, 95-99, 101, 111, 115, 117, 123,
    127, 129, 131, 134-35, 138, 140,
    142-45, 153, 157, 159-61, 180,
    183-84, 186-88, 190, 193, 197, 206,
    210, 216-18, 220, 230-31, 237-38,
    240-42, 244-45, 251
converts/conversion, 23-26, 31, 36,
    39-40, 44, 49, 99, 121, 137, 152, 183,
    203
cosmology, 105, 109-10, 136-38
Council of Chalcedon, 31-32, 156
Council of Nicaea, 30
creation, 98, 111-12, 120-21, 125-27,
    129-32, 166-78, 181, 187, 221, 228,
    238
crosscultural interpretation/
    hermeneutics, 103, 105-6, 115, 200
Cuban Revolution, 67, 181
Dalits, 58, 123-24, 244
"Declaration of Cochabamba," 71, 83,
    94
demons/demonic. See spiritual world
denominations, 82, 95-96, 100-101,
    144, 158, 181, 184, 211
diaspora/dispersion, 191
    Asian, 197, 206
    Jewish, 20, 40
dreams/dream interpretation, 37, 82
dualism, 166, 174
ecclesiology, 83, 199, 222, 249
Ecuador, 15, 68, 84, 87

Ecumenical Institute for Contextual Theology, 142

ecumenism, 31, 33, 100, 121, 123, 150-51, 198-99, 243, 246-47

Edinburgh 1910 Missionary Conference, 89

education, 14, 25, 50, 74, 96, 121, 150, 185, 198, 204, 222, 230, 238, 243

Egypt, 26, 31-32, 148, 151-52, 157-58

Enlightenment, 33, 40, 48, 54, 138, 174, 204, 228, 238-39

eschatology, 69, 108-9, 152, 221-22

ethics, 68, 72, 90, 93, 103, 105, 107, 110-15, 150, 191, 221, 248-49. *See also* morality

Ethiopia, 29-31

European Christianity, 27, 30, 32-33, 40, 42, 46, 60, 73, 76-77, 95, 104, 136, 138-39, 151, 153-54, 193, 213, 217, 220, 237-38, 243

evangelicalism, 11-12, 15, 48, 51, 53, 55-59, 67-69, 71-84, 88-90, 92-95, 97-98, 100, 102, 118-19, 123, 128, 140, 144-46, 148, 151, 154, 156-59, 168-69, 174, 179-81, 184, 190-93, 195, 200-208, 211, 219-20, 222, 237, 242, 248-49

evangelism, evangelization, 21, 67-69, 73-74, 76, 80, 84, 89-90, 94-96, 98-99, 120, 123, 132, 153, 167, 180-81, 186-87, 192

exile, 62, 182, 186, 188, 190-91, 202, 206

the Fall, 120, 125, 131, 173, 185

feminism, 91

feminist theology, 28, 212, 216

First Nations. *See* Native North American

Gentiles, 21-24, 40, 111-12

Global South, 10, 237-38, 240, 245-46, 249-51. S*ee also* Majority World

globalization, 50, 104, 182, 192, 196, 198-99, 206, 251

gospel, 9-10, 28, 36, 39, 42-43, 52, 58, 74, 76, 79, 91-92, 95, 97, 99, 104, 107, 110, 118-19, 127-28, 138, 140, 159,

167, 181, 187, 202, 207, 210, 219-20, 222, 231, 242

in Africa, 29, 135-38, 140, 142, 145

and Americanization, 181, 191

in China, 107

and culture, 9, 11, 20, 25-26, 28, 33, 43, 47, 52, 58, 74-75, 104, 191

in India, 118-20

in Latin America, 67, 91-92, 96-98

in the Middle East, 159-60

prosperity, 243

social dimension of, 73, 76, 95, 212

transmission of, 40

Great Commission, 69

Greek theology, 25, 28

heaven, 100, 107-10, 113-14, 131, 171, 173, 199, 207, 212, 222, 235

Hellenism, 21-24, 33, 44

heresies, 36-37, 45, 118, 142, 213

hermeneutics, 12, 40, 56, 59, 71-72, 76, 97-98, 102, 106, 134, 203-4

African, 134, 138, 143

Asian, 197

crosscultural, 105

evangelical, 204

inculturation, 58-59

liberation, 77

Majority World, 57, 62-63, 138, 252

Middle Eastern, 155, 157, 159, 161

postcolonial, 59-61

of translation, 58

Western, 61

Hindu/Hinduism, 61, 116-20, 122-24, 127-30

HIV/AIDS, 126, 250

Holy Spirit, 20-21, 24, 28, 32, 37, 39, 82-84, 88, 96-97, 99, 109, 111-12, 120, 132, 152, 169, 171-73, 175-78, 188, 207, 232, 234-35, 243

humanization, 123, 126

hymns, 28, 87, 97, 169, 179, 181, 184. *See also* music

idolatry, 41, 128, 173, 220-21

image of God, 113, 130-31, 225, 229

imago Dei. See image of God

immigrants, immigration, 101, 180-82,

184, 188, 191-92, 199, 201-2, 206,
208, 242
incarnation, 22, 28, 31, 53, 68, 87, 98,
101, 117, 129, 135-36, 138, 161, 179,
199, 207, 228, 234, 259
India, 13, 58, 60, 116, 118, 127-28,
243-44
   church in, 123, 125
   language in, 29
   religion/theology in, 116-32, 243-44
indigenous culture, 47-48, 58, 60,
88-89, 92, 96, 98, 105, 115-16, 134,
136, 138, 168-69, 210
individualism, 13, 62, 193
International Congress on World
Evangelization, 73, 95
Iran, 30, 148
Iraq, 30
International Fellowship of Evangelical
Mission Theologians, 94-95
International Fellowship of Evangelical
Students, 67-69, 95
Islam 26, 29, 32, 155, 157, 160-61, 183
Israel, 20-21, 23, 25-26, 31, 132, 148,
152, 157-58, 161, 188
Jerusalem, 20-23, 30, 221
   Council, 23
Jesus Christ, 10, 20-24, 41, 43, 45, 48,
57, 68, 73, 86-87, 95, 98, 108-10, 113,
117, 119-22, 127-29, 132, 135-36, 139,
144-46, 149, 159, 168-69, 177, 199,
203, 213-14, 232, 234-35, 244
   as Ancestor, 58, 199, 244
   as Creator, 58
   as Dalit, 58, 123, 244
   and Hinduism, 117, 119-22
   and Islam, 160
   as Liberator, 244
   as Life-Giver, 57
   as Lord, 21-22, 31, 58, 72, 98
   as Mediator, 57
   as Messiah, 22-23, 31
   as Son of God, 53, 135, 160, 199
Judaism, 22-24
Judea, 10
justice, 12, 51, 62, 76, 89, 94, 96, 98,
101, 132, 142, 186, 190, 212, 214,

218, 230. *See also* social justice
justification, 112, 129
Kairos Document, 142
King James Bible, 38
kingdom of God, 21, 72, 79, 91, 94, 96,
99, 101, 109, 123, 199, 215, 221, 227,
231-34, 236
Korea, 196, 198, 203, 242-43
Korean American Theology, 196, 198
land, 51-52, 60, 87-88, 92, 175, 221,
229
language, 9-10, 22-23, 27, 30, 33,
35-39, 42, 46-48, 52, 55, 88, 103-6,
110, 113, 128, 134-36, 146, 153,
155-56, 165, 175, 185, 191, 204, 207,
216, 239
   Arabic, 148-51, 153-56
   Aramaic, 10
   Buddhist, 29
   Chinese, 29, 106
   Confucian, 207
   Coptic, 30
   Greek, 22-23, 30, 154
   Indian, 29
   Latin, 27
   sacred, 104
   Spanish, 179, 190
   Syriac, 28, 30-31, 150, 154-55
   Western, 150
Laotian American theology, 202
Latin America, 9-10, 12, 15, 17, 27, 32,
33, 51, 54, 67-70, 72-73, 75-80, 84,
88-91, 93-96, 98, 100-101, 181,
185-87, 189
   biblical interpretation in, 15, 62, 94,
97, 186, 188, 249
   Christianity in, 9, 15, 70, 88-91,
93-96, 100-101, 179-80, 184-85
   church in, 76-79, 89-90, 92, 94, 186
   cultural context of, 51, 54, 67-69,
71-72, 77-78, 80, 82, 84, 91,
95-98, 100, 180-92
   evangelicalism in, 11, 15, 55, 69-71,
73, 75-76, 80-84, 88-90, 92-95,
184, 190-93
   missionaries in, 70, 80, 181, 192
   Pentecostalism in, 84, 88, 90,

182-84, 187-88, 190-91, 193
  Protestantism in, 72, 76-77, 84,
    88-90, 179-87, 189-91, 193
  Roman Catholicism in, 72, 76-78,
    81-82, 89-90, 93-94, 100, 179-80,
    183, 249
Latin American liberation theology, 11,
  76, 79, 88, 94, 124, 181, 184, 212,
  244
Latin American Theological
  Fellowship/Fraternity, 11, 51, 53, 71,
  88, 93-98, 101, 186, 189
Latin American theology, 10-12, 15,
  27, 51, 55, 71-101, 124, 179-93, 220,
  237, 240, 244
Lausanne Congress, 73-74, 98
Lausanne Covenant, 11, 15, 55, 73-74,
  95, 101
leadership, 20, 30, 37, 62, 68-69, 74,
  76-77, 81, 92, 95-96, 112, 146, 156,
  161, 175, 183-85, 211, 218, 250-51
liberation theology, 10-11, 54-55, 72,
  75-82, 88, 90, 93-94, 124-25, 140,
  142-43, 181, 184, 186, 210-16,
  218-19, 244
logos, 25, 48, 79, 103, 108, 110
Madras Group, 117-18
Majority World, 9-10, 13, 39, 50,
  52-54, 56-63, 62, 95, 143, 237, 242,
  248-51. *See also* Global South
marginality, 11, 51, 62, 81, 114, 124,
  186-88, 190-91, 193, 196, 199, 235,
  237
martyrs, 81, 89
Marxism, 67-70, 79, 218
medicine, 126
mestizo/mestizaje, 62, 182, 186, 192
Mexican Revolution, 181
Middle East, 148-49, 151-61
Middle East Council of Churches/
  MECC, 149, 151
minorities, 10, 13, 50, 53, 63, 79-80,
  93, 112, 184, 192-93, 208, 220, 242
mision integral, 11, 55, 90
missiology, 52, 73-77, 80-82, 90, 96,
  99, 186-87, 199, 202
  "Church Growth missiology," 74

mission, missionaries, 9, 11, 13, 19, 21,
  28-29, 31-33, 36, 40-41, 42-44,
  46-49, 52, 68-69, 70-71, 73-74, 76,
  78-80, 83, 89-91, 93-96, 99, 111, 115,
  121, 123, 127, 129, 135, 145, 160,
  168-69, 180-181, 184-88, 190-93,
  219, 225, 239, 241, 243
missionary movement, 9, 255
morality, 105, 108-11, 113-14, 143, 150,
  208
mother tongue, 9, 35-36, 38, 48-49
multiculturalism, 10, 22, 49, 75, 122,
  127, 131, 182, 192, 208
music, 10, 87-88, 92, 96, 98, 184, 211,
  226. *See also* hymns
Muslim culture, 127-28, 155-61
mythology
  Greek, 22
  Western, 241
Native North American
  community, 10, 165-66, 171
  worldview, 170-72, 176
National Committee of Negro
  Churchmen, 211
Native North American theology, 51,
  58, 75, 165, 169, 187
neocolonialism, 61, 77
neo-Pentecostalism, 90
Nestorianism, 31-32
New Testament, 12, 20, 24, 29, 32, 35,
  40, 58, 69, 74, 103, 113-14, 122, 127,
  149, 151, 160, 191
Nicene Creed, 36-37
Niceno-Constantinopolitan creed, 21
North America, 10, 13, 27, 32-33, 51,
  60, 68, 73-74, 77, 79, 81, 93, 97, 101,
  158, 198-99, 206, 208, 210, 214-15,
  227, 237
  academy in, 238, 243
  Christianity in, 100-101, 243
  church in, 242
  evangelicalism in, 203-7, 242
North American theology, 104, 153,
  205, 207, 220, 237, 240
Operation Wetback, 181
orality, 82, 177
Organization of African Instituted

Churches, 144
paganism, 21, 24, 44, 192
Palestine, 20, 158
Pan African Conference of Third
  World Theologians, 143
patristic period, 103, 151-52, 154
Pentecost, 20-21, 104, 172, 207
Pentecostalism, 37, 81-84, 88, 90-92,
  96, 144, 179, 181, 183-84, 187-88,
  190-91, 193, 207. *See also* neo-
  Pentecostalism
persecution, 21, 29, 36, 86-87
Persia, 30-31, 148, 155
Peru, 54, 68, 72, 78, 83-84, 90, 96
Platonism, 25, 103
pluralism, 29, 41, 47-48, 50, 52-54, 61,
  81, 122, 152, 198, 204, 247
Pneumatology, 83, 172, 207
poor, 13, 50-51, 55, 77-79, 81-82, 91,
  98, 142, 182-84, 187, 214-15, 217,
  235. *See also* poverty
postcolonialism, 10, 59-61, 104, 200,
  202, 250
postmodernism, 83, 190, 202, 204
poverty, 12, 50-51, 55, 62, 76, 99, 143,
  186, 220. *See also* poor
praxis, 55, 78, 81, 88, 99
prayer, 36-37, 55, 89, 130, 171, 177
"preferential option for the poor," 78,
  142, 187
proselytes. *See* converts/conversion
publishing/publication, 68, 72, 74,
  76-77, 81-82, 84, 96, 99, 118, 148-53,
  157, 160-61, 169, 186, 189, 196, 200,
  202, 237, 248, 251-52
race/racism, 35, 40, 104, 120, 180, 182,
  192-93, 202, 211-12, 214, 218-22, 242
rationalistic theology, 78, 240
reconciliation, 142, 167, 212, 214
redemption. *See* salvation
Reformation, 12, 27, 36, 62, 90, 103, 204
Reformed theology, 70, 142, 167, 196
relativism, 52-53, 57-58, 246
resurrection, 29, 68, 108-10, 112, 132,
  214
"Rethinking Group." *See* Madras
  Group

revelation, 43, 54, 63, 103, 108-11,
  119-20, 130, 132, 135, 141, 159, 214
  biblical, 57-58, 79
  general, 61
salvation, 20-21, 109-10, 122, 123,
  125-27, 129, 132, 141, 167-69, 171,
  173-74, 218, 226, 236, 245
sanctification, 112-13, 222
scholasticism, 78
Scripture, 9-11, 20, 25, 27, 51-53,
  55-63, 69, 75-76, 81, 84, 89, 102-11,
  114, 119, 126, 130-31, 134-35,
  144-45, 150-53, 160-61, 165, 168,
  171, 185-86, 204-5, 208, 211, 213,
  219, 229, 245, 247
  Arabic, 150-51, 160
  authority of, 11, 40, 73, 97, 102,
    145, 247
  and colonialism, 59-61
  commentaries on, 151-52, 160, 249
  Hebrew, 103
  Hindu, 117, 119
  interpretation of, 50-54, 56-57,
    59-63, 83
  Mandarin. *See* Union Version
  perspicuity of, 62
  reading of, 62, 71, 75-77, 185, 246
  translation of, 35-49, 52, 150, 160
  scholarship of, 50, 152, 158
  and society, 50
  sufficiency of, 48
  and Western culture, 104
seminaries, 14, 63, 70, 150, 153, 156,
  169, 185-86, 196, 203-4, 243, 248,
  250-51
sin, 24, 46, 109-10, 117, 125, 130-32,
  135, 145, 174, 205, 225, 231, 245
social justice, 55, 77, 190
Society of Biblical Literature, 200
socioeconomics, 123-24, 126, 218, 220
sociology, 74, 79, 84, 152, 188, 202,
  205, 229, 233
sola scriptura, 48, 204
South African Council of Churches, 142
South African Truth and
  Reconciliation Commission, 142
Spain, 69, 73, 81-82

Spanish-American War, 180
Spirit of God. *See* Holy Spirit
spirit world, 29, 36-37, 39, 81, 126, 130-31, 137, 166, 174-75
spirituality, 70-71, 82, 96, 101, 108, 123-26, 131, 152, 166, 168, 171-72, 175, 177, 183, 190, 199, 203, 227, 230, 234, 242, 247
Sudan, 29, 31
suffering, 29, 92, 123, 125, 173, 234
syncretism, 45, 121, 203
temple, 19, 23-24, 32, 87
Third World. *See* Majority World
translation, 10, 21, 35-41, 43-49, 52, 58, 68, 103-4, 106, 108, 134, 136, 138, 150-51, 153-56, 160-61, 179, 184, 185
Trinity, 22, 25, 28, 172, 207-8, 249
Union Version, 104, 114
United Bible Societies, 81
United States, 62, 73, 78, 80-81, 83, 92, 94, 100, 179-82, 184-87, 189-93, 212, 219, 222, 232
Vatican II, 76, 78, 81
vernacular, 31, 36-37, 41-42, 44-45, 47-49, 146
Vietnam, 198-99, 200, 203
Vietnamese American theology, 199-200
virtue, 23, 32, 79, 110-15, 248
West/Western, 46, 51, 95, 206
    academy, 63, 67, 111, 156, 206, 237-41, 243-45, 247, 249-51
    Christianity, 14, 27, 30, 32, 46, 114-15, 119, 153-54, 171, 174, 242, 247

church, 9-10, 30, 32, 156, 169, 241
culture, 10, 27, 32-33, 48, 50, 104-5, 119, 124, 126, 130, 139, 153-54, 167, 169, 173, 221, 241
evangelicals/evangelicalism, 11, 144, 151
hermeneutic, 50, 52, 54, 56-57, 61, 63
language, 42, 50, 150
missionaries, 28
philosophy, 170-71
religion, 107
Western theology, 11, 13, 25, 27, 33, 48, 50, 54, 61, 103, 117-19, 154, 156-57, 166, 168, 171, 174, 213, 237-42, 244-46, 249, 251
Westernization, 36, 104
witchcraft, 37, 81
Wheaton College, 14-15, 84, 250
Wheaton Theology Conference, 14-15, 84
womanist theology, 211, 216
women, 50, 62, 84, 89, 91, 98, 100, 121-22, 128-32, 140, 143-44, 173-74, 215-17
World Alliance of Reformed Churches, 142
World Congress on Evangelism, 69, 73
World Council of Churches, 72, 123
World Evangelical Alliance, 144
World War I, 181
World War II, 70, 78, 181
worship, 26, 28, 81, 83, 89, 128, 130, 146, 155, 179, 183-84, 192, 207, 220, 226, 229, 233